DATE DUE

DEC 7 1994		

Brodart Co.   Cat. # 55 137 001   Printed in USA

MONEY ON THE RUN

Canada and How the World's Dirty Profits Are Laundered

MARIO POSSAMAI

VIKING

VIKING
Published by the Penguin Group
Penguin Books Canada Ltd, 10 Alcorn Avenue, Toronto, Ontario,
Canada M4V 3B2
Penguin Books Ltd, 27 Wrights Lane, London W8 5TZ, England
Viking Penguin, a division of Penguin Books USA Inc., 375 Hudson
Street, New York, New York 10014, USA
Penguin Books Australia Ltd, Ringwood, Victoria, Australia
Penguin Books (NZ) Ltd, 182-190 Wairau Road,
Auckland 10, New Zealand

Penguin Books Ltd, Registered Offices:
Harmondsworth, Middlesex, England

First published 1992

1 3 5 7 9 10 8 6 4 2

Printed and bound in Canada on acid free paper ∞

Canadian Cataloguing in Publication Data

Possamai, Mario
Money on the run

Includes bibliographical references.
ISBN 0–670–83843–8

1. Money laundering – Canada.   2. Commercial crimes – Canada.
3. Duvalier, Jean-Claude, 1951–   .   I. Title

HV6771.C3P78 1992   364.1'68   C92-094124-9

Owing to limitations of space, all acknowledgments of permission to
reprint previously published material will be found on pages 289-90.

Dedica
Ai miei genitori Rosa e Luigi, il mio fratello Alec e il
mio defunto zio Mario: con coràggio, onore e dignità
hanno costruito una nuova vita in una
terra straniera.

ACKNOWLEDGMENTS

One day in the mid-1980s, while I was at The Canadian Press, I decided to write a feature on money laundering, thinking it could be completed quickly. After all, this seemed to be a simple, straightforward topic. How wrong I was. Little did I realize at the time, but I was embarking on a research project — eventually involving hundreds of interviews in more than 10 countries — that would last into the next decade, and culminate in a book. It could not have been completed without the help and encouragement of many people, including one of the first experts I interviewed in 1986, Rod Stamler, then a Chief Superintendent at the RCMP.

I'd especially like to acknowledge my debt to a number of sources who proved essential — especially in researching the Duvalier and Ceausescu chapters — but asked not to be identified. I hope this book bears out the faith and trust they placed in me.

I'd also like to express my thanks:

Particularly to Susan Teskey, Linden MacIntyre and Oleh Rumak of CBC Television's "the 5th estate." A special word of gratitude to Liviu Turcu and Mircea Raceanu in Washington and Petre Bacanu in Bucharest — their support and generosity proved crucial. My hope is that their courageous efforts will one day be rewarded by the emergence of a truly free and democratic Romania. Thanks also to executive producer Kelly Crichton and senior producer David Nayman of "the 5th estate."

To Brian Sargent, who graciously shared valuable insights and observations into money laundering picked up during an impressive career at the RCMP.

To lawyer Colin Campbell, whose cool head saved many a day.

To Paul McGrath of CBC Television's "The Journal," who was generous not only with access to his extensive files and library, but also with his recommendations on the manuscript, and his encouragement.

To James Dubro, who first took an in-depth look at John Pullman in the 1970s in the "Connections" series. He shared valuable information on this intriguing figure and also first suggested that I examine the Prohibition-era activities of the Bronfmans.

At the RCMP in Ottawa, to Assistant Commissioner Norm Doucette and Inspector Bruce Bowie, who generously made time for what must have seemed an endless (and often tedious) stream of questions and requests. Thanks also to Chief Intelligence Analyst Robert Fahlman and Helen Booth, Chief Librarian at the Canadian Police College. Also, Sergeant Pierre Belanger and Corporal Andy Baird of the RCMP's Access to Information Section.

At the Metropolitan Toronto Police, to the late Sergeant Craig Law, Inspector Bill Blair, Sergeants Chuck Konkel and Don Denley, Detectives Frank Besenthal, Ken Yates, Dave Caravella and Bill Henderson.

To Michael Bliss, Neil Brooks and David Perry, who reviewed some chapters and provided invaluable comments and advice.

At CP, to Jim Poling, Vice-President, Editorial, and Ian Donaldson, General News Editor, who encouraged my research into Jean-Claude Duvalier — even when it must have all seemed quite quixotic. Also at CP, I'm grateful to Gordon Grant, Paul Mooney, Roberto Russo, John Ward, Dean Beeby, Clyde Graham, Peter Buckley, Paul Woods and Gord McIntosh.

At the *Toronto Star*, thanks to Shawn McCarthy and Tony Van Alphen, who while at CP, generously shouldered my duties so that I could pursue my inquiries into Carlos Lehder. At the *Ottawa Citizen,* Jim Coyle. At the *Globe and Mail*, Graham Fraser.

In Toronto, thanks to Don Blakeman, who agreed to discuss what remains a painful episode in his life; Andrew Mitrovica; Catherine Wismer; Stevie Cameron; Chris Anderson, Sonny Saunders, and Jack Burnett of the Royal Bank of Canada; Rick Marshall of the Bank of Nova Scotia; Pat Adams of Probe International; Mihaela Antanea; Ben Eng; and Cynthia Reed.

In Montreal, thanks to Sergeant Marc Bourque of the RCMP, Michel C. Auger, of *Le Journal de Montréal*, for his help during the Duvalier series, Normand Lester of Société Radio-Canada, and Tom Naylor.

In Ottawa, thanks to Liberal members of Parliament Sheila Copps and Don Boudria, Senator Norm Atkins, Fred Gorbet, Dalton Camp, Frank Kirkwood, Professor Blair Neatby, Geoffrey Pearson, Margaret Beare, and Richard Clippingdale. At the National Archives of Canada, thanks to Antonio Lechasseur.

In Washington, thanks to Jack Blum, Bill Ruzzamenti, Nestor Ratesh, Jerris Leonard, Chuck Saphos, David Funderburk, Michael Orndorff, David Wilson, David McKean and Vladimir Tismaneau. In Florida, Ernst Mueller and Wendel Wellman. In New York City, James Harmon, Greg Wallance, Robert Morgenthau and Daniel Cotton. In California, Tom Perdue and William Cassidy. In Michigan, Art Langeveld and William Cunningham.

In Austria, Hans Pretterebner, Dennis Silvestri and George Jahn. In Switzerland, Suzanne Wolfe, Dumitru Mazilu, Mario Casella, Jorg Kistler, Mihai Lupoi, Daniel Zuberbuhler, Jean Ziegler and Stefan Weber. In Italy, Paola Biocca, Dott. Silvano Montanaro and Dott. Ivano Nelson Salvarani. In Germany, Manfred Engelmann, Dr. Heinz Gunther Husch, Peter Rothen and Dr. Klaus Rose. In France, Philippe Madelin and Alexandra Laignel-Levastine. In Romania, Octavian Brenzai, Dan Bada, Eugen Serbanescu, Adrian Gaspar and Cornel Nistorescu. In Israel, Yossi Melman.

My thanks also to reporters who first probed some key areas covered in this book: William Marsden of the Montreal *Gazette*; Philip Mathias of the *Financial Post*; Peter Moon of the *Globe and Mail*; Robert Hutchison, formerly of the *Financial Post*; and Richard Cleroux, formerly of the *Globe and Mail*.

A special thanks to the book's editor, Meg Masters at Penguin Books, and the copy editor, Kathryn Dean — for shaping and polishing an unruly manuscript and riding herd on a wilful author. Also at Penguin, thanks to Cynthia Good, Brad Martin, Scott Sellers, Karen Cossar and Lori Ledingham for their support: No first-time author could have been made to feel more welcome.

I'm especially indebted to Iris Skeoch. Without her vision and faith, this book would never have been written.

Deborah provided incomparable support and invaluable suggestions and comments on the work-in-progress. She also showed superhuman patience living with a cantankerous author. My parents Rosa and Luigi and brother Alec provided a never-ending supply of encouragement. And Deborah Black provided the "special" coffee cup.

Finally, my regrets to anyone whom I may have inadvertently neglected to mention.

Mario Possamai
June 1992
Toronto, Ontario

CONTENTS

MONEY ON THE RUN

■1 RINSING BABY DOC'S LOOT

On September 23, 1986, a member of a noted Swiss law practice strolled into the Royal Bank of Canada's gold-tinted headquarters in Toronto's financial district. His name was Alain Le Fort. And at the tender age of thirty-three, he had the distinction of being the youngest partner in Patry, Junet, Simon et Le Fort, a well-to-do Geneva firm that had been retained by at least one major Canadian bank. To round out his training, he'd even had a brief stint at the Chase Manhattan Bank in New York. Needless to say, little distinguished the fluently bilingual Le Fort from the scores of other blue-chip customers who complete multi-million-dollar transactions at the Royal Bank's central offices every working day. Little, that is, except for his confidential mission and his unsavoury client. For Le Fort and a handful of other lawyers were key figures in the kind of money laundering scheme that gives police officers and bankers sleepless nights — the kind that's virtually undetectable, practically unstoppable and completely legal, despite the 1989 legislation intended to crack down on the practice. Worryingly for Canadians, the operation also underscored the disturbing, if unwitting, role this country and its financial institutions can play in the

1

burgeoning world of tainted money. To grasp the full measure of Le Fort's visit — and the tangled web of ensuing events — we must begin seven months earlier in one of the world's most impoverished countries, a place that Graham Greene once called "the nightmare republic."[1]

A silver-grey BMW, escorted by carloads of army officers, sped through the darkness of Port-au-Prince, the forlorn capital of Haiti, in the early hours of February 7, 1986. The driver was a stout black man whose face bore a strangely blank expression. With him was a striking, lighter-skinned woman in a white turban, her face frozen into its typical arrogance. Few Haitians would have failed to recognize them, for Jean-Claude "Baby Doc" Duvalier, the rapacious President-for-Life, and his testy wife Michele were the most hated people in the Western Hemisphere's poorest nation.

On this February night, something momentous was afoot. Instead of going on a leisurely drive, the couple was heading straight for the airport. Earlier, a cargo plane had reportedly taken off, crammed with jewels, antiques and art from the presidential palace. A starkly lit U.S. Air Force jet now waited on the tarmac, ready to whisk the notorious couple, along with close family and a handful of favoured cronies, into exile. The Duvalier clan's twenty-nine-year rule — a blood-stained era in which the regime's thugs had murdered as many as fifty-thousand people — was drawing to a close. That the final chapter would be played out at the airport seemed appropriate enough. It bore the name of the dynasty's much-dreaded founder, Jean-Claude's late father, François "Papa Doc" Duvalier.

For months, Haiti, a barren country occupying the western third of the Caribbean island of Hispaniola, had been anything but calm. In late 1985, after years of fear and misery, its citizens had begun to lash out. Anti-government demonstrations mushroomed. So did the violence, which reminded one foreign correspondent of "the streets of Tehran in the weeks before the 1979 revolution that toppled the Shah."[2] The notorious security forces responded in their customary fashion —

killing dozens of Haitians. At one point, the government, which was increasingly losing control, closed all schools, depriving many children of their only meal of the day. Intended to quell the growing discontent, the move had the opposite effect. Protests gained momentum; food shortages worsened.

The once iron-fisted system of terror, so carefully nurtured by Jean-Claude's father, began to lose its grip. Tellingly, the Tonton Macoutes, the regime's ruthless militia whose members sported dark sunglasses, red neckerchiefs and blue denim uniforms, failed to reassert control. Attempts to whitewash the situation also failed. Not even the hiring of American public relations firms "at a rumored cost of around $7 million*" could improve Haiti's international reputation.[3] Finally, even the United States, once a stalwart ally thanks to the Duvaliers' unabashed anti-communism, could no longer stomach such a brutal regime.

American pressure mounted to have Jean-Claude step down, and on February 6, 1986, he finally capitulated. Secret plans for the departure were quickly set in motion, though it wasn't easy to find a country that would accept him. Greece, Spain and Switzerland gave blunt "no's." France finally agreed to take him in, though it did so reluctantly and on the understanding that it would be just a temporary refuge. Michele, for her part, took charge of the packing, personally supervising the stuffing of valuables into myriad Louis Vuitton suitcases.[4] Duvalier himself made sure there was enough cash on hand by getting "$100,000 [US] at the government-owned National Credit Bank."[5] That night, they bade farewell to their impoverished country in typical fashion — with an extravagant bash for their intimates at the presidential palace. Duvalier also took the time to write three cheques to himself on official government accounts. They totalled $169,000 US.[6]

A few hours later, they went to the airport. "Only a group of foreign journalists and cameramen saw the family drive

---

* All figures are in Canadian dollars unless otherwise noted.

through a side gate on to the tarmac . . . in a motorcade of half a dozen cars and four military pick-up trucks, which carried baggage and armed soldiers," wrote reporter Phil Davison. "Baggage was also crammed into one small taxi, driven by a lone chauffeur."[7] The scene was worthy of *People* magazine's breathless prose: "The Duvaliers drove through a gauntlet of photographers. Baby Doc, at the wheel, was characteristically impassive, but Michele, wearing a chic white turban, flicked the cigarette she held in her long fingers and exhaled theatrically for the paparazzi."[8] At around 3:45 A.M. on February 7, the American Air Force C-141 jet lifted off from the airport, carrying the well-outfitted Duvaliers into exile. (Though the United States had imposed a two-suitcase limit, Michele took along eighteen bulging valises and her husband ten.)[9] Jean-Claude and Michele appeared composed to the end. Perhaps the champagne they'd sipped at their midnight party had soothed their nerves. More likely, they had the peace of mind of knowing they would have few financial worries in their new life.[10]

That morning, jubilant Haitians awoke to a once-in-a-lifetime party savoured by millions. As one journalist described it, the Duvaliers' departure sparked "wild, carnival-like celebrations in the streets. . . . Youths stood on their heads, shaking their legs in glee, while others jumped and wriggled in sheer delight as cars and pick-up trucks raced through city streets, packed with men and women waving and making V-for-victory signs."[11]

Officials assessing the damage caused by three decades of Duvalier profligacy found less to cheer about. The cupboard was so bare that there was scarcely enough money to cover the army's expenses for one week.[12] According to some sources, government bank accounts held a paltry $500,000 US. People had suspected Jean-Claude Duvalier of liberally dipping into the country's finances, but no one imagined that the slow-witted strongman, who had been derisively dismissed in his youth as "Tête-Panier," or Basket-Head, could have been so thorough. Ordinary Haitians, most of whom lived on less than $100 US a year, demanded to know what had happened to the tens of millions of dollars that entered state coffers each year. So did the National Governing Council, which succeeded the Duvalier regime. It faced the unenviable task of rebuilding a primarily agricultural country where soil erosion and poor farming practices had rendered one-third of the land unusable.[13]

Particularly galling for the council was an agreement it was forced to reach with the Dominican Republic on March 17, 1986, to settle a huge Duvalier debt. Every year, Baby Doc had been paid a bounty for each Haitian sent to harvest sugar in the neighbouring republic, which covers the remaining two-thirds of Hispaniola. Some 19,000 Haitians usually went, living under such deplorable conditions that human rights groups condemned the practice as "slavery." For the 1986 harvest, Baby Doc had pocketed an advance of some $2 million US. As soon as it had been received, the money was reportedly shipped offshore by a trusted courier. Upon his overthrow, the accord was suspended and no Haitians went to work in Dominican sugar fields. Yet the debt remained.[14]

The council — perhaps spurred by the Dominican debt episode — acted decisively to investigate the Duvalier finances, forming a seven-member commission in April 1986. To coordinate the international search for the missing assets, an American law firm, Stroock and Stroock and Lavan, was hired. It retained a small army of attorneys and investigators from the legendary New York firm of Kroll and Associates, who fanned out on both sides of the Atlantic. The early findings were promising. Based on initial calculations, the council reckoned that more than $360 million US had been stolen and funnelled abroad — more than twice the government's annual budget. Some estimates put Duvalier's total plundered wealth at $900 million US. Among the purported irregularities: suspicious Duvalier debts to the National Credit Bank, totalling $5.6 million US; $6 million US in missing payments to the state car insurance agency; and a mysterious monthly payment of $60,000 US allotted to the palace for unexplained "military expenses."[15] Of particular interest were Duvalier's five palace accounts. According to the *Washington Post,* his "finance ministers wrote cheques to those accounts over the past five years totalling as much as $600,000 [US] a month." Some of those cheques were strangely classified in government records under the listing "no explanation." One was for the equivalent of $90,000 US.[16] Clearly, this was just scratching the surface. Thus began the hunt for Duvalier's fortune.

Few would credit Jean-Claude Duvalier with being particularly bright. But he did have one nefarious skill — one that marked him as his father's son. He knew how to suck blood from a stone. Certainly, dictators like the late Ferdinand Marcos of the Philippines, overthrown in 1986, or Nicolae Ceausescu of Romania, deposed and executed three years later, had reportedly looted larger sums. But few others could have stolen so much from a country with so little. To fully grasp Haiti's privation, suggests the British newspaper, the *Economist,* fly along its border with the Dominican Republic: "On the Dominican side, the ground is covered with green tropical vegetation. On the Haitian side, it is brown and dead." Indeed, large tracts are dotted with tree stumps, the remains of the vast forests that once covered Haiti. More than 90 percent have been cut down to produce charcoal, which provides the bulk of its energy needs. The resulting erosion is leading to what some call "an irreversible ecological disaster."[17] In fact, some pessimistic scientific assessments expect the whole of Haiti to turn to desert in twenty-five years.[18] The health statistics of this nation of seven million are just as gloomy. Estimates of infant mortality are as high as 110 per 1,000, with between 7 and 15 percent of babies dying in the first eight weeks from umbilical tetanus. The result: Fully one-third of children die before their fifth birthday.[19] The prospects are little better for those who reach adulthood. Four of five people cannot read. And the life expectancy is a little over fifty.[20] By any economic yardstick, Haiti is one of the most impoverished nations in the world.

It was not always thus. Though it's hard to imagine, this desperate country was once the lush crown jewel of the French empire. Saint-Domingue, as it was known, was widely referred to as "the pearl of the Antilles" — a worthy title for the world's most profitable colony. By some estimates, one of every five French citizens in the second half of the seventeenth century depended on trade with the colony for their livelihood.[21] Moreover, it helped France earn much of its keep, contributing an estimated two-thirds of all French colonial revenues in the late 1780s.[22]

What made this all possible was the most brutal of enterprises. The island's lucrative bounty of cotton, sugar and coffee was harvested by more than 500,000 slaves working in barbarous conditions on the island's 8,500 plantations. "Saint Domingue was . . . one of the world's greatest markets for the African slave trade," wrote journalist Elizabeth Abbott. Planters found it more economical to work their slaves to death and buy new ones "than allow them to survive and reproduce themselves naturally."[23] Slavery was eventually abolished, thanks to a series of bloody uprisings that culminated in the nation winning independence in 1804. The newly minted country remained comparatively prosperous. According to some estimates, Haiti, as it was renamed, afforded its peasants the highest standard of living in the Western Hemisphere, after the United States. There was enough food to go around, and a manufacturing base was even developing.[24]

This would be one of the infrequent bright spots in Haiti's history. With a few respites, despot followed despot. Cycles of violence and political chaos were repeated. The country's peasants grew inexorably poorer. No matter how hard they worked, they earned less and less. Ruler after ruler took to heart the motto of an early leader: "Pluck the chicken, but don't make it scream." Haitian peasants retorted with their own proverb in the local patois: *Si travay te bon bagay, moun rich ta pranl' lontan.* ("If work was a good thing, the rich would have grabbed it long ago.")[25]

Not even this dismal legacy could have prepared Haiti for

the hardships that began in 1957 when Papa Doc won a disputed election with the army's help. Under the Duvaliers, mismanagement, corruption and greed reached new heights. Children, in particular, paid a high price. In 1958, one in five infants was malnourished. By 1977, the rate was nearly seven in ten, soaring to nearly nine in ten just three years later. The final six years of Jean-Claude's rule alone saw the Haitian economy shrink by about 15 percent.[26]

The poor sometimes ate a strange kind of biscuit made mostly of sand, that filled the belly at least for a time. However, not everyone was suffering. While Haiti was controlled by members of some thirty extended families in 1957, their ranks grew, according to the World Bank, to include about two hundred millionaire families by 1982.[27] They benefited from the rich world's brief forays into the Haitian economy, drawn by some of the hemisphere's lowest labour costs.

Upon his election, François Duvalier wasted little time in establishing a "kleptocracy." Businesspeople soon learned to contribute to his secret accounts if they wanted to purchase lucrative franchises and import licences. But Papa Doc didn't stop there. He also routinely tapped into the Régie du Tabac, the state tobacco monopoly. (So would his son, years later.) The Régie also handled taxes on imports and exports of basic goods and staples — everything from sugar to cotton. As in most poor, Third World countries, this agency was among the government's most important domestic money makers. Thanks to the Régie's broad reach and ever-tightening grip, Haitians were caught coming and going. They earned less for their heavily taxed exports and paid more for imported staples, on which prohibitive tariffs were levied. The system was appropriately called *"peze-suce"* or "squeeze and suck." [28] Even visitors' pockets were carefully picked. As Graham Greene, the late British writer, discovered during a visit in 1963, foreigners paid twice as much for an exit visa as for the document that let them enter the country. The profits trickled into the president's pocket.[29]

But when it came to out-and-out greed and plunder, investigators poring over records left behind by the Duvaliers in February 1986 found that Baby Doc had been more than a match for the light-fingered Papa Doc. Indeed, this was probably the only area where the son not only resembled his father, but clearly surpassed him. In all else, Jean-Claude was hardly a chip off the old block. François — in his sombre dark suits, thick, black-rimmed eyeglasses and prim hats — kept up a punishing schedule at his desk, despite his frail health. When he wasn't peeking from a secret hideway, furtively watching the grisly goings-on in one of his many torture chambers, he was personally attending to every facet of Haitian life. No detail was too small for the notorious country doctor, who'd first made his name by curing peasants of the debilitating tropical disease, yaws.

His son, by contrast, was indolence personified. If his school teachers had had their way, they probably would have noted on Jean-Claude's report card: Makes absolutely no effort to apply himself. Of course, none did. To do so would certainly have cost them their lives. Jean-Claude, obese and painfully stupid, doddled through school. "Only once had Jean-Claude excelled," wrote journalist Elizabeth Abbott. "When the Education Ministry had provided advance copies of the state-administered high school graduation exams."[30] It appears that he got along with his schoolmates, though he was often teased for being a dolt. By his teens, Baby Doc had acquired a coterie of hangers-on, scores of girlfriends, and a slew of expensive habits. Such was the sum of the nineteen-year-old Jean-Claude's life experience when he succeeded his late father in April 1971, becoming what newspapers trumpeted as the world's youngest head of state.

As president, Baby Doc's prodigious spending quickly matched his girth. His official salary of about $24,000 US a year didn't go far, despite the fact that it was the equivalent of what his government spent each year on the health of eight thousand Haitians. [31] Neither did the $1.5 million US or so he received to supplement his expenses. A fondness for fast sports cars, expensive watches and huge, late-night parties saw to that. But if Jean-Claude was an extravagant bachelor, married life sharply increased the demands on his pocketbook and, by extension, on Haiti's coffers. Consider his elaborate wedding in May 1980 to Michele, an attractive divorcée and would-be model. It cost an estimated $3 million US, including $100,000 US for a massive fireworks display. Indeed, some reckon the final tab was closer to $10 million US. Whatever the tally, it was judged by the *Guinness Book of World Records* to be one of the most expensive matrimonials ever. Not even this extravagance benefited the Haitian economy — for little was spent locally. France supplied everything from the bride's white Givenchy dress and matching silk Alexandre headdress to the food and flowers. Likewise, "the treat" that Jean-Claude bought himself just a week before the wedding came from overseas: a Ferrari purchased with $100,000 US drawn from a government account at the central bank. The poor of Haiti weren't totally left out, however. T-shirts bearing a photo of the happy couple as well as supplies of soup and rum were freely distributed. And in a garish display, the poor witnessed the spectacle on television sets especially set up in the slums by the government. "It was beautiful," Michele later gushed to an interviewer.[32]

The wedding set the tone for married life. Home was a huge, two-storey, hermetically sealed apartment in the gleaming white presidential palace — complete with thirty-foot ceilings, gold fixtures and a giant vault for jewelry. To decorate it, flowers were flown in from abroad. Haitian blooms, as eye-catching as any in the tropics, just weren't good enough for the Duvaliers, suggested one former investigator familiar with their lifestyle. And there were regular shopping expeditions to Paris, the final one being perhaps the most extravagant. In late 1985, just as the regime was beginning to flag, the Duvaliers dropped as much as $2 million US during this one spree. Paying for this opulence was simple enough for someone who treated Haiti as a vast, private estate. Like the slavery-based estates on Saint-Domingue of old, it was to be plundered at will.

Duvalier, as the absolute dictator, could write a cheque on any government bank account. In fact, he kept stacks of blank cheques for eight government bank accounts at the central bank, the Banque de la République d'Haiti for just such a purpose. Who was to say this was illegal? Duvalier was the land's absolute lawmaker. Few officials would even know about the withdrawals from government accounts for everything from national defence to auto insurance. Money came in; money went out "at the instruction of His Excellency Jean-Claude Duvalier, President for Life." No comprehensive, independent ledger, let alone computers or auditors, recorded or verified the transactions. Investigators later reckoned that $39 million US was pilfered this way in the 1980s. Similarly, Ministry of Finance accounts chipped in a further $31 million US.

When the exiled Duvalier dismissed allegations that he had pilfered funds from his country's treasury, he claimed that his family personally financed 90 percent of Haiti's social spending. "All heads of state of my country had certain funds at their disposal for implementing policy," he told an interviewer in 1987. The shocking state of the nation's health care system is a grim testament to this method of "policy implementation." For instance, hospital patients were required to provide their own syringes, drugs and dressings. But Duvalier's deceptions went even further. When writing out government cheques, he sometimes appeared to have a philanthropic bent, making them out to "Oeuvres Sociales de la Présidence," or "Social Works of the Presidency." However, reams of cancelled cheques discovered in Haiti and carefully catalogued by investigators make it clear that the huge sums handled by Duvalier went to anything but the social welfare. In late 1982, for example, Duvalier signed over two cheques, worth a total of $35,000 US, to the ubiquitous "Social Works of the Presidency." Not one penny reached Haiti's slums. The first cheque — number 764 and worth about $15,000 US — was drawn on November 17, 1982, from the account of the Haitian State lottery. Eight days later, the lottery forked over a further $20,000 US through cheque number 852. Both were endorsed to Maison Boucheron, Michele's favourite Paris jeweler. In other words, what the investigators discovered was that Jean-Claude's highly touted charity had only one beneficiary — his family. No one knows how Duvalier settled on this artifice, but it does have a nasty antecedent. In Nazi Germany in the 1930s, the Deutsche Winterhelfe purported to be a charity. In fact, it was a secret slush fund controlled by Hermann Goering.[33]

Like her husband, Michele Duvalier had few qualms about siphoning off money ostensibly earmarked for benevolent purposes. For starters, she had her own dummy charity, as did Duvalier's mother Simone, also known as "Mama Doc." Michele went a step further, however. As journalist Marie Brenner discovered, the case involved Bon Repos Hospital, a small maternity clinic that Michele had established. For a woman who fancied herself a kind of Evita — the wife of the late Argentine dictator Juan Perón and legendary patron of Buenos Aires slum dwellers — Bon Repos was a source of pride and joy. Apparently intended as a shining example of Michele's munificence to Haiti's poor, it played quite a differ-ent role. According to Brenner's research, the Haitian govern-ment was supposed to provide $70,000 US each month to the hospital. A cheque was dutifully issued to Michele Duvalier, care of the Bon Repos Hospital, drawn on Ministry of Finance account no. 950G at the central bank. However, virtually all the cheques were deposited in Michele's chequing account — no. 6251. That's the one she used for her personal expenses. Little, if any, went into the hospital's account no. 7485.[34]

Duvalier didn't always try to conceal his dipping-into-the-till behind a fictitious charity — especially if he was pressed for time. Investigators found that in mid-December 1982, for example, he drew $100,000 US from the Finance Ministry's rolling fund account. The cheque, signed by Jean-Claude Duvalier, who may have been caught up in the Christmas rush, displayed a hastily scrawled "cash." It was endorsed to the order of the jeweler, Boucheron. The Duvaliers used a similarly cavalier approach to pay for a hefty bill incurred in

December 1980 at the Caribbean's leading jewelry shop, Spritzer and Fuhrmann in the Netherlands Antilles. Two cheques settled the account. One, written on December 2, 1980, totalled approximately $143,000 US; the second, on December 26, 1980, about $414,000 US. Both were drawn on the National Defence Account by order of the "President-for-Life." The total amount, incidentally, was the rough equivalent of a quarter of Haiti's monthly spending on education.

Month after month, year after year, the Duvaliers spent on a vast scale. And month after month, year after year, Baby Doc and his wife paid the bills by tapping into government bank accounts. At the same time, they were building up their overseas nest-egg. At least $86 million US was transferred to foreign banks in Duvalier's final three years in power. The drain on state finances was paralyzing. As Felix Gaston, deputy governor of the Banque de la République d'Haiti, stated in a sworn affidavit in 1986: "Jean-Claude Duvalier and his wife, Michele Duvalier, personally ordered the transfer of millions of dollars from these accounts to himself, personal friends and family members." None of these cash transfers, he added, related to any governmental purpose or were authorized by any proper governmental authority. All were made "as a result of Duvalier's power as absolute dictator of Haiti."

Not even foreign aid was safe. In 1980, for instance, "the International Monetary Fund gave Haiti $22 million US in budgetary support; $20 million US simply vanished."[35] The Duvaliers even took a cut on millions of dollars in food aid that Haiti received every year from the United States. There was a 93 percent surcharge on each sack of aid flour that went directly to the Duvaliers.[36] Investigators were later able to show that Duvalier earned $4.5 million US from this levy.

Clearly, when the Duvaliers were forced into exile, they did not leave as paupers. At first, France granted them a temporary eight-day visa to tide them over until they found a permanent haven, a task that proved to be futile. No other country would have them, not even desperately poor Liberia in Africa.[37] Officials in Paris stubbornly stuck to the position that the Duvaliers were just temporary visitors, but as the weeks and months passed, it became clear that this was merely a ploy intended, perhaps, to placate French citizens wary of allowing yet another despot to while away his days in comfort in their country. (There'd been a great uproar in 1983 over the sanctuary given to the fallen Central African Republic dictator, Jean-Bedel Bokassa.) The plain truth was that the Duvaliers had found a new home in France — and a comfortable one at that.[38]

Exile in the sunny Côte d'Azur, not far from Cannes, entailed little hardship. The Duvaliers' villa, located in the jet-set village of Mougins, was less lavish than their palace in Haiti, but the mansion did come with its own olive grove, a swimming pool and an impressive iron front gate. The owner of the Villa Mohamedia was none other than the son of Saudi arms merchant Adnan Khashoggi. The location was perfect. The Mediterranean coast was studded with the pricey antique shops, art galleries and tony boutiques crucial to keeping Michele entertained. And if worse came to worst and Michele's shopping needs couldn't be met locally, Paris was within easy reach. There, she was often seen patronizing her friend the jeweler Alain Boucheron, and Givenchy, the up-scale couturier. As for Jean-Claude, when he wanted to indulge his celebrated palate, he needed only take a short drive to a restaurant that was up to his demanding standards: the Moulin de Mougins operated by the celebrated chef, Roger Verge. The fallen dictator had no trouble fitting in. "President Duvalier likes to eat well," Verge once told a reporter. "He has a passion for the table that for me is a high form of civilization."[39] As one investigator cynically noted, the exiled Duvaliers were probably better off than they had been in Port-au-Prince: they had all the benefits of the Haitian treasury with none of the headaches of governing.

Maintaining such a lavish lifestyle chewed up a lot of money, which presented something of a headache to the

Duvaliers' capable financial managers. Certainly, Duvalier had stored up a considerable fortune in overseas bank accounts before his fall. Almost to the end of his dictatorship, couriers had ferried funds into foreign accounts, while local financial institutions had wired money abroad. The problem was that most of these funds weren't easily accessible. This had not been a worry when the Duvaliers were in power, since they could always rely on the ever-accommodating Haitian treasury for cash.

In exile, however, they required a fail-safe system for replenishing their cash supply from their deeply buried fortune. And there was a complicating factor. Things were heating up on the legal front. In Haiti, criminal proceedings had begun against the Duvaliers, alleging embezzlement on a grand scale. The Swiss courts, in turn, froze their bank accounts in April 1986.[40] Haiti's American lawyers were also on the offensive. In June, they went to court to seize a $2.5 million condominium in Manhattan's Trump Towers. Other properties were rumoured to be slated for seizure. All of this meant that the Duvaliers had to retrieve their cash without alerting investigators and without leading them to the safely stored motherlode.

On their own, the judicial developments in Switzerland, Haiti or the United States were not particularly worrisome. Indeed, over the years, deposed dictators have seldom had to repay their stolen loot. The Swiss action, for example, while headline-grabbing, was less consequential than it appeared. Under Swiss law, the banks couldn't tell Haiti how much was in the accounts — until it was proved in Haitian courts that Duvalier's assets had been illegally obtained.[41] Moreover, Haiti's lawyers would have to demonstrate that the frozen funds had been illegally acquired under Swiss law — no easy task. But the progress of the investigators hired by Stroock and Stroock and Lavan, Haiti's American law firm, was greater cause for concern. Poring over banking documents and records dating back to the mid-1970s, they were compiling an exhaustive dossier. It would eventually grow to twenty thousand pages bound in seventeen volumes — a comprehensive exposé of Baby Doc's larceny. Who knew whether that information might actually lead investigators to the Duvaliers' hidden money?

According to investigators' reconstruction, sometime in the summer of 1986 — no one knows when — the Duvaliers' financial advisers developed a strategy for topping up the couple's spending kitty. The idea was to launder enough of the overall fortune to tide the couple over for a few years, or at least until their legal troubles were settled. In practice, this meant converting hard-to-spend assets — in this case, $41.8 million in Canadian treasury bills, a security backed by the government — into an easy-to-use form without disclosing the funds' origins or owners. Often this is done by emulating rich individuals and corporations who reside (formally, at least) in tax havens or conduct business there.

A number of countries around the world have set themselves up as havens. (In the case of successful ones like the Cayman Islands, it's made their citizens prosperous, their neighbours envious.) By imposing little or no tax, havens meet the needs of wealthy residents and corporations of high-tax countries like the United States and Canada. Poorer inhabitants of such countries might try to avoid taxes by participating in a tax revolt; their richer counterparts have a better option, since they can afford to set up shell companies and hire lawyers and accountants to oversee their affairs in tax havens. Thus, they can avoid paying some taxes by depositing income in a haven or channelling a transaction through it. Tax avoidance is not illegal, but "avoidance" in some havens constitutes tax evasion in other jurisdictions, and that rankles high-tax countries who correctly see the havens as drains on their national revenue. Tax havens also appeal to wealthy residents of the usually wobbly Third World, who want to put their assets into stable foreign strongboxes — endeavours which anger their often virtually insolvent governments.

To fend off the prying eyes of such rich and poor countries, havens tend to jealously guard the privacy of their customers

— a feature that also attracts the money of clients like drug dealers and fallen dictators who have more pressing needs for financial secrecy. Commonly, money launderers like to hide their tracks by passing their illegally obtained funds through a series of tax havens which preserve the confidentiality of transactions. For instance, if a launderer wanted the money to end up in the Cayman Islands, he or she might first pass it through Luxembourg and Liechtenstein. In the case of the Duvaliers, a hybrid technique was used. That is, the $41.8 million did eventually end up in bank accounts in Jersey, a haven in the Channel Islands favoured by residents of England. (Not surprisingly, a London lawyer handled much of the technical side of the affair.) To get there, the money went through the normal money laundering process, with one important variation. The Duvaliers wanted their money to end up in Jersey. The intermediaries, however, were Canada and Canadian financial institutions. Though decidedly less glamorous, the chosen route proved no less safe or effective.

"Essentially, Canada was used as a place to break paper trails and to make it difficult to trace [the $41.8 million] properly," said a source with intimate knowledge of the Duvaliers' finances who spoke on condition of anonymity. "When things were at risk, they were sent to Canada and moved around and then [sent] back to where they came from but in a cleansed and different form."

Why Canada? The answer lies, in part, in a still-confidential report jointly prepared in 1988 by the RCMP and the U.S. Drug Enforcement Administration. Though the study focused on the drug trade, it listed the features that appeal to any money launderer: "Canada's stable political climate, reasonably strong currency, and well-developed banking system make it an attractive repository or transshipment point." (This was written before the constitutional fissures of the early 1990s began to tarnish Canada's image as a bedrock of financial stability.)

To put the plan into action, the Duvaliers turned to the Swiss law firm of Patry, Junet, Simon et Le Fort. And, apparently on its advice, they also retained a softspoken British lawyer, John Stephen Matlin of the small London firm Turner and Co. He would act as a kind of technician, handling most of the day-to-day matters — opening bank accounts, setting up anonymous entities, transferring money and ensuring that the Duvaliers' cash needs were met. Jean Patry, the Swiss firm's senior partner, seemed to like keeping his distance from these clients. According to a Matlin memo, he made this abundantly clear on September 30, 1986, when he first introduced Matlin to the Duvaliers. Matlin's summary of the meeting in Nice, France, went like this: "When I returned to Nice airport, JP [Jean Patry] indicated that I was now on my own. His firm will have no further contact with the clients on this aspect."

To be sure, none of the lawyers' actions was illegal. The Duvaliers, after all, had not been convicted of any crime — and no court had ruled that the $41.8 million had been unlawfully obtained. Still, the arrangement, as outlined in the memo, did leave Matlin in the most exposed position — if only to bad publicity — should any problems have arisen.

Like the careful packing of expensive china — and, of course, like the prudent handling of confidential funds — the true ownership of the $41.8 million was masked by wrapping it in layer upon layer of concealment. For starters, there were two sets of attorneys in separate countries — Switzerland and Britain — each governed by their own client confidentiality provisions. The Duvaliers themselves were in a third location. Having to contend with three jurisdictions was, in itself, a considerable hindrance to anyone trying to subpoena documents. And that was in the unlikely event that someone stumbled onto part of the paper trail. But there was more. The banks would provide the most crucial, and mystifying, part of the protective mantle. Four separate institutions were used. The two most important were Canadian. And the funds themselves would move through three different jurisdictions: Canada, Britain and tiny Jersey.

The first step was to take the $41.8 million in treasury bills from the mother-lode and introduce it into the Canadian banking system without raising any suspicion. Patry and Matlin apparently first discussed the matter over the phone on September 10, 1986 — less than two weeks before Patry's junior partner, Alain Le Fort, visited the Royal Bank in downtown Toronto. Matlin summed up the conversation in a handwritten memo: "Where can J.P. [Jean Patry] have assets transferred? Wants securities delivered in Canada."

There was much work to be done, for major Canadian banks tread carefully when dealing with new customers. It's called "Know Your Client," a widely touted method for detecting money launderers by vetting their bona fides. Yet this system failed to prevent the entry of the Duvaliers' money. The problem was that the credentials of the couple's lawyers were impeccable, as were their references. The giant Hongkong and Shanghai Bank, for instance, introduced Matlin to the Royal Bank. Indeed, the Royal Bank went so far as to independently verify the backgrounds and references of Matlin and Le Fort. "I don't know what more you can do," said one Royal Bank official. The bank says it would certainly have turned the business away had it known who was really behind it. That it did not highlights the limitations of a cornerstone of the strategy used by both the federal government and Canadian banks to combat money laundering. (The Duvaliers' $41.8 million would likely have slipped through any Canadian institution.) In the end, nothing distinguished this transaction from similar ones involving top-notch Royal Bank clients. The moral: "Know Your Client" might deter small fry, but not the powerful and the well-connected, or those who appear to be so.

Matlin himself had some doubts about his new clients and their money, and raised the issue when he first met the Duvaliers in Nice. As a terse memo recounts: "I mentioned my firm's position that the assets belonged to them. They both gave this assurance. My request was explained to Mr. D [Jean-Claude Duvalier] in French but I believe he had understood what I was talking about." Despite the Duvaliers' word,

Matlin still had some nagging doubts, as he recounted in a memo: "[Before flying out of Nice airport], I mentioned to JP [Jean Patry] my concern about the ownership of the funds but he assured me that to the best of his knowledge, the funds belong to Mr. and Mrs. D. He mentioned the fact that Mr. D had huge inherited wealth and that Mrs. D was a wealthy lady in her own right before she married Mr. D." That seemed to set Matlin's mind at ease.

Little by little, the plan emerged. Le Fort would physically deliver the $41.8 million in treasury bills to Toronto. Why there? No one knows for sure. Some investigators suggest the securities were already in the city and there might have been some reluctance to ship them elsewhere. Both Haiti's investigators and some RCMP experts who performed a post-mortem were unable to find out where the bonds were purchased or stored prior to delivery.[42] That was not surprising, since Canadian treasury bills — popular internationally for, among other things, the ease with which they're bought and sold — are virtually anonymous. The Duvaliers' bonds could have been purchased anywhere.

On September 23, 1986, nearly eight months after the Duvaliers' flight, Le Fort delivered the $41.8 million in treasury bills to the Royal's securities department at the Royal Bank Plaza. The details had been arranged by Matlin through an official at the Hongkong and Shanghai Bank. A confidential bank memo in its files, dated September 23, 1986, described Le Fort as a Swiss national and the owner of the bonds. From Toronto, the securities were transferred to the Royal's main branch in Montreal and deposited into account no. 129-8827 on behalf of Matlin's firm, Turner and Co. The account was held by the Hongkong and Shanghai's subsidiary on Jersey, which verified the transaction in an October 8, 1986, memo.

Then a bit of clever Turner and Co. bookkeeping complicated the paper trail: the ownership records of the treasury bills were split up from the securities themselves. This kind of thing is a common tactic among international money movers — usually for tax reasons. For example, say you're listed as a taxpayer in Switzerland but have some bonds in Canada. In that case, the ownership records would be held in your tax jurisdiction, Switzerland. But to forgo the expense and bother of actually shifting the bonds across the Atlantic, you could keep them stored in a safekeeping account in Canada, which is, more or less, a kind of secure warehouse. To put it another way, it's like someone who owns a car in Paris but lives in Winnipeg. She keeps the ownership papers in her filing cabinet, but stores the vehicle in a secure parking garage in Paris. Turner and Co. gained no tax advantage or higher interest by splitting the securities. The only benefit was that the spoor grew fainter. The records went to a Turner and Co. account at the Royal Bank in London, England; the treasury bills were shifted into a Royal Bank safekeeping account in Montreal. A bank receipt dated October 30, 1986 confirmed the transaction.

On October 24, 1986, in Nice, the Duvaliers approved the procedure at a lengthy meeting with Matlin, who later recorded the details in a brief memo. It said that more than half the cash, $30.507 million, would eventually go into what Matlin termed account no. 1; the balance of $11.303 million would be deposited into account no. 2. Further, the money was to be changed from Canadian funds into U.S. dollars. Written in Matlin's precise script was the Duvaliers' address, Villa Mohamedia, 204, chemin du Château, 06250 Mougins; their private telephone number, 38–16–32; and a number to call in emergencies, 39–01–69. (Ask for Franz, Matlin was told — Michele's brother Franz Bennett.) Provisions had also been made in case either Michele or Jean-Claude died. Their two children, Nicholas and Anya, would be taken care of. So would Alex and Sasha Pasquet, children of Mrs. Duvalier's first marriage. And the memo listed the Duvaliers' own financial needs, which totalled $390,000 US and would be met through bank drafts. All seemed in order. The Duvaliers gave their OK in a letter addressed to Boncardo Ltd., a corporate front that Matlin had set up on their behalf on Jersey. (Company formation fee: £1,599.05 sterling.)

The next step in the plan was to cash the treasury bills. The process was spread over four transactions in late 1986. Matlin issued the instructions to the Royal's London office, which acknowledged completing the deals in letters dated November 19, December 8, December 24 and December 29. The Royal charged a small amount for this service — in one case just $84.50. Like everything else in the operation, depositing the cash was anything but direct. It was more like a perverse banker's version of the Russian doll-within-a-doll. The money was put into an unusual kind of account — no. 6001–101527–501 — held by the Royal Trust Bank, a wholly owned Jersey subsidiary of Canada's Royal Trust Co. What set this account apart was that it wasn't free-standing. Rather, it was part of a larger account held by yet another financial institution — Manufacturers Hanover Bank of Canada. And it wasn't where you'd expect it to be — in London, Montreal or even Jersey. No, it was at the Royal Bank's correspondent banking facilities in Toronto, a few minutes' walk from where the $41.8 million had been delivered on September 23. Correspondent banking is a holdover from the days when banks didn't have branches around the world. A bank in one country would retain the services of a bank in another (their correspondent bank) so that they could do business in that country without actually having an office there.

Once the money, totalling $30.2 million US, had been deposited in the Royal Trust Bank account in Toronto, it was transferred to two accounts at the Royal Trust Bank in Jersey. They were operated by Matlin's firm on behalf of Boncardo, the Duvaliers' ghost company. There the money quickly earned interest, chalking up $178,000 US between October 31, 1986, and January 12, 1987, in account no. 783617-841 alone.

A little more than three months after Alain Le Fort made his delivery to the Royal Bank in Toronto, the operation was nearly complete. All that remained were some technical details. Topping the list was the couple's ever-present cash needs. Matlin took care of that by asking Royal Trust in Jersey to issue cheques payable to the bearer. Royal Trust had reservations about this because so-called bearer cheques are as good as cash. As their name implies, they can be redeemed by whoever holds them. Royal Trust complied only after Matlin gave guarantees absolving the institution of any liability in case the bearer cheques were lost or stolen once in his possession. The first four bearer cheques — for $25,000 US apiece — were then quickly drawn on the two Royal Trust Bank accounts. Dated January 22, 1987, they were personally delivered to Mrs. Duvalier by Matlin. A few days later, she signed two letters authorizing Boncardo Ltd. to make two payments to Patry, Junet, Simon et Le Fort. One, for $180,000 US, was "to discharge fees for children's schooling." The second, for $20,000, was simply "to discharge notary fees."

When February 7, 1987, the anniversary of their flight to France, rolled around, the Duvaliers were able to breathe a sigh of relief. Lawyers acting for Haiti might be busy tracking down assets and launching court cases on both sides of the Atlantic, but the location of their spending money had been painstakingly concealed. They had hired discreet lawyers in two countries, and they had set up an intricately concealed flow of money through a bevy of banks and accounts, most of them Canadian. The paper trail would send even the most experienced auditor on a long chase. And finally there was the protection provided by Jersey's financial secrecy, which extended over both the Duvaliers' bank accounts and their ghost company, Boncardo. Adding to their peace of mind was the poor track record of countries trying to recover the looted funds of deposed dictators.

Their worries were over. At least for the time being.

■ 2 WHY IS MONEY LAUNDERING SO HARD TO STOP?

L ess than a generation ago, the term "money laundering" was confined to the demi-mondes of big-time crime and international intrigue. Then along came Watergate. With its juicy tales of secret payoffs stuffed into brown paper bags and suitcases of cash funnelled through Mexico, the American scandal of 1973–74 turned "money laundering" into a household word. [1]

The term's linguistic roots, however, are much murkier — rather like laundering schemes and techniques themselves. According to the underworld's hazy lore, it dates back to Prohibition days when the U.S. ban on alcohol created scores of shadowy fortunes. The *nouveau riche* gangsters of the 1920s apparently discovered that the hefty profits generated from illegal booze sales created equally weighty problems — namely, increased scrutiny from both police and tax collectors. What they needed were rock-solid alibis for their bootlegging revenues. Many solutions were tried. In Chicago, criminal entrepreneurs like the brash, flamboyant Al Capone settled on a simple tack — giving their illegal earnings a legitimate veneer by funnelling them through actual clothing laundries.2

Whether the term actually grew out of such schemes is anyone's guess, though it does seem plausible. One of the few Capone contemporaries to discuss the matter was an elderly New Yorker by the name of Joseph "Doc" Stacher. But the former bootlegger's memories weren't recorded until just before his death in 1977, and by then he couldn't recall "who first decided to call the system 'laundering.' " There was nothing fuzzy about Stacher's explanation of the process, however: "to wash clean, by that I mean to make legal."3

His definition is just as valid today. At heart, money laundering involves "passing money through a very secret sieve (like a Swiss bank) or through a series of extraordinarily complicated transactions that disguise its true origin or purpose."4 Put another way, it's a kind of financial filter. Funds to be camouflaged enter at one end and emerge at the other with their pedigrees carefully disguised. Concealment is not enough, however. The ultimate goal is to obscure the origins of those funds so that they can be used without raising the least suspicion. That often involves transferring them to a foreign country and later retrieving them from what seem to be legitimate sources in that country or any other.5

All kinds of people, in all kinds of countries, and in all sorts of circumstances, launder their money. The two most important kinds of laundered funds are "dirty money" and "black money."6 "Dirty money" is a thread linking many of the world's most odious callings. There are dictators and corrupt public officials, for instance, who hide funds stolen from public treasuries, the largest known diversions being in the Third World or in former Communist countries. When the French magazine *Le Point* examined this situation, it discovered a disturbing pattern of financial outflows from the developing world between 1975 and 1985 — a period when the balance sheets of many countries in Latin America and Africa were swamped with debt. During that decade, it estimates, $150 billion US coursed from the Third World into the secret foreign accounts of crooked leaders and officials.[7] Then there are drug barons, residing in lavish estates in places like Colombia, Sicily or Thailand, who legitimize the dirty profits from cocaine and heroin. Among the other members of this group are crooked spy agencies (like those in some former Eastern European nations, who were laws unto themselves); terrorist groups, like the Irish Republican Army, whose coffers are often topped up from extortion and racketeering; and white-collar criminals who profit from stock market manipulations and various forms of fraud.

"Black money," on the other hand, is legally accumulated and typically held by otherwise respectable people. It becomes illegal not in the earning but in the laundering process, which takes two basic forms. There's money that's usually laundered through a foreign country to evade a home country's tax laws — a common reason why so much Italian money ends up in Switzerland — and there's money secretly sent abroad by jittery residents of volatile countries (often in the Third World) that restrict exports of money. Eluding the taxman is a possible secondary benefit, though not the primary impetus for such exports, which are often grouped under the broad label of flight capital. Flight capital can also refer to money legally escaping political and economic uncertainties; for instance, if large sums of money were to bolt out of a Canada collapsing from the separation of Quebec, those funds would also be called flight capital. (It would be interesting to see whether in such dire circumstances Ottawa might clamp down on the current system of unfettered capital flows. Or whether it could.)

The loss of flight capital can be a huge drain on a country's economy. In the 1980s, officials in many Latin American countries — especially Brazil, Argentina and Mexico — lost the battle to stem large exports of money. In the process, as much as $400 billion US flowed out of the region, exacerbating its economic woes. By the early 1990s, however, there

were signs that some of the flight capital was returning —
thanks to the emergence of democracy and political stability
in the aforementioned countries and elsewhere.[8]

Far less stigma is attached to "black money" than to "dirty
money." No country, after all, wants to be seen warmly greet-
ing drug profits or the proceeds of a commercial fraud. Attracting "black money" is another matter. Switzerland and
Luxembourg, for example, do not mind abetting tax evasion
in other jurisdictions. Flight capital is even more widely con-
doned. Most Western bankers don't think twice about accepting the flight capital that officials in destitute countries try to
keep at home in order to prop up their local economy. This is
hardly surprising. The governments of most rich countries
firmly believe in — and clearly benefit from — the free flow
of money, even if, as critics claim, its departure creates hardships among their poorer brethren. In the world of international finance, one man's illicit flight capital is another's
injection of fresh investment.

For a snapshot of the kinds of sums laundered worldwide, all
you need to do is examine some spectacular "dirty money"
fortunes. According to *Forbes* magazine, Pablo Escobar, the
reputed head of Colombia's once dominant Medellin cocaine
cartel, tucked away an estimated $3 billion US.[9] Or consider
Mobutu Sese Seko, the self-styled "Citizen-President" of
mineral-rich Zaire. According to a U.S. Congressional estimate, he's salted away a personal bonanza of $2.5 billion
US.[10] As Jack Blum, a former U.S. Senate investigator, says:
"There is a large black market in money."

How large is anyone's guess, though some stratospheric
estimates touch the $1-trillion-a-year mark. Precise figures are
impossible to generate. Clandestine money movers, after all,
don't publish annual reports. And a similar silence envelops
their favourite playgrounds — tax havens. Havens come in
many shapes and sizes, but their most important legitimate
service is always the same — allowing people from high-tax
countries to discreetly avoid taxes by channelling transactions

or depositing income outside their countries of residence. They aim to meet the needs of clients who live by a simple credo: "To make as much money as possible while paying as little tax as possible — while making sure no one knows you have done it."[11]

A Canadian corporation, for instance, might sell a product to a subsidiary in a tax haven for a low price. The product would then be resold elsewhere for much more — with the bulk of the profit remaining in the haven. Or take a self-employed Canadian engineer who operates mostly abroad. He might work for a corporation he had set up in a haven. Clients would pay his fees directly to the corporation in the haven — rather than to Canada, where a higher tax would have to be paid.

The popularity of such perfectly legal tax-avoidance systems is precisely why havens are so useful in laundering dirty and black money. For without an extensive veneer of legitimacy, there would be nothing in havens to mask murkier activities. For example, the tax-haven company used by the Canadian engineer might be little more than a brass plate on a wall and a slim, uninformative file in a corporate registry. Coupled with the tight financial secrecy laws of most havens, it would be virtually impossible to find out who ultimately owned the company, what kind of business it was involved in and what amounts of money flowed through its accounts. An appealing set of factors to anyone needing to launder tainted funds — like the notorious Wall Street banker, Dennis Levine. In the 1980s, he rinsed $10 million US in insider stock-trading profits through such corporations in the Cayman Islands.

Tax havens maintain high levels of secrecy in order to retain the business of their wealthy customers. Without secrecy, their clients' countries would possibly be able to examine the offshore activities of clients and thereby prosecute them — since, as noted earlier, tax avoidance according to the tax haven might constitute (illegal) tax evasion in a high-tax country. Similar differences of opinion occur over the legitimacy of flight capital.

In spite of the secrecy surrounding funds in tax havens, some experts have tried to take the pulse of particular kinds of "dirty money" flows — especially those involving the drug trade. For example, a confidential report by the RCMP and the U.S. Drug Enforcement Administration in 1988 estimated that "the total amount of drug-related money that passes between the United States and Canada is probably in the hundreds of millions of dollars annually." The results of efforts to measure drug profits more precisely are mixed. A task force of the Group of Seven, the club of the seven most powerful Western economies, including Canada, had a hellish time coming up with a worldwide total. According to one participant who prefers anonymity, the discussions were often heated, with many experts advising against putting a precise figure on such a subterranean commerce. The Americans took the opposite tack and won out. The final report, released in 1990 in Paris, reckoned that every year launderers wash $85 billion — more than twice Ireland's gross national product — in profits churned up by the drug trade in North America and Europe. [12] According to the dissenting participant, this figure is at best a rough approximation; at worst, meaningless.

It is just as difficult to get a sense of the magnitude of the world's furtive money by looking at the huge sums that pass through offshore financial centres. These are special kinds of havens that typically blend attractive tax rates with looser regulations over financial institutions, and modern banking facilities. In a place like the Cayman Islands, that combination attracts some of the world's most important banks, who use the Caymans as a "booking centre," to "book," or register, loans in a low-tax milieu. Not all financial flows passing through such offshore centres are visible, nor are they necessarily illicit. However, according to one estimate in the *Economist*, the British newspaper, more than half the $500 billion that moved from the offshore into Western banks in 1989 was "dirty money" of some sort.[13]

That figure may be inflated; the previously mentioned $1 trillion figure obviously was. But corroborating such a breakdown is a hopeless task. As a federal study into money laundering concluded in 1990: "There is no verifiable method for determining the size of the illicit economy. Estimated figures in this area of illicit proceeds, however carefully calculated, are only guesses. Once stated they take on a reality they do not deserve."[14]

Make no mistake, in money laundering, the edge is clearly on the side of its practitioners. Thus a blunt, irascible, white-haired banker told the Senate banking committee in October 1985. "You can move money around so fast now to so many different places through several legal jurisdictions, some of which have very strict laws against disclosure, that it isn't even funny," said William Mulholland, then head of the Bank of Montreal. Though speaking in general terms, he could easily have been depicting the efforts made one year later to conceal Duvalier's fortune. "I have spent thirty-three years in the financial industry one way or another and one of the main reasons that people create complicated financial structures is to create veils."

Flanked by two aides, Mulholland gloated: "I can hide money in the twinkling of an eye from all the bloodhounds that could be put on the case, and I would be so far ahead of them there would never be a hope of unravelling the trail. I am not kidding you. Technology today means that sort of thing can be done by electronic means. In a day, money can be moved through Winnipeg, Toronto, New York, Miami, the Cayman Islands, the Bahamas and into Switzerland, and I defy anyone to unravel that trail."

Mulholland had first-hand experience. In a voice that still bore the lilt of his American background, he recounted a fraud that he'd helped authorities try to unravel in the United States: "This case involved some money that started in Chicago, went to New York, to the Cayman Islands, to the Bahamas and into Switzerland, just like that. It was a hopeless case. The Cayman Islands authorities stonewalled the investigators, the Bahamian authorities stonewalled them, and, of course, the Swiss didn't even talk to them."[15] (Financial secrecy is so important to the viability of havens like the Caymans and the Bahamas that they breach it only in very special circumstances.)

Money laundering schemes do not have to be this intricate to be effective. In fact, their complexity varies with the need at hand. A low-level drug trafficker would not require an offshore shell company or a Cayman Islands bank account. All he'd need is a simple way of caching his week's take of $2,000 — usually in $10 and $20 bills. The solution might be something as rudimentary as opening ten accounts under ten different names in ten different financial institutions. The one difficulty would be obtaining ten separate forged identities. But that's not insurmountable — especially for the right price and for someone in his milieu. Day in and day out, he would put a small deposit in each of the ten accounts — say $20 to $40 a day, totalling $200 a week. Who would notice such seemingly innocuous money movements?

At the opposite end of the spectrum are more sophisticated techniques involving the buying and selling of goods and services. "There are so many opportunities to move money hidden in commercial transactions that it's most difficult to tell which are legitimate and which aren't," says Rod Stamler, a former assistant RCMP commissioner who's now a forensic investigator in Toronto. "If somebody goes to any trouble at all to disguise the transaction, it's virtually impossible to detect it."

One popular way of secretly whisking disputed funds out of a country is by using phoney invoices. That is, you pay a foreign company for reasonable-sounding services it never provided.

A similar technique is called over-invoicing. In a typical scenario, a foreign business partner overcharges you (the money launderer) for a particular shipment or service. To conceal the fact that you are laundering illicit funds, you might tell your business partner that you're pulling off a tax dodge — an easy-to-swallow alibi, since duping the taxman — legally or illegally — is popular around the globe. (And of course, an illegal tax dodge incurs a lesser penalty than laundering illicit funds.) Or, to tug at your partner's heartstrings, you might say you want to move money abroad because you're afraid the economy will hit the skids and ruin your family.

Thus, a shipment of tractors imported into Canada might be invoiced as costing $2 million instead of $1.5 million. Or a consulting study might be billed for $200,000, instead of $100,000. The discrepancy — the $500,000 in the first example, and the $100,000 in the second — would include a fee to the foreign partner, plus the money you're trying to move offshore. As Stamler noted, detecting such a manoeuvre is very difficult. Who's to say, for instance, that the tractors weren't worth $2 million or the study, $200,000? If the foreign business partner were questioned, she could, at the very least, claim that you overpaid because you were outfoxed by a superior salesperson.

In some cases, the same laundering techniques can be used to wash different kinds of "dirty" and "black" money. As Javier Gonzalez Fraga, former president of Argentina's central bank, put it: "All banks in Argentina are involved in handling black money of some kind . . . and do so using the same channels as drug money launderers."[16] A Peruvian strongman, a Colombian drug dealer, a Brazilian terrorist, and a Venezuelan businessman worried about domestic unrest might perform a similar range of manoeuvres to rinse their secret funds.

They might, for instance, graft their schemes onto the system described earlier that allows multinational corporations to legally reduce their taxes by funnelling profits from a high-tax country to a tax haven. An international company with subsidiaries in Colombia, Canada and the tax haven, for instance, might want to export toys from Colombia to Canada and avoid paying any taxes on the profits made in Canada. Say the toys cost $100,000 and the company expected the deal to put it a further $100,000 in the black. It would first sell the toys to its tax-haven subsidiary for $100,000. The subsidiary, in turn, would market the toys to the branch in Canada for what the toys cost, plus the company's profit — that is, for $200,000. At that price, the Canadian branch would roughly break even, but show no earnings in its annual tax return. The profit — $100,000 — would have been earned, on paper at least, by the subsidiary in the tax haven.

Furthermore, it would be very simple to hide "dirty" or "black" money within such a transaction — through a technique called under-invoicing. As the name implies, it's the opposite of the previously described over-invoicing technique. To launder $10,000 in flight capital or drug profits out of Colombia, the company would top up the shipment to Canada with extra toys worth $10,000 in sales. The additional toys would never show up in documents in Colombia: the invoices would still disclose exports worth $100,000. However, the Canadian subsidiary would be charged $210,000 by the subsidiary in the tax haven — including the $10,000 in profit from the additional toys. That money would never be reported in Colombia. It would remain in the tax haven, unnoticed by Bogotá authorities.

To be sure, such techniques can result in some absurd distortions in the prices of trade goods. Two American researchers analyzed the average cost in 1990 of commodities traded between the United States and other countries. They found indications of huge sums being hidden in commercial transactions. In 1990, for instance, Colombia sold razor blades to the United States for an average of $34.81 apiece — considerably more than the world norm of nine cents per blade. Such an outlandish figure points to an over-invoicing scheme — which inflates the cost of Colombian exports to mask money covertly moving out of the United States. In view of the size of the illicit cocaine trade, one can only imagine what kinds of profits at least some of those razor exports helped to conceal. On the flip side, the researchers at Florida International University came across U.S. sales to Colombia of antibiotics at a staggering 10,254 percent of the world price. That's obviously an indication of the same technique being used in reverse — to shift funds past Colombian currency export controls. Flight capital perhaps?[17]

Much conspires to make money laundering an elusive process to root out. "It's like nailing jelly to a wall," laments one Canadian bank security official. For one thing, no matter how shady the origins of the funds or elaborate the scheme, laundering transactions are not necessarily illegal, though they may, of course, be unquestionably immoral. Jean-Claude Baby Doc Duvalier's $41.8 million is a case in point. Nothing about the operation was illegal: not the financial transactions; not the use of legally constituted front companies and properly accredited lawyers; and not the $41.8 million itself. Though the money was clearly stolen, that was never proven in a court of law. And yet, there's no doubt that Duvalier funnelled the money through Canada for just one reason — to conceal its origins so he could freely spend it.

Another complicating factor is that much of the world is governed by an international patchwork quilt of differing rules and regulations and uneven policing. A transaction that's considered illegal in one jurisdiction may be permitted in another. This makes it difficult to prosecute offenders. For instance, Marc Rich, an international financier based in Switzerland, faces a number of fraud, racketeering and tax evasion charges in the United States. However, the Swiss refuse to extradite him because the charges "are only violations of either currency, economic or fiscal measures."[18] Under Swiss law, such violations in a foreign jurisdiction do not warrant extradition.

The result is a heavenly situation for drug money launderers. "Major traffickers are taking advantage of variations in national laws and regulations to engage in international laundering operations," concluded a 1991 report by the RCMP. "Differences in bank secrecy provisions and record-keeping practices often obscure the audit or paper trail, while diplomatic obstacles and distinctions between national judicial systems restrict international criminal investigations."[19]

These variations make it extremely difficult to tell legitimate transactions from illegitimate ones, as the Metro Toronto police discovered during their investigation of a small,

Toronto travel agency. Their probe began when it was discovered that in just two months, the agency had handled $16 million worth of business — a whopping eight times as much as a comparable storefront agency would transact in a whole year. That wasn't all that was odd about the volume of money. The $16 million had arrived in cash — not the way most people buy their airline tickets or Florida vacations. Then there was the money's peculiar destination. From Toronto, it was transferred first to New York, then to Argentina and finally to Colombia, home of the world's biggest cocaine exporters.

If the thought crossed your mind that this agency may be in the business of hiding drug profits, you wouldn't be alone. The late Craig Law had a similar suspicion. Law — burly, intense and middle-aged — was a Detective Sergeant in the Metropolitan Toronto Police's crack Intelligence Unit. He was also its top money laundering expert.

"We looked at the amount of money going through it," he said. "It was like multi-million dollars . . . and it didn't represent the number of [travel] tickets being sold."

We spoke in Law's cramped, windowless cubbyhole at the Intelligence Unit in March 1992, a few weeks before his death. In nearby offices decorated with mug shots, maps and eccentric mementoes scooped up in countless undercover operations, other hard-driven souls were poring over thick files or beavering away at computer keyboards. Law had spent many years grappling with money laundering's diverse, chameleon-like forms. It had been as much an obsession as a job and, as he explained in the case of the small travel agency, telling the licit from the illicit had been a continuing source of frustration.

"I spent an exhaustive amount of time and manpower looking at this investigation," he said, a note of exasperation in his voice, for it had ultimately led nowhere. Over cups of strong, black coffee, he explained how, in his many attempts to get more information from South American banks — to discover the ultimate destination of the funds — he had been stonewalled every time. Equally frustrating were the travel agency's financial records — which successfully blended the

$16 million with more standard business activities. In such cases of "co-mingled money," he said, it's virtually impossible to distinguish between "what is the legitimate money and what is the illegal money."

In the end, his results were meagre. There were instances of "creative bookkeeping," which is not a crime, and he had "a rough explanation" of where the money was coming from — a bizarre, sparsely documented scheme to profit from the foreign exchange market. But there was nothing tangible: "No matter how much I looked at it, I just couldn't come up with a designated drug offence nor an enterprise crime." Law paused for a moment, his eyes narrowing slightly. Obviously, the case still rankled. "And yet," he said, his voice rising, "I have a little travel agency with multi-million-dollars in cash." He shook his head. "Laundering is extremely difficult to prove."

Ultimately, the factor that facilitates laundering of all kinds — and hinders those trying to expose the washing of "dirty" funds — is a particular quality of money, one that also makes it both useful and indispensable in modern commerce. Money, of course, is many things. It's a handy medium of exchange and a safe, imperishable cache of wealth. Thanks to money, there's no need to haul a horse when going to buy some casks of wine, or worry that it might break a leg in transit.[20] Significantly for merchant and launderer alike, money is also an anonymous, easy-to-transfer store of value — inflation and economic upheaval notwithstanding. Coins that purchased ale in the morning can pay for a book in the afternoon. Coins gained criminally don't look much different from ones honestly acquired. They retain their value no matter how they are used or obtained — or who owned them.

The Roman emperor Vespasian was probably the first to identify this trait of money. One day, he decided to increase his revenues by taxing public toilets. The Romans objected and none more so than his mortified son, Titus, who complained: "The money stinks." Not so, replied the emperor. As proof, he held a coin to his son's nose and asked if it smelled. The chastened Titus agreed that it didn't reek. Yet, noted Vespasian, it's made from urine and faeces.[21] The resulting adage — "pecunia non olet" or, roughly, "money has no smell" — proved so memorable that it survived long after Vespasian's death in 79 A.D.. Right to this day, in fact.

Vespasian's message was a practical one: The most fundamental characteristic of money is not whether it's clean or dirty or black — that is, its pedigree or the way it's processed — but a host of other factors. Can I spend it anywhere in the world or just in my neck of the woods? Will it be worth less tomorrow than today or, in the case of hyper-inflation-sufferers in Latin America, this afternoon? Is it therefore better to horde it or to quickly exchange it for more valuable gasoline, bread or livestock?

The world financial system is similary anonymous. Its merit does not hinge on the relative purity of the money flowing through its arteries. More important are such things as whether it can efficiently allocate capital, quickly settle cheques and adeptly support the international flow of goods and services. Hence, there is an unusual symbiosis between a fundamental characteristic of the world economy (one that helps ensure our collective prosperity) and what facilitates money laundering. Nearly two thousand years ago, this essential neutrality of money is what allowed Vespasian to reap his levy.

He certainly would have marvelled at the many forms that today's money can take, though he would not likely have been surprised by the ease with which legitimate and "dirty" funds can mingle. If his coins bore no smell, the electronic blips that are the workhorses of modern banking have gone one better. Not only are they odourless, they can't even be held or seen. Only a small fraction of the world's money supply exists in tangible form as bills and coins. Most of it lies in silicone-chip repositories as electronic bookkeeping notations stored deep in the computer databases of banks.

Confirming this concept, a Canadian judge ruled in 1985 in the influential Pinto case (named after Luis Pinto, an

American-based money launderer) that "a credit balance is an intangible, merely proof that the bank has certain sums on deposit." A bookkeeping notation, he wrote, is therefore not a tangible asset. This judgment prevented police from seizing tainted funds that Pinto had deposited in a Montreal bank. It led to an uproar in the Canadian law enforcement community and the eventual passage of Canada's anti-money-laundering law, which took effect in 1989.

In spite of this new law, however, it is difficult to compile evidence against money launderers who work the international financial system to their advantage. In just minutes and for a few dollars, you can ship $1 million halfway around the world. Indeed, every working day, tens of thousands of transactions worth hundreds of billions of dollars sail through the world's financial pipelines — ferried on the backs of tiny electronic signals. In Canada alone, electronic money transfers top the $1-trillion-a-year mark. On any given day, the Royal Bank handles between $3.5 billion and $4 billion in foreign exchange and more than $1 billion in securities.

All these transactions fit Vespasian's adage, too. Each tends to look like any other of the same type — much as one dollar resembles another. Money is used to pay for imports and exports — to buy alumina from Jamaica, for example, or to sell Quebec newsprint to Spain. It can also be loaned or invested in another country — to build a bottling plant in Zimbabwe or open a fast-food outlet in Poland. There's speculative money chasing around the world — looking to profit from the tiny differences between the value of currencies in various markets. In foreign exchange trading alone, the daily worldwide turnover is more than $600 billion US. Finally, there's money taking part in the dizzying twenty-four-hour-a-day global trading in shares and financial instruments. Spotting "dirty" and "black" money among the clean in this vast torrent is nearly impossible.

Money laundering is a financially rewarding endeavour for those who can afford the fees and who can stomach having to associate with an often unsavoury crowd. "The notion that providing clandestine financial services to those in need of secrecy can be extraordinarily lucrative is self-evident," says Ingo Walter, the American economist.[22] The high price of these services is why street-corner drug dealers and other minor operators may try to conceal their profits themselves. "Small traffickers often lack the expertise and contacts to engage in sophisticated laundering operations," said an RCMP report in 1990.[23] Some American mobsters, for instance, once eschewed laundering in favour of a simpler pursuit: interring cash. According to *Forbes* magazine, "one retired FBI agent still remembers how the bail money one Mafioso posted smelled musty from long-term burial."[24]

Bigger fish, however, tend to rely on specialists to provide an alibi to cover up their dubious profits. Many are professionals, law and accounting being especially popular backgrounds for anyone wanting to get into the money washing business. A federal report listed some of the attractive attributes of those two vocations: "Unique expertise, high social status and credibility among the financial community, and in the case of lawyers, special solicitor-client privileges that the justice system grants to the legal profession."[25]

Take Gary Casilio, convicted in Calgary in 1991 of trying to launder millions in drug profits. No flies on this former top-notch Vancouver lawyer. As an ex-partner told the Vancouver *Province:* "He had a strong constitution and great stamina. He was very competent at what he did. He's a charming man."[26] But you don't have to be a lawyer to be a proficient money launderer, as Montrealer William Obront proved. The Quebec Crime Commission in the 1970s found that the millionaire meat packer and nightclub owner had sanitized more than $83 million in dirty money through scores of business and corporate fronts.[27]

The Casilios and Obronts of the world ultimately sell just one commodity — financial secrecy. Walter, the American economist and a pioneer in analyzing money laundering, says the cost of financial secrecy "depends mainly on the perceived personal and financial cost of disclosure. The higher the cost, the greater the willingness to pay."[28] In practice, this works out to a percentage of the amount washed, depending on the difficulty of the task and the notoriety of the client. The safest kinds of shady funds might cost 3 to 4 percent to launder; the dirtiest varieties, 10 percent or more.

The origins of money laundering's core product — financial secrecy — are nearly as old as banking itself. Ancient Babylonia, the first banking society, provides the earliest, albeit indirect, reference to financial secrecy. The Code of Hammurabi, named after a Babylonian king who lived around 1800 B.C., sets out a strict condition under which a banker could publicly divulge his private records — only in the case of a conflict with a client. Otherwise, they had to remain sealed.[29]

Refinements began in the sixteenth century with the dawn of modern banking. In 1593 came the first written reference to bank secrecy: "You are not to give information to other people, except to the [depositor], his attorneys and heirs, under penalty of losing office or greater sanction." (This statement appeared in the statutes of an ancient Italian bank that would be at the centre of a huge financial scandal in the 1980s: the Banco Ambrosiano.) In 1693 Louis XIII of France went further, issuing a Royal Decree which stated: "Banking secrecy is absolutely necessary in negotiations involving banking, money-exchange, commerce and finance."[30]

But it is the Swiss who have become best known for financial secrecy. According to the popular version of the story, in 1934 the Swiss passed a tough law on bank secrecy to protect Jewish depositors from the rapacious Nazis. The truth is a little different. As British journalist Nicholas Faith discovered: "Its acceptance depends on a total lack of historical curiosity." He marshalled convincing evidence showing that the Swiss law was instituted for a less noble purpose — commercial self-interest.[31] According to Faith, what mainly motivated the Swiss was the fact that some of their major banks were heading for bankruptcy because foreign funds had been withdrawn in large quantities. The greatest cause of uncertainty among foreign depositors was persistent efforts by the French government to penetrate Swiss financial secrecy and inspect the Swiss bank accounts of its citizens. As he put it: "The case of the Swiss Discount Bank [which went under in 1934] had shown that the rush would be greatly accelerated if foreign depositors' confidence in the impregnability of Swiss banking secrecy was not restored by some positive measure."[32]

Financial secrecy has other, less obvious, side effects. For instance, there are great perils and benefits — depending on which side of the bank counter you're on — in the event of a secret account holder's death. Among the legacies of the twentieth century's two world wars were unclaimed secret accounts that "boosted the fortunes of many European banks . . . the Russian revolution wiped out some of their richest, and most secretive clients."[33] If the holder of a numbered account dies and no one else in the family knows the location and code of the account (or perhaps even of its existence), there is then no one to claim the money. In such cases, a bank is supposed to try to trace the next of kin. But if they too were killed, as happened to many Russian aristocrats in 1917, or to victims of the Holocaust, then the money typically either reverts to the bank or to the victim's country of origin.

In itself, financial secrecy is not such a bad thing. Who, after all, wants the whole world to know what they're worth? What corporation wants its competitors peering into its financial affairs? The difficulty is in differentiating between the kind of secrecy we all want and the kind that protects the profits of a drug lord or a dictator. No easy task. It's at the heart of one of the many headaches faced by banks wanting to fend off money launderers.

Consultant Chuck Morley, a former investigator with the U.S. Internal Revenue Service, knows this first-hand. One of his clients, a multinational bank he won't identify, went through the "Draconian exercise" of sifting through every account to ensure there were no bad apples among its clients.

The scale of the operation was massive: it involved examining thousands of people and firms, and tens of thousands of complex transactions. Indeed, the probe unwittingly proved to be a litmus test of many widely touted approaches to spotting dirty money — since Morley's investigators used the latest techniques and criteria to certify the legitimacy of customers. Many of these techniques were developed by government agencies and banks who advocate deterring money laundering by making a greater effort to discern who their customers are. The results of the operation were mixed — raising doubts about the potential usefulness of the "know your client" approach.

"It was unbelievably difficult to separate the wheat from the chaff," Morley told a U.S. Senate subcommittee. "And we knew the customers in many cases. . . . We would have a foreign exchange, for instance. We would see millions of dollars coming on shore and going offshore through branches of this company. But then you look at that, you say is this drug money or this legitimate money? How do you know the difference? We had a hard time coming up with the answer to that."[34]

So why spend so much time trying to spot the bad apples? Indeed, why worry about money laundering at all? For the simple reason that this chameleon-like trade is a point of vulnerability — since it's essential to those who profit from many of the world's ills.

What if dictators like Jean-Claude Duvalier of Haiti and the late Ferdinand Marcos of the Philippines had not been able to safely salt away their stolen loot? Imagine the food, housing and doctors the Duvalier and Marcos fortunes could have provided for the millions of residents in the fetid slums of Port-au-Prince or Manila.

By the same token, the international commerce in narcotics would be greatly affected if the billions of dollars in annual proceeds could not be cleansed. There was a time when progress in the battle against drugs was measured by the amounts seized. Yet no matter how much cocaine or heroin was nabbed, prices rarely rose. There was always more than enough supply to meet the demand.

That is why today's drug cops favour targeting the systems that allow cocaine barons and heroin kingpins to accumulate and enjoy their assets. Payments to pushers — in return for a snort of cocaine or a hit of heroin — are the drug trade's lifeblood. To concentrate only on pushers and smugglers is akin to "putting General Motors out of business by arresting car dealers," says Jack Blum, the former U.S. Senate investigator.

The potential benefits of effectively attacking those who profit most from the drug trade are appealing. Consider the human cost of the tens of thousands of narcotic abusers living miserably in scores of big cities — from Miami to Montreal and from Venice to Vancouver. Consider, too, the millions more affected by the wider social problems created by the drug trade. The economic harm of illegal drug use in Canada is estimated at $4.6 billion a year, according to the Addiction Research Foundation. And, of course, taxpayers foot the bills for police efforts against drugs and for the pitifully few rehabilitation programs for its victims. Taxpayers and consumers should take note for other reasons as well. They feel the pinch whenever potential tax revenues — no matter how illicitly earned — are siphoned offshore, or when fraudsters rip off businesses and secretly funnel the profits overseas, or when banks have to impose costly, anti-money-laundering measures.

Politicians seem to be listening. Since the washing of drug money is the most talked-about form of laundering, politicians seen to be against it are sure to get votes. A pledge to attack the rinsing of drug profits was a centrepiece of the 1988 summit in Toronto of the leaders of the seven most powerful Western economies. (Mention of battling other kinds of dirty money, including those filling the pockets of dictators, was conspicuously absent. Such are the exigencies of realpolitik.) In late 1990, European finance ministers agreed on a common set of regulations against the rinsing of drug profits. The United Nations, too, is stepping up its efforts.

It is the United States, however, that has led the charge. The issue has been dealt with in a slew of Congressional hearings. Tough laws are in place, including regulations forcing financial institutions to file reports on all cash transactions greater than $10,000. And scores of law enforcement strike forces are up and running. The Americans are leaning on their allies too. Canada, for one, has felt the heat, as some previously confidential diplomatic cables show. Amid U.S. charges that Canada was "a laundromat" for drug money, the Canadian embassy in Washington rushed home a classified cable (released under the Access to Information Act) on October 6, 1989: "America is turning to its friends and allies to join the battle and provide both moral and material support. . . . In terms of our interests, it is important that we be perceived as doing 'our share.' "

As has happened so often in the past, the Americans hadn't been paying attention to their northern neighbour. If they had, they would have seen that Canada was, in fact, trying to pitch in. The government is implementing tighter record-keeping requirements on all financial institutions, and on professionals, like lawyers, who handle clients' money in trust accounts. This will make it easier for police to follow paper trails. And on January 1, 1989, under Bill C-61, money laundering became a crime. Though the law has many weaknesses, it has resulted in some successes, including the fact that more drug assets have been seized since its enactment than before the legislation was in place: $38 million worth in 1989, up sharply from $2.7 million in 1984. During the first three years of the law's existence, $60 million in assets were seized. In one case in May 1990, for example, the RCMP nabbed a Quebec ski resort, four condos, two houses and an assortment of vehicles, including a $100,000 Mercedes-Benz. All the assets — totalling $6 million — had belonged to a successful drug ring operating out of North Hatley, in Quebec's Eastern Townships.

Canadian banks are joining the fray, too, implementing

tougher internal measures against drug money. And they're voluntarily turning over dozens of suspicious instances each month to law enforcement — so many, it turns out, that police are often swamped with solid tips.

So far, however, the overall results in Canada have been less than spectacular. The Mounties have discovered that assets are easier to seize than manage. Seized assets must be properly managed while all parties wait for the court cases that could result in the forfeiture of the properties. That Quebec ski resort, for example, has been a headache to run, despite the breathtaking view and the comfy après-ski lounge. Moreover, despite the rising number of suspicious deals reported to authorities by banks and others, too few Crown attorneys and police officers have been properly trained to follow up on them. Tracking money laundering is extremely labour inten-sive — a major obstacle in an era of government penny-pinch-ing. As one overworked senior RCMP official privately grumbled: What a money launderer can knit together in an afternoon can take a trained investigator a month to unravel.

Among the problems with Bill C-61 is the fact that, unlike legislation in the United States, it does not address the issue of cross-border money movements. Criminals can still shift huge sums in and out of Canada virtually at will. Moreover, police suggest that the burden of proof required for them to freeze assets is so onerous that criminals can dispose of them well before the legal paperwork is ready. Likewise with the profits of some kinds of illicit endeavours, which, paradoxi-cally, can be allowed under Canadian law. Toronto police found this out the hard way. In the late 1980s, they cracked a huge operation to smuggle in illegal Asian immigrants. While the scheme was effectively "taken down" (to use police par-lance), millions of dollars of the smuggling ring's profits remained safely secreted in Hong Kong banks. The money could not be seized because breaches of immigration law did not fit into the cramped legal framework of Bill C-61. "The law is highly flawed," concluded the late Craig Law, former head of the Metro Police Proceeds of Crime section.

If, as some critics suggest, current measures have managed to deter only small-time drug dealers, are there any better solutions? "In an electronic-banking system, banks will always be used to launder money," says the *Economist*, which goes on to suggest that, ultimately, the solution might be to ban all forms of cash.35 This may not be practical, but some financial leaders, including Richard Thomson, the influential chairman of the Toronto-Dominion Bank, support the idea of getting rid of some kinds of cash. Certainly, there are suspicions about the possible use of the Canadian $1,000 bill in money laundering schemes. There are 1.38 million such notes, worth $1.38 billion, in circulation — four times the number of a decade ago. The $1,000 bill is used frequently in the drug trade,36 so it would seem logical to ban the bill altogether. Federal finance officials say privately that their advisory committees, comprising police and bankers among others, opposed such a move. According to their findings, some economic groups would be adversely affected by the elimination of the bill. Fishermen on the East and West coasts, for example, use $1,000 bills on a regular basis when landing large catches. Cash, it appears, will continue to be with us for some time to come.

Seemingly intractable difficulties have also greeted bankers and government officials who've examined how to keep "dirty money" from entering the world's electronic financial pipelines. "How the hell do you deal with this volume of transactions without grinding the whole system to a halt?" asked a senior banker who spoke on condition of anonymity. "Very clearly 99.9 percent of these transactions are lawful. They are legitimate business transactions. Maybe there's a little tax hustle going on — we can't get into that sort of thing. But it's legitimate." He adds that the volume of money and trade sloshing around the world is so great that "once the money gets into the [electronic] system, the identification [of illegal money] becomes very difficult if not impossible."

What to make, then, of a financial world so apparently vulnerable to laundering illicit funds? Are the spheres of clean and dirty money merely opposite sides of the same coin — since both use virtually the same techniques and instruments? Yes, suggests the *Economist*. Though referring to drug trade profits, the British newspaper's conclusion could apply to "dirty" and "black" money as a whole: "The business is simply too vast to be isolated. It has become part of the financial system."[37]

Take this argument further and you hear bankers compare themselves to the operators of utilities and public services. Cedric Ritchie, chairman of the Bank of Nova Scotia, for instance, once described banks as "society's common carrier of money, just as the post office and the phone companies are common carriers of information."[38] For a time, this view was cited by some bankers to explain why they could not act against the laundering of dirty money. That is, a bank's task is to efficiently handle money — regardless of legal or moral issues. But that has changed — thanks, in part, to Canadians being repelled by the thought of their banks being used to wash drug profits. "We can no longer turn a Nelson's eye to these things and regard ourselves simply as a public utility that is in the business of moving money," said the banker who asked not to be identified. "The public is not prepared to accept that."

In response to such pressure, Canadian banks have tried to reduce their vulnerability. Stated Ritchie: "We accept without question the responsibility to help break the financial chain that supports the drug trade." At the heart of their strategy is a delicate balancing act. It's important to tackle the issue "in a way that will not cause the system to bog down and make people think their privacy is being invaded," says Helen Sinclair, president of the Canadian Bankers Association.[39]

To be sure, their efforts go only so far. In addition to the drawbacks in the banks' approaches, including the "know your client" technique, banks around the world have different standards. Thus, if Bank X in another country allows drug profits to enter the international financial system, there's not much a Canadian bank can do when it receives those funds. By the time it completes a transaction involving those drug profits, it's too late: thanks to Bank X, the dirty money has become virtually indistinguishable from legitimate funds. "Unless there are universal standards, it is going to be tough to catch them," says the unidentified Canadian banker.

Now may be the best time to set up such international standards. The worldwide trend to freer movements of money and goods is accelerating. The Canada-U.S. Free Trade Agreement is but one example; the harmonization of the European Community and the proposed North "American" free trade deal are others. In many regions of the world, borders are melting away, and money, corporations and jobs are increasingly fleet-footed. Power, say many economists, is shifting from individual states to the broad, faceless international market. Whether it is good or bad, there is little hope of halting this development. The implications for the debate on money laundering are far-reaching. As a 1990 federal report warned: "The liberalization of trade restrictions and limits to government regulation will make money laundering much easier by eliminating barriers, while making the transactions seem much more commonplace."[40]

Ultimately, plugging the torrents of drug money and other types of tainted funds may mean constricting the arteries of international banking. Assuming this feat could be pulled off, the cost would be hefty, and in the process, the movement of clean money could be pinched — an undesirable side effect. Among other things, the unfettered, worldwide circulation of funds ensures that exporters and importers are promptly paid. That's a key underpinning of international trade and commerce. At the other end of the telescope, consumers have a big stake in unobstructed electronic money moving too. Otherwise, they would not be able to withdraw cash night and day from banking machines around the world. (The next generation of banking machines will even allow consumers to automatically exchange foreign currency. That's a nightmarish scenario for some drug cops.) Whether the price is worth paying — and, indeed, whether any approach will bear fruit — is the kind of question that only politicians and their electors can finally answer.

■3 THE TRICKS OF THE TRADE

I may have handled more Canadian $1,000 bills than anybody else in this country." The amiable, softspoken man crosses his legs and relaxes in a wood-panelled room in a handsome Victorian house in midtown Toronto. It's not an idle boast; simply a statement of fact. And an understated one at that. Indeed, there's much that's unassuming about this round-faced man with the bronzed look and easy demeanour. Until June 1987 Donovan Blakeman was the administrator (not the owner, he quickly points out) of a thriving real estate concern that had joint projects in Barrie, a city north of Toronto, and in bustling Kitchener, Ontario. It also had land development in Florida and a substantial stake in First Trust Corp., a trust company in St. Kitts in the Caribbean. Flourishing, yes. But an unusual sort of business too, one that frequently took Blakeman to some of the world's most secret tax havens — and that received its "project financing" in a decidedly unconventional manner. Large-denomination bearer cheques — the kind that can be cashed by whoever has them — would be slipped into the mail-slot of his Toronto home. He never knew who delivered them. Then there were the large quantities of cash — in briefcases or in paper bags

— that he'd quietly pick up in bars or other locations.

For nearly five years, Donovan Blakeman, forty-seven, successful real estate investor and retired lawyer, was also Donovan Blakeman, expert money launderer. He helped bleach the profits of an international drug ring that boasted revenues of as much as $100 million between 1982 and 1987, the year it was cracked. He was no ordinary practioner of the craft either. His was the most complex drug-money-laundering scheme ever fully unravelled in Canada. And as drug cops will readily admit, it would probably never have been uncovered if the importing end of the operation had not been compromised. "It could have gone on forever and ever," says Blakeman himself.

So impressive was his handiwork that the RCMP uses his intricate scheme, complete with a baffling corporate blueprint dubbed the "Spaghetti Jungle," as a textbook illustration of the big-time washing of Canadian drug money. A federal study concluded that the Blakeman case "deserves special attention due to the sheer number of companies used, the diversity of laundering techniques associated with these companies, and the amount of money laundered through this method."[1]

"I was doing everything," admits Blakeman. "I was running the businesses. I was transporting the money. I did the works. Maybe that's why I'm a textbook case." For his troubles, Blakeman received a fee of $1,000 a week, an extra $1,000 a week against future profits, and expenses. He was also supposed to receive 25 percent of any profits made from the investments he administered. Alas, police detection meant there were ultimately no earnings.

Consider the breadth of his structure. There was a multitude of shell companies. Eleven of these anonymous entities — little more than brief registration forms in corporate registries — were in the Channel Islands. A further fifteen were in other discreet havens: Liberia, the British Virgin Islands, the Grand Caymans, the Netherlands Antilles and Switzerland. For good measure, Blakeman set up fourteen working corporations in

Canada and controlled myriad international bank accounts. An impressively nebulous corporate structure, one certain to perplex anyone trying to unravel it. And just the ticket to launder the burgeoning profits of his employer, Timothy Neeb — a boyish-looking one-time real estate agent in the London, Ontario, area. Neeb's organization was a major player in the lucrative marijuana and hashish market in southern Ontario in the mid-1980s, and Blakeman acted as Neeb's management consultant. Neeb didn't just want to rinse his illicit profits offshore. What he required was much more difficult and complex — to create a legitimate identity in Canada as a prosperous businessman.

"These things are like a jigsaw puzzle," says Blakeman, who retired from practising law in 1979 and was formally disbarred in 1990. "You put the thing together piece by piece to satisfy the requirements of your client."

Neeb's organization imported truckloads of marijuana from the Guadalajara region of Mexico. Some went to British Columbia; most headed to Ontario, crossing the U.S.-Canada border hidden in secret truck compartments. Much of the marijuana was distributed from a farm warehouse north of Toronto. To pay suppliers, couriers delivered millions of dollars in cash, some sewn into T-shirts, to Mexico. In a four-month period in 1986 alone, purchases of 35,000 pounds of marijuana were paid for with $22 million US in cash. The RCMP cracked the ring — an operation called "Outrage" — when an erstwhile partner of Neeb turned informant after being arrested in 1986. Neeb was sentenced to thirteen years in prison in 1990.

His money manager, Blakeman, was arrested in England in June 1987 and pleaded guilty to laundering charges in 1989. At the time, Blakeman's hotel safe contained $250,000 in cash under his name — a retainer for a lawyer he was hiring. The Crown recommended that his term be reduced because of his "substantial assistance" in the investigation. Though he was sentenced to two years in prison, he was released after serving ten weeks because of ill health. Blakeman says he didn't know where the money came from: "I never asked. That was the nature of my crime. I never asked. The fact is I should have."

Blakeman didn't oversee every aspect of the laundering operation. Others handled the drug ring's biggest money-handling headache — processing the prodigious volumes of cumbersome cash that it raked in. Physically disposing of cash — a common problem in the drug trade — is known as the placement stage, or wash cycle, in the laundering process. And it can present a difficulty for even the biggest kingpin. According to a 1989 U.S. court affidavit, Pablo Escobar, a founder of Colombia's Medellin cocaine cartel, once had so much trouble exporting $400 million US in cash that the money is said to have rotted in a basement hideout in California. Though this anecdote from a U.S. government informant was never verified, it underlines the scale of the predicament.

"Cash is heavy and takes up a substantial amount of space," says Peter Djinis, an attorney with the U.S. Department of Justice. "And unlike drugs, which can be replaced at much less cost, once cash is seized by authorities, all profit and expenses by the trafficker are lost in one fell swoop."[2]

Every streetcorner drug purchase is bought with cash, usually in small bills. Similarly, when the local pusher settles accounts with his supplier, he uses cash, often in the small bills recently garnered on the street. As profits rise from the street, this trickle of cash swells, fed by myriad drug deals, until it becomes a torrent heading for specialists like Blakeman.

The U.S greenback is the currency of choice in the drug trade. By one estimate, the small bills generated each year by U.S. drug sales weigh in at a hefty 26 million pounds.[3] What helps conceal this large amount of cash is that there's already a huge unregulated pool of U.S. currency. According to the Federal Reserve Board, the American central bank, as much as $100 billion US is held outside the borders of the United States and is thereby beyond its control. This pool exists, in part, because for the past four decades the American dollar has been more valuable than local currencies in many areas of the world. In numerous countries, merchants prefer to be paid in American greenbacks. Only with great reluctance will they accept the locally constituted and virtually worthless rouble, lei or gourde. For residents of such countries, American dollars stuffed in mattresses or buried in metal tins are a form of insurance against the vagaries of a nasty life. If you need a medical specialist in Bucharest or are desperate enough to want to slip away from Vietnam in a leaky boat, American dollars will turn the trick.

Not surprisingly, a subterranean financial system has emerged to soak up and recycle this underground U.S. cash. In Latin America, for example, you'll find scores of cambios, or unofficial money exchange houses. They're popular with all kinds of people because many Latin American governments tightly control exports of non-local currencies. Exporters in Colombia, for instance, are required to use their U.S. dollar earnings to buy twelve-month government bonds. There's a stiff financial penalty if the bonds are redeemed immediately.[4] Thus, businesspeople purchasing foreign goods and services prefer to exchange local currency for American funds at a black market cambio. They do the same if they want to stash away some money abroad in case the local situation deteriorates. There's no paper trail, and the taxman isn't tipped off. This godsend for businesspeople is also a boon to drug dealers. They are suspected of being major suppliers of U.S. funds to underground cambios — providing a handy way of disposing of the huge caches of U.S. dollars earned in the giant American cocaine market. [5]

In Canada, the cash-burdened launderer has no recourse to a handy neighbourhood cambio. Sooner or later, he must take the plunge and inject his carefully accumulated stacks of bills into the conventional financial network. The easiest route was taken by a brazen American trafficker who entered a Vancouver bank on June 26, 1986, lugging three cash-stuffed cardboard boxes. They held $806,000 US, including 25,700 twenty-dollar bills. But there was more in a pocket of his pants

— a further $4,000. 6 Few traffickers would be as nervy today, since banks are now much warier of large cash deposits.

To dodge the problem, traffickers now hire a large number of innocuous couriers to make numerous small transactions. Known as "smurfing," this technique is named after the well-known television cartoon characters. Elderly women have been employed on occasion. But no one was more inventive than Gary Hendin, a now-disbarred lawyer from St. Catharines, Ontario. Hendin's sometime smurf was a fifteen-year-old boy who delivered parcels of money — $250,000 all told — to a bank on his bicycle. One former Colombian money launderer told me his squad of smurfs would be busy working nine to five, Monday to Friday, making small deposits at many bank accounts in the Toronto area.

Cash-rich businesses like car washes and gas stations are also terrific for concealing drug cash. An increase in cash bank deposits can easily be explained as a rise in business, as long as taxes are properly paid, of course.

The Neeb organization's solution? Unassuming female couriers would collect the cash from other money handlers, usually at suburban Toronto malls or industrial complexes. Then they would haul the gym bags jammed with ten- and twenty-dollar bills, often to an unwitting Toronto currency exchange, Friedberg and Co., in the Bay Street financial district. There, most of the cash would be turned into easy-to-transport bearer cheques. The rest was converted into $1,000 Canadian bills or $100 US bills, a process known as refining, since it reduces the volume of the raw, street-generated cash. They were then turned over to Blakeman, who did the rest.

How did Blakeman know what to do? After all, no law faculty offers a course in "Concealment of Illicit Funds: An Introduction." Says Blakeman: "You just sort of feel your way through it." Indeed, the basic principles are quite simple. "There's only a few ways that people can get money," says Blakeman. "They can earn it, they can borrow it or somebody can give it to them. So if someone's got illicit cash that they have to launder, they would have to arrange for it to come into their hands in one of those ways: earn it, borrow it or have someone give it to them as a gift or inheritance or something like that. The last one isn't particularly easy. If it's a question of borrowing it or setting up some sort of business where you could ostensibly earn it, then you have to establish a lending entity or a business. And every business uses a bank. So you have to find a bank that will accept your deposit of cash . . . I actually consider that the easy part. People actually walk into banks all over the world and just deposit the cash."

Blakeman would himself transport the bearer cheques and cash to bank accounts in such places as the Island of Jersey, the Cayman Islands and St. Kitts. Fourteen bank accounts were at Brown Shipley (Jersey) Ltd., a merchant bank on Jersey. Interestingly, the Brown Shipley manager was suspicious of Blakeman's large currency deposits. "Why the cash?" he asked. Blakeman said there was a simple explanation: some investors in his real estate developments preferred to deal in cash. The bank manager seemed placated, though he wanted some references. Blakeman gave him two in Toronto: his lawyer and his bank manager, which satisfied the Brown Shipley manager. That taken care of, the huge cash deposits were allowed to continue.

(A similar exchange occurred between a Vancouver lawyer charged with money laundering and the manager of the local branch of the Bank of Credit and Commerce Canada. According to an RCMP affidavit, manager Irshad Karim questioned the lawyer about some suspicious U.S. cash transactions. The reply: "I'm a lawyer and I'm doing this for clients." The bank decided not to pursue the matter for fear of "losing a lucrative foreign exchange client."7)

Blakeman recalls that he wasn't an unusual visitor to tax havens: "I remember going to the Cayman Islands one day . . . I get into a lineup [at a bank]. There's six people in front of me, all with plastic bags or paper bags. They all made cash deposits. I flew into the Channel Islands [another] day with two African guys. Each had a suitcase. And each carried the suitcase onto the plane and . . . had bought an extra ticket so they could put that suitcase down. I have no doubt that they just got off a plane and walked into a bank, which accepted the deposit."

Blakeman was using the safest way to move cash and easy-to-convert financial instruments to a foreign country, suggests Rod Stamler, the former RCMP assistant commissioner. "This system leaves no paper trail within Canada." What makes it so foolproof is that unlike the United States, there's no legal requirement in Canada for declaring cross-border shipments of cash. Blakeman recalls often going to an airport and putting a briefcase full of cash through an X-ray machine. The security guards would gasp at seeing the money, but would let him through: "No bombs, no guns and that's it. There's absolutely no exit requirement at all."

Once deposited, the funds would be shifted and funnelled through various accounts owned by a bewildering number of corporate fronts. Thus the drug profits acquired a new identity. Drug cops call this wash cycle layering — "transferring the funds among various accounts through a series of complex transactions designed to disguise the trail of illicit proceeds."[8]

Hiding the origins of criminal profits is just part of the money laundering cycle. "The next stage involves the return of the funds [from a haven] to make it appear that they were legitimately acquired," says Stamler. Otherwise, drug dealers can't enjoy the fruits of their labour. Hence Blakeman's complex corporate structure: it was necessary for implementing another often-used and hard-to-detect technique: loan-back laundering. The money deposited offshore was funnelled back to Canada and to the United States through a combination of real and shell companies in the guise of loans or investment capital. Neeb's two main corporate entities were Erintree Inc. in Canada and Greenbrook in the United States. None of the loans, however, was directly linked to Neeb or Blakeman, even though the borrowed money belonged to the drug organization. The idea was to create the impression that Neeb, the drug ring's kingpin, was relying on foreign investors to bankroll land developments.

"When you set up your business you're specifically trying to hide the ownership of the business," says Blakeman. To do this, Blakeman looked for jurisdictions that allow the owner-ship to be concealed. That is, places where companies can be incorporated and the shares issued to a nominee or places that allow the ownership of bearer shares. Many financial havens offer such services.

"Once you've got that established, the business is either going to lend the money to you or put it up as collateral for a bank loan. Or the business is going to be active and you're going to run it and receive a salary for it. Once you've serviced those broad parameters, it's just a question of finding the peo-ple in the bank. They want the cash deposit. That's the busi-ness they're in. And they turn a blind eye to it. The guys who set up the corporations or the guys who sell the corporations, they turn a blind a eye to it. The guys who hold shares in trust for you, they turn a blind eye to it."

This peculiar form of sightlessness is rampant in tax havens, Blakeman says. "Go to one of the management com-panies [in a tax haven] that look after these things and look at the name-plates outside their office. You see the names of hundreds and hundreds of corporations that these people manage. And probably 99 percent of them are managed on the basis of secrecy. In actual fact, it's all money laundering of some construction. Whether it's taxes or criminal activities or embezzlement."

Blakeman was skilled at establishing a legitimate-appear-ing structure. As he wrote in a May 1987 memo to Neeb: "I believe we have succeeded in creating the 'look' of two busi-nessmen who went abroad to find backing for projects that already had a natural relationship with both of us . . ." One of their projects was a real estate investment in West Palm Beach, Florida. Other Blakeman-managed assets included a condo-minium development in Kitchener, Ontario, and a housing subdivision in Barrie, Ontario. The purchase of a project's land, for instance, would be financed with a mortgage from one of its offshore companies. Any profits or interest payments would be duly recorded and shipped back offshore to one of the entities belonging to Neeb's organization.

Police were fascinated by Blakeman's preoccupation with financial institutions. In September 1986, some $3 million was invested in First Trust Corp., the St. Kitts trust company. Of that, $2.6 million was in preferred shares which paid interest of 9 percent. That same amount was subsequently loaned to Penmarric Ltd., a Liberian-registered "Spaghetti Jungle" company, also at 9 percent interest. As a forensic accountant stated: "In normal business, it is unusual that there is no spread between the rate of interest paid and interest earned. Having equal rates allows the lender no earning power for administration and profit." In other words, since borrowing and lending at the same percentage makes no commercial sense, such transactions can have but one objective — to conceal or obscure. This kind of deal is a red flag commonly used to spot money laundering.

No charges were laid against First Trust, which appeared to be an unwitting participant in the laundering operation. Though there is probably no better way to wash dirty funds than through your own financial institutions, Blakeman says he was more interested in their profit potential as legitimate businesses than as money laundering conduits. So potentially profitable was the stake in First Trust that in 1987 Blakeman began to look into purchasing a Savings and Loan in Atlanta. His May 1987 memo stated: "They are an S and L with five branches and a mortgage company based in Atlanta that services over a billion dollars in mortgages. There is also a construction division." The purchase never came about; Blakeman was arrested shortly after penning the memo.

The memo also provided a glimpse of Blakeman's prodigious efforts to avoid incurring the taxman's wrath. As he stated in his May 1987 note to Neeb, which was seized by police in Blakeman's home: "The original purpose of the overseas companies was to use them as a step in routing cash back into your hands that you could not otherwise use. This was possible because the tax legislation in both Canada and the U.S. provided a combination of loopholes and mechanisms that made investing in North America attractive to foreigners.

"These were natural methods for foreigners to bring investment into both countries and get their funds out, free of tax. The basic idea in both countries was to bring funds into various projects at normal to high interest rates. The interest could be paid out free of withholding taxes and at the same time would be an expense for Canadian or U.S. tax purposes that would reduce taxable profits in these countries."

A veritable army of lawyers and accountants were used in Florida and Canada to provide tax advice. Recalls Blakeman: "We had meetings all the time. We'd say we had foreign investors who wanted to bring their money in, and then asked what was the best way to do it. These people all gave us written opinions because the initial request was about foreign investors who wanted to do a real estate deal in Florida." This expensive tax planning was for naught, however. Neeb's three main Canadian corporate entities were eventually convicted of tax evasion.

Blakeman is now trying to rebuild his life. He admits making a mistake, and he has paid a stiff price besides his jail term: a nearly fatal heart attack in jail, disbarment, and his impressive house up for sale. It is also difficult to shake the shadows of his previous life. Neatly piled on his front porch are dozens of document boxes containing Neeb's corporate records. Blakeman wanted to burn them — and hence make a complete break with the past — but he cannot. Under Canadian law, he has to hang onto them for ten years. Revenue Canada delivered that message to him personally. Blakeman is also very wary of discussing the ins and outs of his former profession, and for good reason. He's already had a couple of inquiries from people wanting to tap into his expertise. Thanks, but no thanks, is his firm reply.

An accountant (or Neeb or Blakeman, for that matter) would have appreciated the quality of the ledgers: they were meticulously kept. Neat columns detailed shipments: the quantities, the delivery dates, even the most minor costs and expenses. Other columns recorded money owed, payments made, debtors in arrears. The records of a thriving importer? Sort of. They were the records of the Company, a Colombian-run ring that for a brief period in 1990 supplied about 30 percent of the cocaine sold in Ontario and Quebec. Before it was shut down by police in December 1990, the Company had made an estimated profit of about $100 million over a three-year period. While Blakeman worked for a Canadian-run organization, the Company's money handlers sanitized the profits of the other major force in the Canadian illicit drug business — the criminal multinational. Their painstakingly kept ledgers chronicle the activities of an appropriate business structure in Canada — the branch plant.

How proficient were the Company's launderers? The ledgers tell the tale. They're "remarkable," says Bill Blair, a tall, polished inspector with the Metropolitan Toronto Police. He examined a single-year set of accounting books that the Company kept in Toronto. Parallel ledgers were in Colombia, where much of the world's cocaine is produced and then exported. There's a touch of respect in his voice as Blair describes what he found. Rent a car? It's documented in the Company's ledgers. Pay out $50 in expense money? It's in the logs. Send a bundle of money off to be laundered? It, too, is checked off. "It's kept nicely in the books," says Blair. "A shipment of 122 kilos comes in. It shows you who got it and all the expenses that the organization took responsibility for. As the drugs come out, they're debited to your account. As you make payments, you come back out to a balance. The amounts are staggering."

The Company was a typical Colombian organization. Money and drugs never mixed. Says Blair: "The people involved in the money collection, counting, storage, smuggling or laundering are totally separate from the part of the organization which involves drugs." Even the various segments of the laundering side were isolated from each other, so the money-handling eggs would not all end up in the same basket. More than one group performed each stage of the laundering, and none shepherded the dirty funds through all the wash cycles. "It's a cellular kind of operation. If you pull one arm off, they quickly grow a new one," says Blair.

The Company's bookkeeper, a Colombian woman with a degree in accounting, used an innocuous townhouse as a stash house. She was recruited in the United States specifically for the Toronto branch plant. Not only did she mind the ledgers, she also collected some of the money. On a single day, she'd gather hundreds of thousands of dollars in cash and bring it back to the townhouse she shared with her sister and another woman. Says Blair: "They'd bundle the money all up and put it in the trunk of a car. One of the women would drive it to another address." From there, a separate money-laundering cell would take over. Their task was to convert the Canadian funds into U.S. dollars, the drug trade's currency of choice, a difficult operation to perform in the United States. Indeed, changing Canadian funds into American dollars is such a preoccupation in the drug world that some money launderers virtually specialize in it. A Vancouver lawyer, for example, between March 1985 and July 1987, exchanged "a total of $3.1 million from Canadian currency into U.S. funds on 18 occasions, with amounts ranging from $56,000 to $396,000."9

The Company used a number of currency exchanges in Toronto for this purpose. To smuggle the U.S. cash south of the border, they often used a fleet of white Ford pickup trucks — complete with ingenious hidden compartments — which had brought in the cocaine in the first place. "They were bringing them up filled with cocaine into Ontario and Quebec and then cleaning them off and filling them up with money," says Blair. The subsequent laundering stages were handled in the United States. The profits eventually reached Colombia.

As members of a criminal multinational, the Company's money movers were akin to expatriate employees of a global concern temporarily posted to this country. Theirs was a simpler task than the one faced by Blakeman and his employer

Neeb. The Colombians had no need to shift drug profits abroad and then repatriate them under a carefully crafted legitimate facade. Their sole goal was to safely ferry the earnings abroad. But they did share the need for an institution to act as a conduit into the world financial system.

If a money launderer in Canada had his druthers, he'd prefer to use one of the Big Six Canadian banks. Not only do they dominate the marketplace, accounting for the lion's share of all transactions in Canada, but they also offer a variety of international services — something trust companies and credit unions tend to lack. To a money launderer, the Big Six chartered banks are a kind of one-stop shopping for just the kinds of services he needs: currency conversions and such travel-friendly financial instruments as bank drafts, certified cheques and money orders. Most of all, the Big Six control the country's electronic financial arteries. Through them, a customer in Vancouver, for instance, can easily shift funds to his bank's branch in, say, the Bahamas or the Cayman Islands. There are also the coast-to-coast networks of cash-dispensing machines linked through the Interac system. And there are embryonic computerized systems to allow corporations to automatically settle their accounts with other companies.

Especially attractive to launderers is the fact that banks have unique access to key international wire-transfer systems. Each day these systems handle some $1 trillion US worth of business. Foremost is the New York–based Clearinghouse Interbank Payment System, or CHIPS. It is basically a set of powerful Unisys computers in a blue-tinted room in Manhattan that allows worldwide transactions in U.S. dollars to be completed. (In case of disaster, a duplicate CHIPS system in another building can spring into action in seconds.) For example, if a Montreal aluminum company is buying Jamaican bauxite under a U.S.-dollar-denominated contract, CHIPS would convey the payment to the seller. Special wires hook some 140 banks in New York, including branches of major Canadian institutions, into the CHIPS system. They not only handle their own clients' needs, but also represent thousands of other banks worldwide. How does it work? Consider that Montreal company buying bauxite. When the payment was due, its bank — presuming it was a CHIPS member — would send a message to its New York branch. If it wasn't a member, it would call a correspondent facility in the Big Apple. Either way, a message would be flashed to the CHIPS computers, which would transfer the funds to the bank representing the Jamaican supplier. All this would be done in the blink of an eye. To the launderer's advantage, CHIPS wire transfers can be relatively anonymous. And, not surprisingly for a system that handles such high daily volumes, there's little supervision over the transactions.

As a federal study on money laundering concluded: "The electronic wire transfer represents one of the most effective and popular means to launder the proceeds of crime."[10] And it cites the following example drawn from RCMP case files: "From a branch of the Bank of Tokyo (Canada) in Vancouver, a launderer for an international drug trafficking ring wire transferred funds to three different banks in Japan. Part of the money then went to Thailand to purchase heroin. In all, $302,000 out of $563,000 identified by police as the proceeds of crime was laundered through this route."[11]

Much effort has been expended (mostly by American officials) to find a way of monitoring wire transfers through major systems like CHIPS. They've had little luck. So far at least, proposed methods for spotting shady transactions seem more likely to grind the system to a halt.

"The more checks and balances you put into any activity, the greater the risk that you will slow down the process," says Inspector Bruce Bowie, the RCMP's top expert on money laundering. "And nobody in the area I work in is interested in seeing the worldwide financial community brought to its knees because of overly restrictive measures governing wire transfers. It's a problem that no one in the world has an answer to. The volume of money being transmitted around the globe on a daily basis is so incredibly large. The requirement for speed is so fundamental and people have become so accustomed to rapid financial transactions that I don't know how it's going to be addressed."

It is not only major financial institutions that have access to wire transfers. Larger cities boast countless outlets, including currency exchanges and storefront cheque-cashing firms, that can wire money abroad and receive it. So many, in fact, that it's virtually impossible to regulate the practice. Bill Blair of the Metro Toronto police came across one case where a Colombian cocaine ring wired $100,000 to a contact in Toronto. The conduit: a mom-and-pop variety store in a working-class neighbourhood. "They paid their $3 and the wire arrived," says Blair. "In it came. How can you hope to monitor that? It's just impossible."

Banks may be attractive, but as the Big Six have made efforts to fend off money launderers, they're also increasingly difficult to penetrate. Hence, launderers are turning to currency exchanges, part of a relatively unregulated industry favoured by smurfs working for major Colombian cocaine dealers and marijuana smugglers like Neeb, among others. Many exchanges can convert large amounts of cash, no questions asked, into bearer cheques or other, more convenient currencies. Blair recalls the case of one Colombian money-handler who was doing most of his business through a currency exchange for tourists operated by the Ontario government. It was located near a major highway in southern Ontario. Blair says the launderer "had a business right near there. His wife was going over and doing about $60,000 a day. Nobody was doing anything illegal."

Some currency exchanges even acquire an unusual reputation in the underworld. (Again, this does not necessarily mean that they engage in illegal activities or condone them.) One day, for example, there was a bizarre robbery outside one exchange in downtown Toronto. A man with a large duffel bag was held up at gunpoint by two bandits. The victim fled. So did the two robbers. But they were caught by some alert policemen. Inside the bag was $180,000 in cash. When police interrogated the pair, says Blair, "the two bandits explained that everybody knows that you just go down to [this exchange] and hang around until somebody arrives with a big bag. It will be cash. It will be drug dealers. And you rob them and it'll never be reported."

New Canadian legislation forces currency exchanges to keep records of all cash transactions for at least five years, thereby giving police a paper trail. Whether this will block this apparent loophole is anyone's guess.

Launderers are not restricted to using only money in their schemes. Other wealth-bearing instruments, such as gold and gems, can also be used as a medium of exchange, though in recent years the yellow metal has lost some of its lustre for legitimate investors. No longer is it the first resort of the panic-stricken — as was shown by the muted reactions on the gold markets to Iraq's invasion of Kuwait and upheavals in the former Soviet Union in the summer of 1991.[12] Nevertheless, it remains an attractive vehicle for washing dirty money. For one thing, it's easy to buy and sell in Canada with no questions asked. For another, it's widely accepted and easily cashed around the world. In its physical form, gold comes in bars, wafers or coins, or it can be purchased through certificates issued by financial institutions or bullion dealers which give the holder title to a specific amount of the yellow metal. In either form, the buying and selling of gold comes under little scrutiny and requires only minimal identification. Says Brian Sargent, a former RCMP white-collar crime specialist: "If you as a gold dealer want to sell me $40 million in gold, very little information has to change hands for that transaction to take place." There are no government regulations and hence no restrictions on gold imports and exports, and no records of transactions are kept. Perfect for anyone wanting to hide drug proceeds. Concluded a federal report on money laundering: "The lack of government regulation specifically aimed at gold allows criminal launderers easy access to this precious metal as a laundering vehicle. Thus, gold which has been purchased with illicit money in Canada can circulate freely inside and across Canadian borders."[13]

How often is gold used as a laundering vehicle? No one knows for sure. But there are some troubling indications. Says Sargent, who helped prepare the federal study: "What I understand is that there's a lot of gold that moves out of Canada under fairly suspicious circumstances. Not a lot of questions are asked. That's a problem."

Also unregulated within Canada is the buying and selling of gems, which are especially attractive because of their portability. Unlike gold, however, gems must be declared when entering or leaving the country. According to the federal study, "Sophisticated launderers will simply declare the gems and pay the applicable duties and taxes. There is little reason for gems to attract suspicion of a Customs officer, and the declaration of the gems gives this laundering vehicle further legitimacy."[14]

Securities are another alluring laundering vehicle. Fingers have been pointed at the Vancouver Stock Exchange as a particular favourite for money launderers. However, as a federal study concluded, "police cases do not identify any specific stock exchange in Canada as being overwhelmingly used as a laundering vehicle."[15] It is true, however, that stocks and bonds can easily become the final repositories for already cleansed drug money. And anonymity can be ensured through the use of third-party investment advisers or shell companies in tax havens. Securities dealers are becoming more attractive as they perform more and more banking-like functions — including providing chequing accounts. This development is part of a worldwide process that's seen the blurring of boundaries between different kinds of financial institutions. The result: brokerages are seen as a potential alternative to dirty-money-wary banks.[16]

What makes the securities industry especially enticing is that techniques used to hide securities violations — including shell companies and tax havens — are similar to those employed by drug money launderers. Telling one kind of infraction from the other can be nearly impossible. Consider a recent case investigated by the Ontario Securities Commission. It centred on a brokerage industry veteran, who created a complex series of fictitious bond trades involving a chain of intermediaries. The pivot was that offshore mecca, the Cayman Islands. The purpose of most of the faked deals was never disclosed, but the result was certainly unusual: hundreds of thousands of dollars covertly moved from Canada to a mysterious company in the Caymans. There were no indications that the case was anything but a securities violation. Yet a federal panel's examination of a number of similar instances raised a disturbing scenario. "The securities industry," it concluded, "must contend with the fact that it is used as a laundering vehicle for not only the proceeds of drug trafficking and other enterprise criminal offences but also traditional security-related illegalities. . . . When used in conjunction with one another, it is often difficult to delineate between the securities infraction and the effort to launder illicit proceeds."[17]

Enforcement of the kinds of infractions which might also conceal dirty money are usually handled by provincial regulators. Since regulators' primary objective is to uphold securities laws — not to spot tainted funds — the risk of such a violator being prosecuted on a laundering charge is much reduced. Even if the violator is indicted, it would likely be under a provincial securities act, which provides far more lenient penalties than the Criminal Code. In many cases, the violator simply reaches a settlement with the securities regulator, which slaps him on the wrist.

Bonded couriers, too, are vulnerable to being used by money launderers. With their armoured trucks and other secure facilities, they can efficiently and quickly transport cash around the world. Most bonded couriers are careful about who they do business with. Many won't pick up cash at a private residence, for example. But they, too, can be fooled by corporate fronts. Says Sargent: "If you've got a corporate entity that's controlled by a criminal organization . . . if you make the entity look legitimate, then [the bonded courier] would do it quite unwittingly." Moreover, such couriers transcend boundaries fairly easily because they're bonded. And they move a huge quantity of goods across borders. Sargent goes on: "For any customs service to check every single piece of goods that moves across the border is impossible. They'll do spot checks and that kind of thing. But if you're moving currency or negotiable instruments, you can do so fairly safely [using a bonded courier]."

Wire transfers, bonded couriers, financial havens, currency exchanges — such modern-day vehicles are not the only ones used by major drug traffickers to launder profits. Some even exploit remnants of ancient banking systems that have survived to this day. Often called underground banks, these ethnically based, informal money-handling channels are found in many parts of the non-Western world. Though not inherently illegal, they have attracted some contemporary launderers of dirty money and black money for a variety of reasons. First, they tend to offer clients greater confidentiality and discretion than the increasingly dirty-money-shy modern banks. Second, it is difficult for Westerners to investigate them, partly because of cultural differences that can lead to ethnocentric misinterpretation.[18] In practice, says William Cassidy, a leading American authority on the underground banks, Westerners have had trouble differentiating "the criminal transaction from the technical violation . . . the relatively innocuous culturally specific transaction from the overt act in the continuing criminal conspiracy."[19] This obstacle is not insurmountable, suggests Cassidy. His sensible advice to investigators: "Apply common sense and elbow grease and a generous measure of fairness in dealing with the traditions and customs of foreign people."[20]

No one knows how old these parallel monetary systems are,

but some are reminiscent of the kinds of family-run (often by Florentines) merchant banks that began to dot Europe in the Middle Ages. According to Inspector Bruce Bowie, the RCMP's money laundering expert, some "pre-date conventional banking systems as we know them."

The ancient precursors of today's underground banks were created to meet a commercial need. During the Chinese T'ang dynasty, for example, trade between the provinces and the capital grew large enough to require more convenient forms of payment between distant points than transporting shipments of mediums of exchange like gold or silk. The resulting system, known as "flying money," was quite efficient and ingenious. Whenever a southern merchant made a sale to the imperial court, he would not necessarily bring the money home himself. Instead, he would deposit it with his provincial governor's representatives in the capital. They, in turn, would use the money to pay the taxes the province was to pay to the central government. To complete the transaction, the province would pay the merchant an equivalent amount of money when he got home — hence the term "flying money." Both governor and merchant benefited. The provincial administrator had an effective means of remitting his tax quota on time; the merchant had a worry-free method of patriating his profits.[21] From such early roots, informal systems for lending, exchanging and borrowing money have evolved and thrived to this day.

Among other things, they've provided invariably secret, always unofficial means of moving money from place to place — thereby filling people's age-old needs to safeguard savings in the face of political upheaval or overly stringent currency regulations. In Uganda in the early 1970s, for instance, scores of East Asians are said to have used such traditional banking arrangements to secretly whisk money away from the East African country, which was then ruled by the despotic Idi Amin. More recently, in neighbouring Tanzania, an underground structure allows residents to get around that country's tough foreign currency controls and its bias against private property. It's called "bedroom banking," because the banker is commonly thought to keep the money tucked under his bed.[22]

Similar systems operate between Western Europe and the Middle East. They allow "guest workers" to bypass currency regulations and clandestinely remit to families at home the wages earned in the factories of Germany or Belgium. Funds move the other way too. A Middle Eastern businessman once told me that his wealthy father used such a service to pay for his education in Europe.

"These systems of banking were not set up to facilitate criminal activity," says Bowie, "but criminals are very prone to using whatever devices are available to facilitate their aims. The use of such a system doesn't necessarily signify criminal intent." Bowie compares it to the relationship between money laundering and tax havens like the Cayman Islands, which were established for legitimate purposes. "Because the infra-structure is already set up to facilitate confidential movement and ownership of money, [tax havens are] absolutely perfect for drug traffickers."

The best-researched sorts of traditional financial practices are Asian-based. In the ethnic Chinese communities that speckle the northern Pacific Rim, for instance, funds can be shifted through networks of gold shops, money changers and trading companies without going near a modern bank or using an electronic wire transfer. Many are operated in separate locations (and countries) by members of the same extended Chinese family.[23] Likewise in the Indian subcontinent, where researchers have identified two prominent varieties of infor-mal banking. The "Hawala" system, centred in northern India and Pakistan, takes its name from the Arabic word *hawala,* which means "transfer," "consignment of property" or "assignment for payment." The "Hundi" system, found in central and western India, takes its name from a local term for "money order."

Such traditional financial practices differ in terms of the eth-nic groups they serve and the principal geographical location where they originated. But their methods of operation are, in many ways, quite similar. Much as in the days of the ancient "flying money" system, current setups can move money efficiently, safely and anonymously without actually transferring physical money. They can also exchange gold or diamonds into currency and convert one currency into the customer's choice of legal tender.[24] What makes them attractive is not just confidentiality and discretion, but also their reasonable rates, suggest some police studies in the United States and Britain. Hawala bankers in Britain, for example, often offer better exchange rates and lower commission fees than most above-ground banks, and Chinese bankers are said to charge the same fee no matter what size the transaction. All in all, underground banks are perfect for handling many kinds of confidential funds, whether you want to move money away from an unstable political situation, hide profits from the taxman or simply conceal drug proceeds.

How would it move money from Toronto to Singapore? "I'd approach the individual in Toronto who is a representative of [one] underground banking system," says Bowie, describing a procedure not unlike that used in T'ang dynasty China. "I would pay him 'x' amount of dollars. My intention is to transfer the money from Toronto to Singapore, let's say. I'd pay $500,000 to the local representative in Toronto. Then through cable, telephone or other communication means, the local representative would contact an associate in Singapore with instructions that when Mr. X appears, that representative is to pay him $500,000. It's really very, very simple; very, very convenient." At some later date, the Toronto and Singapore representatives, often members of the same extended family, would settle their accounts. Commonly, this would be done when a client of the Singapore representative required $500,000 in Toronto. The money would never physically cross any borders.

Informal banks often rely on coded means of identification and verification — a feature bound to entice both drug dealers and those worried about domestic upheavals.

Customers can authenticate themselves through simple receipts known as chits, which can be anything from bus tickets to specially torn post cards. Alternately, there are the so-called chops, intricately carved signature stamps made of wood or other materials that are said to defy duplication. A chop's inked imprint on a letter, for instance, can verify the authenticity of someone about to receive a payment from abroad at a family-run gold shop. A perfect device for maintaining anonymity.

Underground banks operate on trust. If money goes astray, the customer has little recourse to law enforcement authorities, especially if his or her motives were the least bit clandestine. Increasingly, suggests a federal study, stronger measures are being used to keep everyone honest, at least in "Hawala" schemes: "This system used to rely on the trust between family or clan members. However, as the Hawala system spreads, there is more evidence that fear of violence operates to keep the partners honest."[25]

There's little doubt that underground banks do launder drug profits, but there is no reliable yardstick to measure the extent to which they are used. A 1983 study by the U.S. Drug Enforcement Administration reported that "Wire intercepts placed on some of the major gold shops and trading companies by both Thai and Hong Kong police document large transfers of suspected drug money." Based on a number of cases involving the Chinese banking system, the report concluded: "With a vast majority of the Southeast Asian heroin trade controlled by Chinese organizations, this underground banking system, coupled with a web of commercial contacts in a variety of multinational Chinese business connections, creates a challenging law enforcement problem."[26] A 1988 RCMP report added: "It is believed that this particular system is responsible for the transfer of a great deal of heroin money in Southeast Asia."[27]

Because of the pervasive secrecy (and culturally specific customs) of many underground banking channels, police have had a tough time following the drug money moving through them. One rare success occurred in the early 1980s when police in Canada, Hong Kong, Singapore, Thailand and the United States combined efforts to trace the laundering of several million dollars. The RCMP learned that couriers first carried cash earned in the drug trade in Canada and the United States directly to Hong Kong, where it was deposited into a regular bank. The funds then entered a Chinese-based underground banking system by being transferred to an import-export company in Hong Kong. When it received the money, a corresponding credit appeared at a sister firm in Singapore. Instructions from the company in Singapore generated a further credit in Thailand, the site of the last transaction. "Cash was paid to an unidentified individual and it was suspected that the funds were moved northwards to the benefit of one of the major drug syndicate leaders." At that point, the trail went cold.[28]

Unravelling even the simplest kind of money laundering scheme — let alone an underground bank transaction or a scheme like Blakeman's — is not easy, as Bowie of the RCMP made clear to me in the fall of 1991. We were in his spartan office in the depths of the RCMP's sprawling headquarters in Ottawa. When I asked about the difficulties of mounting a money laundering inquiry, he visibly winced: "It's a horrendous undertaking to do a full-blown financial investigation on an individual target." Tacked on a wall was a photocopy of Blakeman's "Spaghetti Jungle." And he used the case — in which about one million individual documents were accumulated — to explain some of the inherent problems. Let's take an instance, he said, where the Crown prosecutor plans to make full disclosure of the evidence to defence lawyers. And let's say there are twelve defence counsel and one million pieces of documentation. "To produce 12 million photocopies that are readable and are catalogued so that they make some sense to the recipient is in itself a fairly significant undertaking," says Bowie. "It strains available resources — and that's just the disclosure."

And then there are the problems of getting information from tax havens. "These countries have different legal systems. We just can't go into another country and begin doing an investigation. We have to rely on legal conventions and treaties. That takes time. It's not unusual, for example, to wait one or two years for documentation from a country like Switzerland. During this period of time, that phase of our investigation may be stopped."

To be sure, a complex investigation in which police have to visit a number of different countries is time-consuming and expensive. But that's not all, says Bowie. "The longer a case goes on and the greater the volume of documentation that is accumulated, the greater are the difficulties in simply managing the investigation." Adding to the pressures on law enforcement is the rising number of potential cases. They come from both regular police work, and increasingly, from banks tipping off authorities to suspicious transactions.

A lot of work — sometimes for naught. In cases with complex international components, as in the instance of the drug money that ended up in Thailand, trails periodically go cold and the investigations have to be dropped.

■ 4 DIRTY MONEY NORTH OF THE FORTY-NINTH

J ohn Kerry is a tough-minded U.S. Senator with a penchant for muckraking and feather-ruffling. No one ever accused him of pulling his punches. Not when he was blowing the whistle on the scandal-plagued Bank of Credit and Commerce International a full three years prior to its collapse. Nor when he was challenging Manuel Noriega's links to U.S. spy agencies long before most people had ever heard of the corrupt, former Panamanian strongman. If there were drug dealers to expose, shady CIA dealings to uncover or terrorists to finger, you could be sure that Kerry would boldly take the lead. So imagine the Canadian government's surprise on September 27, 1989, when it learned of his latest target. That day, Kerry took aim squarely at Canada, charging that its laws were so lax that high volumes of U.S. drug profits were heading north of the forty-ninth parallel for easy laundering.

In part, what helped make Canada into an attractive haven, he said bluntly, was that its banks did not have to report large cash transactions, as their American counterparts had to. (This is still the case.) To support his claim, he disclosed portions of a confidential and refreshingly frank money laundering report jointly prepared in June 1988 by the RCMP and the U.S. Drug

Enforcement Administration (DEA).[1] It, too, referred to anomalies in Canadian law and concluded that hundreds of millions of dollars of "drug-related money" probably pass between the United States and Canada every year. Among the remedies, Kerry insisted, Canada could embrace the American system of mandatory reporting by banks of large cash transfers. Kerry's attack and his proposed solutions sent tremors through official Ottawa. And for a brief period, the issue moved to a prominent spot on the national political agenda.

Whether or not one accepted Kerry's conclusions and recommendations, the study was revealing. It found that:

• "U.S. traffickers have been known to move the actual cash generated from drug sales to Canada for deposit in Canadian banks to avoid the U.S. reporting requirements. Since Canada has no exit reporting requirements for cash, the easiest way to move currency out of the country is simply to have a courier carry the funds directly."

• "Canada does not fit the profile of the typical financial haven nation, yet it has been a repository for drug monies in recent years as a result of certain anomalies in Canadian law."

• "These monies are easily transported across the border between Canada and the United States. The risk of detection is not high in view of the enormous movement of vehicles and people through the many border points on a daily basis. As a result, Canada has been a popular destination for drug monies."

The report's findings were neither new nor especially controversial. It merely reiterated what Canadian police officers had been saying (not always publicly) for years — that criminals were drawn to Canada by the same features that attracted legitimate immigrants and foreign investors. As RCMP Inspector Bruce Bowie would later tell the House of Commons Finance Committee: "It is the attributes that make Canada a good place to do business, I suppose, that also make it attractive to either move moneys through Canada or have our country as a repository of illegal moneys. It is a relatively good place to invest in, not only for legitimate businessmen."[2]

New or not, the Kerry disclosures caught the Canadian

government off guard and entirely on the defensive (if only because Prime Minister Brian Mulroney had taken full credit for putting money laundering on the agenda at the 1988 Group of Seven summit in Toronto). The Canadian media, too, had some shaky moments. Even though Kerry's assertions received prominent play in Canadian newscasts and newspapers the next day — "U.S. Drug Millions Find Haven in Canada" was a typical front-page headline [3] — most news outlets had to rely on U.S. wire service reports. The bulk of Canadian reporters in Washington simply had not attended the September 27 hearing of Kerry's subcommittee, which until then was little known in Canada.

In Ottawa, officials quickly tried to undermine both the report and Kerry's views. Word of the revelation sent federal bureaucrats scurrying to get details on the until-then-obscure report — and to cobble together a creditable reply. A diplomatic cable sent from Ottawa to the Canadian embassy in Washington the next day and classified "protected," captures the flavour of Canada's flat-footed response. Trying desperately to poke holes in Kerry's claim, the cable, released under the Access to Information Act, tried to tackle the assertion that the report had been widely read by MPs. It lamely attested: "Staffer for Sen. Kerry is incorrect to suggest that report was circulated in Parliament. RCMP contact confirmed that [member of Parliament] John Nunziata (L-York South) requested copy of the report...however, request was declined because of the [confidential] classification of study."[4]

The House of Commons briefing notes — prepared for Cabinet ministers by the Department of External Affairs and also classified "protected" — were no better. The suggested replies to Commons questions, released under the Access to Information Act, were limp: "Canada is deeply committed to fighting drug trafficking in all its aspects.... The report refers to Canada as only one of several countries through which laundered currencies are circulated." Nowhere did the proposed replies confront the report's findings or Kerry's allegations. Ministers and spokespersons merely attempted to undermine by carefully criticizing minor points — a tried-and-true stratagem among politicians everywhere. They talked derisively of Kerry's selective quoting from the report. They called the report "ancient history." They repeatedly focused on their core argument: that the report had been pre-pared before the passage of the bill which made money laun-dering a crime on January 1, 1989. This legislation, they suggested, had cleared up any hint of legal anomaly that may — the emphasis on the word "may" — have attracted laun-derers. Gilles Loiselle, the junior finance minister, firmly stated in the Commons: "The report is based on data which is not relevant anymore." He, too, skipped over some key ques-tions. Was the report's data accurate? Was the report on the mark? And finally, was Canada indeed a haven?

Most galling for Ottawa (and for Canadian bankers) was Kerry's suggestion that Canada adopt American-style cash transaction reporting — something that federal officials had examined but dropped as unproductive and too costly after much lobbying by bankers. Indeed, as a confidential Ministry of Finance memo, dated November 27, 1989, and released under the Access to Information Act, put it: "The U.S. Trea-sury department has been unable to demonstrate the effective-ness of the . . . system other than with anecdotal evidence."

Still, some Canadian police officers were privately admit-ting that much of the report was "a fair assessment." Yes, Canada and the United States are "used increasingly as repos-itories for large amounts of drug proceeds." Yes, hundreds of millions of dollars in drug proceeds probably move between the two countries each year. And yes, it's easy to smuggle currency across the border.

Kerry, for his part, had not found a smoking gun. But his staff had discovered some provocative indicators: Canadian banks were repatriating twice as much U.S. cash as they were receiving through legitimate sources. In the first ten months of 1989, for example, Canadian financial institutions had sent $4 billion in American currency south of the border. Only

$1.2 billion US had, officially at least, gone the other way. As Kerry told a Senate subcommittee hearing: "So you have to say 'What happened?' Did Canadians suddenly empty their mattresses of U.S. dollars and decide to put them in the bank? That's a huge disparity."[5] Kerry suggested the only plausible explanation was money laundering activities. According to that view, the $2.8 billion gap represented dirty money that had been cleaned and injected into the banking system. Certainly that conclusion was consistent with the experience of some major U.S. drug investigations: excess cash tended to point to concentrations of drug money laundering. When the cocaine trade exploded in Florida in the late 1970s, drug cops noted a coinciding rise in the amount of surplus cash deposited in banks in the state, especially in Miami. In 1979, for example, the Federal Reserve Bank in Miami — one of the twelve regional financial institutions of the Federal Reserve Board in Washington, the American central bank — reported a $5.5 billion surplus, which was greater than the combined surpluses of every other Federal Reserve Bank branch in the U.S. [6]

For official Ottawa, the other shoe dropped in February 1990 when Kerry's subcommittee on narcotics, terrorism and international operations issued a report based on the fall 1989 hearings — complete with a pointed reference to Canada and the gap of $2.8 billion US. The findings were particularly irksome to Canadian officials, since they had spent months trying to clear up what they considered to be some of Kerry's misconceptions. Yet despite Ottawa's best diplomatic efforts, the report listed Canada "among the jurisdictions most commonly used to launder drug money from the United States." To their chagrin, federal officials had no hard data to counter Kerry's figures or conclusions — to prove, in other words, that Canada was not a sanctuary for U.S. drug profits. For one thing, Ottawa had no means of gauging the cross-border traffic of cash, since exit and entry declarations are not required for such transactions. Hence, like Kerry's central assertion that Canada is a haven, the unexplained $2.8 billion gap remained unchallenged by facts.

The federal banking regulator, for instance, does not specifically look for evidence of U.S. drug profits passing through Canada. When I asked Michael Mackenzie, the Superintendent of Financial Institutions, whether Canada is a sanctuary for such dirty money, he frankly responded, "I don't know." A more authoritative answer isn't likely either — at least from the data his staff gather. "We don't examine the deposits of every bank," says Mackenzie. "We are informed that the banks claim to know who they deal with. But let's face it, you've got a lot of nominee accounts" (in which the owner of a bank account preserves his anonymity by opening it in the name of someone else, say his lawyer). His office's chief task is not to stop money laundering but to monitor and ensure an institution's financial health. In the words of Mackenzie's former deputy, Donald Macpherson: "It is important to make a distinction between the issues that are of primary concern for our office — that is, the solvency of the institution we are dealing with — and the impact that stories, reports, rumours and what have you about money laundering and other activities may have on the confidence of the institution. The allegations that the bank may be used as a vehicle by money launderers in most cases is not in itself something that will lead to the insolvency of the institution."[7]

There's simply no mechanism in Canada for identifying how big the problem might be, says Brian Sargent, a former RCMP white-collar crime specialist who was instrumental in formulating the 1990 federal report on money laundering. As part of the study, Sargent analyzed all major Canadian cases in which the washing of criminal proceeds played a role. But the federal study was hampered by the same data-gathering voids that restricted the scope of Canada's response to the Kerry report.

"You have to guess" about the magnitude of the problem, says Sargent, now a forensic investigator in private practice in Ottawa. "There have been cases that the RCMP have looked at where large volumes of money move through this country or into this country or out of this country in a short period of time. In a lot of cases, those were detected quite by accident. I don't believe that those are isolated cases. I believe that's probably closer to the norm."

That shady funds flow from the United States into Canada should come as no surprise. Historical links between American and Canadian criminals have long nurtured the U.S. under-world's impression of Canada as a financial sanctuary, suggests Rod Stamler, the former RCMP assistant commissioner. This conception has helped make Canada a kind of financial magnet drawing tainted U.S. funds north. In the 1930s, for example, Huey Long, the crooked Louisiana governor, was rumoured to have hidden part of his cache in Canada.[8]

"During Prohibition," explains Stamler, "you had crime groups working across the border dealing with illicit alcohol. There were groups in Hamilton and St. Catharines and that part of Ontario as well as Montreal and elsewhere working back and forth across the border. Prohibition in the United States created some kind of connection in terms of Canada being a safe haven. So proceeds and profits came from these activities. They were unlawful in the United States. They were perhaps lawful in Canada."

Canada is attractive for quite obvious reasons, geography being one of the principal ones. After all, Canada sits next to the United States, the world's largest economy and the number one destination for Canadian exports. And the U.S. is also the world's largest market for narcotics, which are arguably organized crime's most lucrative cash cow.

"When you look at the illicit drug market in the United States, where are the profits going?" asks Stamler. "Some are going offshore to facilitate the continuation of the drug trade. You can't have an international drug trade without money flowing.

"The values of the drug trade are in the billions of dollars in the U.S. Some say it's $100 billion. But let's say the profits are $20 billion. Even $10 billion. Even $5 billion. That's a lot of money. . . . You've got billions and billions of dollars that have to move. . . . where does it go?"

Stamler pauses a moment. Put yourself in the criminals' shoes, he suggests. Sending it to Mexico is far from appealing, since it lacks Canada's efficient — and stable — financial infrastructure. Funnelling it out through American financial institutions is getting dicier and more costly — thanks to tougher U.S. anti-money-laundering statutes. Flying directly from the United States to a tax haven is not simple anymore either. Airport X-ray machines can easily spot cash, and in the U.S., unlike Canada, cash is subject to exit reporting regulations. What's left? "Canada is the logical place to be used for laundering money. It's the easiest."

Sargent, the former RCMP money laundering expert, agrees: "There's a freedom of movement between the countries which makes it very attractive if you're somebody who wants to get something out of the United States or into the United States surreptitiously." Not only can people easily cross the largely undefended frontier, but so much traffic passes between the two countries through so many border points that it is unlikely for anyone to get nailed for carrying illicit cash.

Free trade is also reducing the already limited amount of scrutiny of goods crossing the border, a fact which causes especially great concern in the United States. A confidential federal memo dated November 27, 1989, and released under the Access to Information Act, to then Finance Minister Michael Wilson, emphasized that there's "the perception by U.S. Treasury officials that the Canada-U.S. Free Trade Agreement will increase economic and financial ties between Canada and the U.S., thus leading inevitably to more attempts to launder U.S. drug profits in Canada."

As noted earlier, phoney invoices or related schemes can easily be used to hide dirty money within the vast amount of legitimate trade between the two countries. The purchase of Canadian real estate by a foreign investor could achieve the same goal by using a "double-pricing" system. Say a small apartment building is actually worth $5 million. It is officially purchased for $3 million using licit funds. The vendor, unofficially, receives a further $2 million in dirty money. Then, after making some cursory improvements to account for the profit, the buyer sells the building for a little over $5 million. He has to pay tax on the roughly $2 million in profit, but that money has been made legitimate through an ostensibly genuine real estate transaction. (Of course, this method can also be used within Canada to hide domestically earned unlawful profits.) Once here, the highly efficient Canadian banks can whisk those U.S. funds (as long as they're adequately disguised) anywhere in the world.

Says Sargent: "Canada, I think, has become a transshipment point not only for the obvious, the drug problem. Because of the large undefended border, it's become a transshipment point from a money laundering perspective."

Certainly, police cases in which foreign criminal funds flow through Canada are far from rare. In 1989, for example, 73 percent, or roughly $23 million, of all cash and assets seized by the RCMP were generated outside Canada. "In every case except two, the illicit revenues originated in the United States. The two exceptions were seizures of proceeds originating from Colombia. These two seizures, however, account for $16.5 million (or 52 percent) of the $31.6 million seized by the RCMP in 1989."9

Italian investigators have turned up several instances in which Canada was used as a laundering conduit. For example, an August 1988 report by the Guardia di Finanza, the Italian fiscal police, outlined one route used to launder heroin profits earned by some Sicilian mafiosi in the United States. The dirty money was refined — small bills exchanged for crisp hundreds — at casinos in Atlantic City and sent to the Bahamas. The funds were then routed through Canada before heading to Europe. Departing from Canada, the couriers would arouse much less suspicion than if they'd come directly from the haven-rich Caribbean.10

Documents discovered following the slaying of criminal financier Michel Pozza in Montreal in 1982 pointed in a similar direction. Among his personal effects, police found a credit note for $5 million drawn on account no. 118–963–8 at a branch of the Canadian Imperial Bank of Commerce in Montreal. The account had been registered to the sons of Vito Ciancimino, a major figure in the Sicilian Mafia. And the funds were thought to be heroin profits "washed into real estate deals in Canada." They had been transferred to Cimasol, a shadowy entity in Liechtenstein. A relative of Pozza was a Cimasol director.[11]

U.S. investigators have also stumbled onto a fair number of cases with Canadian money laundering connections. Take a kickback involving the International Brotherhood of Teamsters, for example. Until recent years, "the Cosa Nostra, with the aid and connivance of a corrupt union leadership, had controlled and operated the union as a lucrative racketeering enterprise for decades — using, for example, the Teamsters' richest pension fund as a mob bank to finance hidden investments in Las Vegas casinos," says Otto Obermaier, U.S. Attorney for the Southern District of New York.[12] Kickbacks from such loans were routine. One payoff in the late 1970s was "laundered through Canada," says an American investigator who worked on the case which, to his regret, never reached the courts. "It was pretty big money. . . . That never did come out. It was money moving to Canada. Once money goes across the border, you lose track of the money."

That prospect appealed to a once-rising star in the Southland Corp., which runs the 7-Eleven convenience store chain, and a former New York City councilman. What brought executive Eugene DeFalco and politician Eugene Mastropieri together in 1977 was a bid to head off a New York State tax ruling. It could have cost Southland hundreds of thousands of dollars — and bit deeply into DeFalco's profit-dependent paycheque. The solution presented itself one evening in January 1977 over dinner at a steak house on Long Island. The well-connected Mastropieri told DeFalco — then in charge of Southland's New York State operations — that there were few problems he couldn't settle, especially if they involved the state's tax commission. According to DeFalco's testimony, Mastropieri smiled when asked the cost of such problem solving. To answer, he leaned forward, as if he needed a little more privacy, and said: "This may require heavy entertainment." DeFalco knew exactly what that meant: bribes to the right people. He replied: "That was possible, we had entertained before."

To pay the bribes, a secret slush fund of $96,500 US was set up and laundered through Canada, a country the participants seemed to regard as a lethargic backwater. As one conspirator told DeFalco: "There would be no way anybody could ever find out about the money being up there." The money itself came from Southland's own coffers. It was hidden in a legal bill — citing unspecified "professional services rendered" — submitted by Mastropieri. Even though the bill was undated and contained no description of what services were provided, Southland duly issued a cheque on July 7, 1977. And the amount was deducted from Southland's 1977 tax return as a legal expense. The result, said the case's prosecutors in 1984, was that "the Treasury of the United States unknowingly shared with the Southland Corp. the cost of bribing public officials in New York state."[13]

The actual laundering operation was quite simple. Six days after the cheque was issued, DeFalco sent it to an intermediary — John Kelly — who, in turn, gave it to Mastropieri. The councilman then deposited the funds into his New York law firm's escrow bank account. And he gave Kelly a cheque for the same amount — $96,500 US — drawn from that same account. On July 18, 1977, Kelly flew to Toronto, opened an account at a Bank of Montreal branch and deposited Mastropieri's cheque. About a month later, DeFalco and Kelly flew to Toronto. DeFalco, at this point, got greedy. He decided to help himself to part of the slush fund. So, he, too, opened an account at the Bank of Montreal. Into it, he transferred $20,000 US from Kelly's account — to be held as a corporate slush fund. He kept $28,500 US for his personal use. The remaining $48,000 US stayed in Kelly's account to pay Mastropieri and to cover any taxes that the transactions might incur. In the end,

no bribe was actually paid to a New York State official, but the
scheme was exposed in the United States. (It didn't cause a rip-
ple in Canada.) DeFalco pleaded guilty. A jury in New York
found both Mastropieri and the Southland Corp. guilty in 1984
of separate criminal conspiracy charges in the case. Southland
had claimed that DeFalco had made the whole thing up to hide
his own embezzlement. Summing up the case, U.S. prosecutors
dubbed it "a sordid story. . . . In the annals of the conduct of
American public officials and publicly held corporations, this
was not one of the finest moments."[14]

Most U.S. examples involved drug money. In 1981, for
instance, American officials arrested Isaac Kattan, an important launderer who worked for Colombian cocaine traffickers.
Over a four-year period, he had washed about $400 million US
in cash. And to do this, he had used foreign bank accounts not
only in Panama, Switzerland and the Bahamas, but also in
Canada.[15] Another instance emerged from the so-called Pizza
Connection case, in which Italian-based criminals used
innocuous U.S. pizzerias in the 1980s in a complex heroin-
trafficking scheme. Some of the dirty cash was shipped north
of the forty-ninth parallel. Investigators were told that a member of the heroin network, Phillip Salamone, "customarily
transported currency from New Jersey to a location in New
York State, where another individual smuggled the currency
across the border into Canada. The ultimate destination of the
money was believed to be Sicily."[16]

Another case centred on the notorious Panamanian
subsidiary of the Colombian-based Banco de Occidente.
It pleaded guilty in August 1989 in Atlanta to helping
Colombian cocaine barons wash millions of dollars in drug
profits through the use of wire transfers. On the day the
charges were laid in March 1989, the Panamian bank whisked
about $63 million US to its accounts in Germany, Switzerland
and Canada. More than $13 million ended up in the bank's
account at the Swiss Banking Corp. in Toronto. Those funds
were subsequently seized by the RCMP and then transferred
to U.S. accounts of the Banco de Occidente which had

been frozen and were supervised by American drug cops. After the guilty plea, the Panamanian bank was ordered to forfeit $6 million. Ottawa received $1.2 million as payment for Canadian involvement in the successful conclusion to the case.

Or consider a shadowy Vancouver company known as the Canada-Asia Finance Group Ltd. In the early 1980s, it offered a special service to U.S. drug dealers — arranging for large amounts of cash to be sanitized and laundered through Hong Kong. It even had the hubris to advertise its services in the *Wall Street Journal* and the *Miami Herald*. The ads read: "Many multinational corporations know the benefits of confidential banking outside of North America. No reporting requirements. Total secrecy. Guaranteed results."[17] The fee: $10,000 and 5 percent of each month's deposits. Two under-cover U.S. agents posing as Miami-based drug traffickers cracked the scheme. They were offered red carpet treatment, including special confidential accounts at a San Francisco branch of a Hong Kong bank and tips from bank officials. To get U.S. cash reporting arrangements, the agents were told "to divide their deposits into specified smaller amounts, to vary their pattern of deposits and to 'build in some odd figures so that the whole lot could not add up to a round sum.' " Just to make sure the two clients weren't confused, bank officials gave them a diagram explaining the flow of funds.[18]

Canadian investigators were also finding important links in U.S. drug-profit laundering schemes in some of the country's smaller centres. In Windsor, RCMP charged a Detroit doctor in 1989 with laundering $384,000 in U.S. drug profits. In Winnipeg, police seized an overflowing safety deposit box in 1990. Inside were 80 envelopes. Each held about $5,000 in cash. The $400,000 had been sent north of the border in the late 1970s by an organization that had imported 100 tons of marijuana into the United States from Colombia.[19] In yet another case, "traffickers operating in the United States used nominees to open bank accounts and purchase real estate in the Toronto area. From the Canadian accounts, substantial amounts in U.S. currency were then transferred to a bank in Liechtenstein. Safety deposit boxes were also kept in Toronto banks to hide large sums of cash.''[20]

Investigators have paid a lot of attention to money laundering activities in Montreal. It was the site of the influential Luis Pinto case, which led, in part, to the enactment in 1989 of Bill C-61, Canada's money laundering law. (Pinto was the American-based Colombian who washed millions of dollars in drug funds in the early 1980s.) The President's Commission on Organized Crime in 1984 reported that in addition to his favoured institution, the People's Liberty Bank in Covington, Kentucky, Pinto also looked to Canada. His Canadian assets were traced to a Royal Bank of Canada branch in Montreal, where an account in the name of Agropecuria Patasia Ltd. held about $600,000 US in drug proceeds. But the money was never recovered — because of the 1985 court ruling that under existing laws, a credit in a bank account was not a tangible asset and therefore could not be seized.[21]

Little has changed in Montreal since Pinto's day, suggests the man who investigated the case, RCMP Sergeant Marc Bourque. "It's happening right now as I'm talking to you," says Bourque, a burly, veteran prober of the city's dirty money fraternity. "I can show you guys who are laundering $1 million, $1.5 million, $2 million a week. They've been doing it for the last six months." (These launderers do not all hail from Quebec. Police in Toronto say privately that some local crime groups prefer to cleanse their profits in Montreal.) If there's a touch of exasperation in Bourque's voice, it's not surprising. He's something of a legend in North American law-enforcement circles — and not only for the Pinto case. He's better known as the hard-nosed investigator who single-handedly pieced together the largest laundering scheme involving the Sicilian Mafia to be exposed in North America. Mention the case to officials at the Drug Enforcement Administration in Washington and they are free with their praise. The case is much more bittersweet for Bourque, since it was never pursued in Canada.

Sitting in a small, beige-coloured room at RCMP offices in Montreal, Bourque pats a thick blue file from his case records. He flips through it. Page after page of bank drafts. Records of bank accounts. Columns of cash deposits. "Five years' work," says Bourque, his voice tinged with a mixture of pride and regret.[22]

As Bourque tells it, the tellers at the Montreal City and District Bank branch (now part of the Laurentian Bank of Canada) were suspicious from the start. For one thing, the bundles of U.S. cash didn't smell right. One recalled that the bills had a musty odour. Tellers were suspicious, too, about the group of three Italian-speaking men — sometimes there was a fourth — who delivered the bills. They'd arrive on a regular basis lugging a suitcase full of small-denomination U.S. bills and head directly for the manager's office. The sums were enormous. On November 5, 1981, alone, deposits totalled $404,400.

The funds were counted in the staff kitchen and then sent off by armoured truck. And the deposits were quickly turned into U.S. bank drafts. "We didn't feel right about this," cashier Denise Maille told a December 1990 hearing into the incident. "It looked shady."[23] Her instinct was right. Between October 20, 1978, and April 25, 1984, the men made a total of $15.395 million US in deposits at the branch at 4057, boulevard St-Jean, and the Montreal City and District was not their only bank. About the same amount of U.S. cash was deposited at the National Bank of Canada branch at 9048, boulevard St-Michel, between September 13, 1979, and September 13, 1982. It, too, was turned into U.S. bank drafts. So was the $1.21 million deposited between October 10, 1984, and November 6, 1984 at the Forexco currency exchange at 360, rue St-Jacques and the $3.6 million delivered between May 11, 1981, and November 9, 1981, at the Hellenic Trust at 5756, avenue du Parc.

The deposits were unusual, to say the least. Says Bourque: "There's not one legitimate business in the whole island of Montreal — not one — that can generate half a million U.S. every week. In Canadian funds, there are plenty. In U.S. funds, there are none." Maybe no legitimate Montreal business could generate such a quantity of U.S. cash, but a major heroin smuggling network could. In fact, according to Bourque's investigation, all $35.598 million US was earned this way.

All of the earnings were garnered and then sanitized by Montreal-based members of the notorious Cuntrera Sicilian crime family. Top members of the family were indicted in the United States in 1990, though some, including scion Pasquale Cuntrera, continue to operate from their sanctuary in Venezuela — their home base since the 1960s. From there, they typically smuggled Asian heroin into the American market through Montreal. The profits followed the same route out of the U.S. "The Cuntreras are maybe the most significant heroin smuggling family involved in the United States," concludes Thomas Raffanello, a DEA special agent.[24]

Bourque's eyes widen and his speech quickens as he describes his investigation. It began in June 1985 when police in Montreal seized 58 kilograms of heroin and arrested four people. A search of their houses turned up no other drugs, but police noticed "a lot of wealth" in the home of one of them — Gerlando Caruana. Bourque was amazed at what he found: jewellery, tony furniture, the trappings of "a millionaire lifestyle." On Caruana's night-table were two watches with a combined value of about $25,000. The problem was that Caruana had declared an income of only $23,000 the previous year. "On $23,000 you can't buy $25,000 worth of watches," says Bourque. A check of Gerlando Caruana's eleven bank accounts turned up nothing suspicious, but then came a stroke of luck. A bank teller told Bourque: "You shouldn't be looking at *his* bank account. Look at his brother's." Bingo! Bourque had hit paydirt: "What we found was that at one particular bank [brother Alfonso Caruana] had laundered some $15 million. What he'd do is come in with the U.S. cash, convert the cash into drafts and the drafts would be sent to Switzerland."

Little by little, Bourque put together the case. The tellers were helpful. Some told him about getting so fed up with counting the small bills that they told the launderers: "From now on, you bring in the bills sorted out and we want them in

$5,000 bundles. We're wasting our time. We're spending half a day counting your money." The ever-cooperative launderers complied, says a smiling Bourque. Building a court case was easier said than done, however. Bourque had to prove that the $36 million US had been earned from the heroin trade. He couldn't use the 58 kilograms of heroin confiscated in June 1985 as proof of that — since the $36 million US Bourque was tracing had been laundered before the drug seizure.

He was helped by Italian police, who put him in touch with Tommaso Buscetta, the rough-hewn Sicilian mafioso who'd turned informer in 1984. He pointed Bourque to a possible source of the profit — a sixty-kilogram heroin deal — and eventually, Bourque was able to show that the Cuntreras had handled one thousand pounds of heroin. How much did they earn from this? As importers, Bourque calculated, they'd garnered about $50 million US. "Of the $50 million, we saw $36 million being laundered. The rest was spent." Then he followed the money trail to the Swiss bank accounts where the $36 million US in bank drafts had been deposited. From there much of the money ended up in the accounts of known Sicilian heroin traffickers. Moreover, Bourque was able to show that the Caruana brothers and the other Montreal representatives of the Cuntrera crime group had no legal source for this money. "Money doesn't just fall off trees," says Bourque. "Where did the money come from? You see a guy who arrives in Canada in 1965. He has $100 in his pocket. All of a sudden, a few years later, he's a millionaire. And he doesn't declare any revenues. Where does the money come from? I was able to prove that there's no legitimate business in the whole of Canada that could generate this kind of cash flow."

Five years after he began his probe, Bourque's work was over. Or so he thought. He took his case to Quebec justice officials, who turned it down. Not enough trained personnel, they said. Besides, a case this big was too costly. Bourque went to see federal justice officials. Would they prosecute the case? "Put it down in writing," was their initial reply. Bourque responded with a 3,500-page court brief, but again was greeted without enthusiasm. They told Bourque: "There are five cases such as yours being considered. We only have the personnel to work two. So we're going to discard your case." The case was never pursued in Canada, though Bourque's evidence was used in court cases in other countries. The irony sits heavily. "Evidence that was rejected in my country — that was legally obtained — was accepted in Italy, Germany and the United States." Equally discouraging was the fate of the money. Says Bourque: "It went from Switzerland down to South America, back into Canada and into different real estate. I could show you shopping centres they own here. Houses. But we can't proceed because the Justice Department won't proceed. I can show you a $3 million house. I can't even touch it."

Why didn't the banks tip off the police? Bourque has a theory. At one bank — he won't say which one — the launderers had to deposit the funds into a Canadian account before they could purchase the U.S. bank drafts. That meant two currency conversions — one to get the U.S. funds into the account and another to turn them back from Canadian currency into American greenbacks, which were then used to buy bank drafts. "This in-and-out transaction would mean 4 or 5 percent interest. . . . That's why the bank didn't phone the cops." What about charging the banks? Bourque looked into that too. "Forget it," the Justice Department told him. "You don't have a case." Part of the problem was that money laundering was not a crime when the transactions occurred. There was no law under which any bank could be charged.

For Bourque, the bottom line is that a promising case that paid dividends in other countries had little to show in Canada — despite his best efforts. And his experience underscores what he feels is Canada's vulnerability to money laundering.

To be sure, money laundering is now a crime in Canada, a move that addresses the most glaring anomaly pinpointed in the 1988 DEA-RCMP report. And under new federal rules, Canadian financial institutions and others who handle money, including lawyers, are required to retain records of large cash transactions for up to five years — and to tip off police if they come across suspicious transactions. (Chartered banks had already been doing this on a voluntary basis.)

But Bourque does not believe this makes enough of a difference. In his view, money laundering continues unabated: "It happened last week. It's happening today. It's going to happen tomorrow. We just don't have any teeth." Proof, he says, is in the lack of successful prosecutions under the new law, though officials in Ottawa chalk this up to inexperience. "We'll get better as time goes on," they say. Others, including Bourque, are not so sure.

According to many critics, the Canadian legislation is so cumbersome that it does not deter either foreign money launderers or domestic ones. For one thing, said the late Craig Law of the Metropolitan Toronto Police, seizing assets is no simple matter. In fact, the odds are stacked in the criminal's favour. Take, for example, a major operation against some Toronto cocaine traffickers. In September 1991, Law's officers began examining about two hundred properties thought to have been bought with drug profits. That was eventually whittled down to just sixteen, the properties with sufficient equity to make forfeiture worthwhile. But because of the requirements of Bill C-61, the restraint order was not obtained until five months later, in January 1992. Said Law: "The extent of this affidavit is tantamount to supplying the necessary evidence to convict the person of trafficking. The burden of proof is very great."

During those five months, the accused could have sold all sixteen properties and the police would have been powerless to stop them. That they didn't was due to the dire state of the Toronto real estate market. "If this had happened several years [ago]," said Law, "the properties would have been sold and therefore our restraint order would have been really worthless." Even though none was sold, some properties lost value anyway. And since being arrested, some of the accused stopped making mortgage payments — sharply lowering the equity in the real estate. In some cases, the lenders have foreclosed on the properties.

"The onus, I believe, is a little too great on my proving the whole case in the restraint order," he said. "The time it takes me to prove this in the restraint order allows the criminal to stop his [mortgage] payments or sell it."

In Law's view, that was not the only drawback of Bill C-61. Immigration Act violations, for instance, are not among the offences it covers. Thus, as noted in Chapter 2, someone who profits from illegally smuggling in immigrants does not have to worry that profits from the operation will be seized. Similarly, the law does not list firearm violations. As Law put it: "Here [in Toronto] we have a city where last year we had a very high murder rate and we have a terrible increase in gun calls. Yet the people importing firearms into the city and selling them — and making a profit from this — cannot be attacked under Bill C-61."

Moreover, there are no moves to regulate cross-border movements of currency, a major problem cited in the 1988 DEA-RCMP report. And Canadian financial institutions are still not required to file reports of all large cash transactions — as their counterparts must in the United States. Canadian government officials and bankers say such a program is not needed. They argue that the current system already provides the kinds of "benefits claimed by more cumbersome and intrusive mechanisms" — by, among other things, giving police a large number of promising tips and leads.[25] They argue that the American approach has not proved cost-effective. Certainly, it has yet to achieve the potential touted by its architects — of creating an early-warning system for suspicious money movements. And it is not, by itself, the answer: the vigilance of individual financial institutions remains of great importance in the United States — as in Canada. Nonetheless, the American reporting system has imposed severe headaches — and higher costs — on money launderers.

In the U.S. investigation called "Operation C Chase," for instance, undercover agents in 1988 assured a drug money launderer they could evade the reporting requirements and thereby sharply lower his operating costs. Even though the launderer trusted the agents and firmly believed they were in the business of washing dirty money, he could not accept their guarantees. In fact, the launderer remained "paranoid about being identified by the government's . . . forms for large currency deposits" — so much so that he insisted on more expensive measures to elude the reporting requirements.[26] Without similar regulations, launderers in Canada have much less reason to be paranoid — a factor bound to make this country more attractive. After all, criminals, like water, seek the path of least resistance.

Sargent believes that Canada will continue to be in a dangerous situation unless its laws are made as stringent as those in the United States. Case after case has shown that criminals — and shady institutions like the Bank of Credit and Commerce International — are drawn to less regulated jurisdictions. He says: "Because of our proximity to the United States, we have to look at their legislation . . . and act accordingly. Because if we don't adopt the same mechanism that they adopt, then we're at risk."

To understand the risks, consider the kinds of cases that slip through unchallenged — like a strange multi-million-dollar transaction involving two controversial Americans, Dallas Bessant and Jerry Tidmore. The transaction was perfectly legal under Canadian law. It was also the sort of deal that is specifically structured to be transacted in Canada in order to avoid U.S. regulations.

Bessant's claim to fame was that he was Treasurer of a purported Indian tribe in Texas called the "Sovereign Cherokee Nation — Tejas." It was nothing of the sort. As a U.S. Senate committee stated in 1991, the entity was "neither sovereign, nor Cherokee, nor a nation. . . . It [was] a sham, run by a group of white or Anglo Americans for the sole purpose of financial self-enrichment."

Together with Tidmore, Bessant operated the U.S. Dominion Financial Corp., a Texas-based firm owned by a cryptic offshore shell company in the Caribbean. The two men were apparently very trusting souls who wouldn't think twice about making complex business deals with total strangers. Or so they tried to convince U.S. investigators. Sometime in the summer of 1988, they got a phone call from a mysterious Mr. Leo Gray in Toronto. Out of the blue this Mr. Gray, whom they claimed never to have met before, proposed a curious deal worth $362 million US, saying he wanted "an offshore intermediary." You've come to the right place, the credulous Texans told him. Since nothing about Mr. Gray or his transaction seemed out of the ordinary to Bessant and Tidmore, they flew to Toronto on September 12, 1988, and completed the deal. At Toronto's Lester B. Pearson International Airport, they were met by officials of the Toronto branch of Bankers Trust of New York. Also on hand, the two claimed, was the enigmatic Mr. Gray. In quick order, Bessant and Tidmore opened accounts at Bankers Trust. They then transferred $362 million US — which they said appeared to be under Gray's control — from the Caymans to their freshly opened accounts. From there, the money quickly moved out again into two mysterious shell companies: International Financial Trust Holdings Corp. and North American Intermediaries. All this occurred within a few hours on the same day. Bessant and Tidmore never left the Toronto airport. Their fee: $70,000 US.

The transaction came to light in 1991 when U.S. Senate investigators looked into the activities of Bessant and Tidmore's circle of associates. The pair volunteered little when questioned. Who was behind the deal? they were asked. Mr. Gray, Bessant replied. Who was Gray? Well, Bessant didn't really know: Gray simply called one day from Toronto. After the deal was completed, he was never seen again. And, claimed Bessant and Tidmore, they were never involved in other deals involving any of these same corporate entities.

So what was it all about? Why did they come to Canada to do such a deal? No one knows for sure. But the Senate investigators have a pretty good idea. Subpoenaed from Bessant's accountant was a letter to Leo Gray from a Toronto law firm. It apparently provided an opinion on the possible tax implications in this kind of a deal. According to investigators, the letter appeared "to lay out the entire transaction in a hypothetical scenario for the apparent purpose of avoiding Canadian tax laws. In addition, another letter from Bessant's Turks and Caicos Island law firm appears to corroborate this interpretation of the deal." To what end? U.S. Senate investigators say the transaction "appears to have been an attempt to avoid Canadian tax laws and possibly U.S. money laundering statutes." Their conclusion: "It leaves the impression that the entities involved were part of an ongoing operation on behalf of Mr. Gray and others to regularly transfer large sums of funds through offshore intermediaries in order to avoid [American currency] reporting and tax laws."27

The actual nature of the transaction will likely remain a question mark. This kind of deal, admits one investigator, is so nebulous and complex that there's little chance of unravelling it, no matter how many people work on the case. Canada's money laundering law, which came into effect a few months after the $362 million US transaction, would neither have prevented it — nor helped decipher it.

Adding to Canada's vulnerability, says Sargent, is the lack of scrutiny built into federal programs to attract foreign investors. A case in point involves the late John H. O'Halloran, a legendary political fixer and government party bagman in the Caribbean island nation of Trinidad and Tobago. As *Globe and Mail* reporter Robert Matas discovered, O'Halloran moved to Canada in 1982 under a federal program designed to attract investors with the money and expertise to create jobs and wealth in Canada.28 In fact, O'Halloran's main purpose was to find a place to hide dirty money — in his case, nearly $4 million in bribes and kickbacks accumulated during more than two decades in public life. Canada was not just a way station for his dirty money. Rather, O'Halloran saw it as a place to enjoy a nest-egg already laundered through places like Switzerland, the Cayman Islands and Liechtenstein. O'Halloran did this until he died of cancer in Toronto in 1985. His funds found a safe refuge in a familiar repository — Toronto-area property developments.29 Unlike many such cases, this one ended happily. In

1990, after a lengthy investigation by Toronto accountant Robert Lindquist, Trinidad received $4 million as compensation from O'Halloran's son.

This is a cautionary tale for the federal government in its efforts to attract wealthy foreigners. In theory, immigration officers have the power to evaluate the source of a prospective applicant's funds. In practice, there is little scrutiny — especially if the immigrant is an entrepreneur with enough money and a viable business plan. Said the 1990 federal study into money laundering: "The question of an immigrant's source of funds is addressed in vague terms, and there are no mechanisms for identifying what are and are not legitimate funds or for verifying net worth statements."[30]

Investment Canada, the federal agency that is supposed to regulate foreign investment, is similarly lax. According to the study, Investment Canada's top priority is to promote foreign investment — not ensure that it's clean. Concludes Sargent: "Canada wants to encourage, as much as possible, foreign investment. What's legitimate foreign investment and what's not? Those are things we have to come to grips with."

In this kind of survey of selected cases, it is impossible to quantify the extent to which Canada is used to launder dirty money. Neither can the magnitude of the problem be delineated. It is more like a marker in a misty landscape. But as the federal money laundering analysis discovered in 1990, the situation in Canada is worrisome: "It is estimated that over 80 percent of the police cases examined as a part of this study incorporate an international component. This is in marked contrast to United States estimates which indicate that only 10 percent of illicit drug money generated in the United States moves into international circles. . . . The involvement of Canada in the global money laundering networks cannot simply be attributed to Canadian criminal enterprises. First, the criminal enterprises are as international as the laundering schemes are. . . . Second, cases reveal that illicit money which has been generated elsewhere (most notably in the United States) has entered Canada for laundering purposes with few connections with indige-nous-based criminal enterprises. Canada is thus inextricably tied to the global laundering network."31

In the narcotics trade, for instance, drug cops are able to intercept no more than a small portion of all shipments. There is no reason to think that authorities can nab a bigger percent-age of drug profits moving through Canada. In fact, there is little to suggest that law enforcement agencies have as good a grip on cross-border movements of disputed funds as they do on drug shipments themselves. In the absence of currency-transaction reporting requirements, clean and dirty money can freely move across the border. Thus, there's no way of mea-suring "the flow of funds (legitimate or otherwise) into and out of Canada."32 And even if cash is discovered in suspicious circumstances, "Customs Canada has little legal recourse. . . . Other law enforcement agencies, such as the RCMP or local police, would not necessarily be contacted [either], as no law would be broken at the border crossing."33

Drug cops will also readily concede having more financial cases than they can handle — enough to overwhelm forces with vastly larger resources than any in Canada. If that weren't bad enough, they also acknowledge their difficulty in tackling really complex schemes. They are typically ham-pered by a dearth of funding, staff and forensic accounting expertise, and by the aforementioned weaknesses in Canada's anti-money-laundering legislation. They are also hindered by a lack of political commitment. On a national scale, surprisingly little expertise and few personnel are devoted to tackling this kind of crime — apart from the RCMP's already stretched resources and the Toronto police's equally overworked financial sleuths. Local and provincial forces have an extra disincentive to devote impor-tant resources to tackling money laundering. All seized assets go into federal coffers, even if the successful investi-gation was by a local or provincial force. The late Craig Law pointed out the injustice of this setup: "Surely if a police force enforces the law, and there is an asset to be gained, then the taxpayers who paid the original salaries ought to be reimbursed out of some of the seized assets."

There are signs that things may improve. In April 1992, Ottawa said it planned to spend $33 million over five years setting up special experimental units in Vancouver, Toronto and Montreal to target drug profits. The units will bring together the RCMP, provincial and municipal police forces. The three cities are good choices — since almost all seizures in 1989 (the latest available figures) of drug proceeds "generated abroad were made in Montreal, Toronto and Vancouver."[34] Moreover, federal officials are said to be looking at the prospect of sharing forfeited assets with the provinces. Yet such tinkering pales in the face of the task at hand.

"Money laundering investigations are labour intensive, time-consuming, they require a level of expertise," says Sargent, the former RCMP investigator. Stating publicly what many of his former colleagues can only say off the record, he says: "I don't think at this point in time that law enforcement agencies in Canada are very prepared from both a financial standpoint and from an expertise standpoint to get into these kinds of investigations." Then, in remarks that recall those of Donovan Blakeman, who set up the "Spaghetti Jungle," Sargent said: "The bad guys use lawyers and accountants. They use people who are experts in tax and corporate structure. The police need the same kind of ability.

"If you don't have it, all you'll end up doing is catching the stupid money launderer — the guy who does things in very basic terms."

■ 5 DOING LAUNDRY: CANADIAN BANKS IN THE CARIBBEAN

W ith his glassy stare, long, scruffy hair and fondness for military fatigues, you'd think Steve Yakovac would raise eyebrows wherever he went. Not so. At least not in the late 1970s in Nassau, the laid-back, sun-drenched capital of the Bahamas. And not at its most prominent financial institution, the Bank of Nova Scotia. No one at the bank, it seems, was much troubled by the sight of the American college dropout who described himself as "a long-haired hippie, a pseudo-revolutionary" or by the cash he delivered in a bulky scuba equipment bag. In one shipment on September 1, 1978, he brought in a deposit that tipped the scales at 54 kilograms. To count it, two tellers were kept busy all afternoon — for which the bank charged a 1 percent fee. By quitting time, they'd toted up $994,765 US in cash, including 44,160 twenty-dollar bills.

Yakovac was a jack-of-all-trades for Carlos Lehder (full name: Carlos Enrique Lehder-Rivas), a flashy Colombian businessman in his late twenties with a penchant for bombastic outbursts and woolly radical politics. Initially at least, Lehder passed himself off as a visionary developer bent on turning a hook-shaped Bahamian island, Norman's Cay, into a luxury resort. He was nothing of the sort — and he had quite other designs on Norman's Cay (and its two-thousand-metre runway). Lehder was, in fact, a charter member of Colombia's notorious Medellin cartel. During much of the late 1970s and 1980s, it controlled the bulk of the white powdery stimulant entering North America. For a time, large quantities of the cartel's exports, at least 3.3 tonnes of cocaine between 1978 and 1980, went through Lehder's transshipment base on Norman's Cay.

This was a huge operation and a costly one. Through his Bahamian-registered firm, International Dutch Resources Ltd., most of the island's residents were bought out. (One left the day he was given a suitcase filled with $100,000 US.) Less cooperative souls were more brusquely scared off. Operating expenses were substantial. Special hangars had to be built to store cocaine and airplanes. Sophisticated communications systems and navigational aids were installed to facilitate night landings by aircraft. Then there were the forty or so machine-gun-toting mercenaries, many from East Germany, who guarded and manned the operation. (Their amusements weren't cheap, either — including wild peacocks for target practice and gargantuan feasting.) There was also a steady demand for aircraft. (Five wrecked planes, including a DC-3, soon littered the waters around the island.)[1]

By and large, the Norman's Cay operation was bankrolled through Lehder's Scotiabank accounts, and he went to great lengths to make his business dealings (and his financial transactions) appear consistent with his stated intentions for the island. "He had a lot of normal chequing accounts," Rick Marshall, Scotiabank's international counsel, said in a 1988 interview. "A lot of the activity was what you'd expect of a guy running a yacht basin or trying to build a yacht basin on Norman's Cay."

Lehder himself was captured in a shootout in Colombia in 1987 and was quickly extradited to the United States — the only major figure in the cocaine trade to have suffered this fate. He was convicted in 1988 in Jacksonville, Florida, and is now serving a sentence of life plus 135 years. Yakovac, who testified against Lehder, is now living under an assumed name under the U.S. Witness Protection Program. The Medellin cartel itself has gone into decline, supplanted by rivals based in the Colombian city of Cali.

More than a thousand pages of records subpoenaed from the Bank of Nova Scotia helped seal Lehder's fate. The sums were substantial. Between May 1978 and January 1980, when Lehder's Scotiabank links ended, more than $11.4 million US, including $9.055 million in cash, flowed through three accounts. "I think it constituted the working capital of his operation, exclusive of the purchase of the product, which would take a lot more working capital," said Marshall at the time.

Yet much about the accounts was suspect, concluded Wendel Welman, a money laundering expert at the U.S. Internal Revenue Service, who analyzed Lehder's Scotiabank records. The pattern of Lehder's deposits, for instance, was not what you would expect from typical commercial dealings. "The periodic nature of the deposits didn't reflect normal operations [of an ordinary business]," he told Lehder's trial in 1988. Welman said the financial outflows — woven through a complex web of transactions — were equally dubious. Many took advantage of the Canadian bank's vast international network. Tens of thousands of dollars, for instance, were routinely wired between Scotiabank branches in Nassau, Miami, Panama and New York.

In a similar vein, scores of cheques — for suspiciously large, round numbers — were sent to shady entities in Colombia and Panama. On December 17, 1978, for instance, four cheques of $50,000 US apiece were shipped to a certain Alberto Acevedo in Panama. On April 26, 1979, six more cheques — this time for $20,000 US apiece — were sent to one Emilio Zuleta in Medellin. Authorities were unable to discover the purpose of those payments, though for others this was much easier to discern: on October 23, 1978, one payment of $504,100 US was sent to the Cessna Aircraft Co., the manufacturer of the type of small, agile plane favoured by cocaine smugglers.

Lehder's actions apparently bred no misgivings at the Canadian bank, partly because he seemed to have above-board references and connections. His company, International Dutch Resources, had been established with the help of a British banker, Ian Davidson, who lived in Nassau. And Lehder himself had been authenticated by a well-known local financial institution, Guardian Trust. (No relation to the Canadian firm of the same name.) Davidson, by coincidence, was also Guardian's manager. He was a very helpful sort, too. On Lehder's behalf, he delivered millions of dollars in cash to the Scotiabank, including a single deposit of $1.25 million US. And, for a time, he was a corporate officer of International Dutch Resources and other Lehder entities. One had the fanciful name Titanic Aircraft Sales. Later, a Bahamian commission found Davidson's efforts to explain his ties to Lehder wanting. It concluded: "The impression that Davidson attempted to create was that of a disinterested trust company executive who unfortunately became associated with a drug smuggling organization. We did not find him a credible witness."[2]

And what of the Bank of Nova Scotia's view of Lehder? "In the late seventies no bells went off [at the bank] as far as I can determine," Marshall said. "What the bank learned from this incident and others like it is that in this day and age it's a lot more difficult than it used to be to know your customer." This proved to be a far-reaching lesson both for the Toronto-based institution and for the Canadian industry as a whole.

Canadian banks dominate the Caribbean, and Scotiabank is the biggest single Canadian presence in the region. The roots of this preeminence go back centuries — to Canada's first mercantile links with the region. The earliest likely date back to the mid-1600s, when Jean Talon, the Intendant of New France, made an ultimately unsuccessful bid to foster trade with the West Indies.[3] His hopes were not realized until long after he'd left the scene. In the next century, it was the rival British who reaped the profits, not the French. Under the British, commerce between what is now Nova Scotia and the West Indies became well established — so much so that by the mid-1700s a Halifax merchant, Joshua Mauger, could readily supply his distillery with molasses and sugar imported from the West Indies. In return, he sent back fish and lumber — commodities that would long remain the backbone of Canadian exports to the region.[4] By the late nineteenth century, the trade links were lucrative enough to attract Canadian bankers to the Caribbean.[5] First off the mark was the Bank of Nova Scotia, which had a branch in Jamaica in 1894, before it had one in Toronto. A little later the Merchants' Bank of Halifax "followed American troops into Havana during the Spanish-American War, [and] developed a thriving business financing Cuban-American trade." The Merchants' Bank later changed its name to the Royal Bank of Canada.[6]

Since then, Canadian financial institutions have tended to be the retail and corporate banks of choice in many parts of the Caribbean. In the Bahamas, for example, they handle about 80 percent of the country's business. Canadian banks succeeded in the West Indies for the same reasons they have thrived around the world. They are large, efficient and trustworthy, with huge international branch networks and the latest in computer technology. Little is beyond their scope. They can do anything from financing a hotel development in the Netherlands Antilles to helping a Jamaican immigrant in Toronto wire money home to family members in Kingston.

For nearly one hundred years, the banks' Caribbean outposts were a point of pride (and profit). But in the 1970s and early 1980s, some also became a source of embarrassment: many cases emerged in which Canadian banks (and especially Scotiabank) had been used to launder shady funds, usually drug profits.

This occurred, in part, because the Caribbean is bloated with tax havens — the Cayman Islands, Bermuda and the Bahamas, to name a few. Indeed, the financial sector is one of the area's two bedrock industries. (Tourism is the other.) Canadians can take some credit for this. It was a Calgary lawyer, Jim Macdonald, for instance, who deftly turned the Caymans into the region's preeminent tax haven. His contribution: drafting legislation that drew on the best features of more established rivals like Bermuda. As Macdonald told journalist Martin Keeley in 1979: "I had a few philosophical ideas on how you make a tax haven work. There was nothing particularly magical about it."[7] Today, citizens of the Caymans are among the most prosperous in the Caribbean. Its 548 financial institutions represent "a who's who of global banking [and] hold assets of some $400 billion US, a fivefold jump in the past decade, placing it just behind Switzerland, as an international banking centre."[8]

Nearby, in the Bahamas, much credit is similarly given to a former Canadian finance minister, Donald Fleming. After resigning from public life in 1963, he helped Bahamian authorities close "most of the loopholes through which confidential client information could be obtained."[9] The success of such Caribbean havens is built on low tax rates, tough financial secrecy laws and generally lax regulatory environments. As we'll see in the next chapter, these attributes have lured both a well-heeled clientele of tax-flinchers and a much murkier crowd.

Two other factors are also worth noting: geography and a buccaneering heritage. As a handy bridge between North and South America, the region is a perfectly situated staging area for all kinds of illicit traffic. Hence, a tradition in the West Indies of shady figures earning large amounts of shady revenues. And hence the risk that even the most well-meaning financial institution could get tangled in questionable endeavours — simply by doing business there. Montreal economist Tom Naylor, an influential money laundering researcher, once compared it to the perils of playing near a cesspool. Anyone who does so, he said, has "no cause for complaint if somebody throws a rock in and they end up getting splashed."

As far back as the mid-1600s, the island of St. Eustatius, or

Statia as it was then known, was a funnel for evading taxes and smuggling goods between England and France, the era's two great colonial powers. French sugar, for instance, found its way to English buyers after being illegally repacked into English barrels on the island. In the 1770s, Statia's British merchants went one better — providing arms for the rebellious American colonies battling Her Majesty's troops (who were also, incidentally, the merchants' compatriots).[10]

This tradition continued into the twentieth century. During Prohibition, bootleggers in the Bahamas and elsewhere in the region took advantage of its location to smuggle (often Canadian) liquor into the United States. According to local lore, one such base had been Norman's Cay.[11]

In the early 1960s, American criminals, like Meyer Lansky, looked to the Caribbean for another reason. The communist takeover in Cuba had deprived them of a freewheeling (and corrupt) site for their casinos, creating the need for accessible alternate locales. The Bahamas soon met a portion of that demand, thanks, in part, to the efforts of a rotund, enterprising Canadian. His name was Lou Chesler, a one-time Toronto mining promoter who'd been involved in some stock deals with Lansky. Along the way, Chesler, who died in 1983, also tried his hand as movie magnate. He helped bankroll such eminently forgettable Hollywood fare as *Panic Button,* starring Jayne Mansfield, and *Main Attraction,* with Pat Boone.[12]

More significant were Chesler's groundbreaking (and shady) efforts to install organized-crime-tainted gambling in the Bahamas. Reporter Paul McGrath of CBC-TV's "The Journal, " who has extensively researched the contemporary history of the Caribbean offshore, calls Chesler "one of the small handful of men initially responsible for corrupting the Bahamas with the introduction in the 1960s of mob-run casinos." Chesler made a name for himself by piloting the Lucayan Beach luxury hotel project in the early 1960s. It relied on a bizarre $11 million loan from Atlantic Acceptance Corp., a Canadian financial institution. "It was more like a gift than a loan, commented one accountant who assessed the transaction some years later," wrote journalist Catherine Wismer.[13] That Chesler got a marvellous deal was not surprising, since he also happened to be close to one of its controlling shareholders. Atlantic Acceptance collapsed in 1965 under the burden of such imprudent lending. But it had already served its purpose: the casino at Lucayan Beach opened on January 22, 1964, to a gala celebration. Wrote organized crime expert Hank Messick: "The international jet set was on hand to give the event some class, but Meyer Lansky's veterans were in complete control."[14]

Another disreputable Canadian, the late Paul Volpe, left his mark on the gambling business in neighbouring Haiti, says Toronto author James Dubro. In the early 1960s, Volpe — a major figure in organized crime in Toronto — helped turn the island's lone casino "into a very profitable operation, selling everything from food to medicine on the premises."[15]

In the late 1970s, Lehder and his partners ushered in perhaps the most remunerative illicit trade to touch the West Indies: cocaine. By the middle of the next decade, the Medellin cartel was said to smuggle up to fifteen tonnes of cocaine into North America and Europe each month. So profitable was this business that some of its leaders were described in 1987 as "probable billionaires" by *Fortune* magazine.[16] The Caribbean played an important two-way role in this development — acting as the conduit for drug shipments heading into the United States and for the tens of millions of dollars in drug profits coming out. Cash, for instance, was often packed into the very planes that delivered drug shipments — and then cleansed in banks scattered throughout the West Indies. By any measure, the cocaine trade — and, to a lesser degree, the less lucrative marijuana business — had a dramatic impact on the region's banks and on their cash balances.

Consider the tiny Bahamian island of Bimini. Its lone financial institution, a branch of the Royal Bank of Canada, was best described as "an overgrown hot-dog stand."[17] Yet for a time, it did the kind of business that would have done a branch many times its size proud. In 1977, it transferred $544,360 US in cash to the Bahamian central bank. Five years later, this had surged to $12.292 million US — nearly $4 million US more than the balance of payments surplus for the Bahamas as a whole. The central bank could not establish that these amounts had come "from any ordinary business transaction," especially since Bimini was a relatively poor island of just two thousand people. (It had once also been a favourite watering hole of the American writer, Ernest Hemingway.) There was just one possible explanation for all this cash. Concluded the 1984 Bahamian commission which probed the island's links with the drug trade: "The large increase in U.S. dollar deposits is directly related to the flow of drugs." [18]

The problem in Bimini was soon addressed. The Royal Bank's board of directors gave bank executives a clear directive: clean it up or shut it down. By 1987, the drug trade had been so reduced that the island's lone bank "did not take in enough U.S. currency to transfer anything to Nassau." [19] This had some negative local effects — "drying up credit on Bimini and starving the whole Bahamian banking system for funds." [20]

Bimini was not an isolated case. In the early 1980s, scores of drug-money-laundering cases surfaced in the Caribbean — the result of an intense, American-led offensive against narcotics profits. Among such cases, the name of one financial institution often arose: the Bank of Nova Scotia. In the drug trade, it seemed (for a time, at least) to have a troubling reputation. As Leigh Ritch, a convicted drug smuggler, testified before a U.S. Senate subcommittee in 1988: "In the early seventies, the Bank of Nova Scotia was the easiest [for washing drug profits], and then it turned to become the very hardest one." [21]

The experience of another convicted American trafficker, Robert "The Dance Man" Twist, had a similar ring. In the late 1970s, he said a well-known Bahamian lawyer recommended he use the Scotiabank. As Twist explained to host Bob McKeown of CBC's "the 5th estate" in a 1986 interview, the lawyer said the Bank of Nova Scotia "was easy to get into and they'd take good care of you. . . . So I went over and met with one of the managers, set up the accounts and told him what I'd be bringing in. And he said fine." Twist said he explained to the bank official that he'd be delivering a few million dollars at a time — in cash and in small denominations.

Bob McKeown: "Did he ask what the money was from?"

Robert Twist: "No, he never asked what [it] was from or anything."

Bob McKeown: "No questions asked?"

Robert Twist: "No questions."22

American Senate investigators heard many similar stories in the early 1980s. Hence, their 1983 staff study into the criminal use of the offshore concluded: "In the Caribbean, one major Canadian international bank has a consistent reputation for encouraging dirty money."23 Though the Senate study did not identify the institution, there was no doubt about its name. As the report of a 1990 federal examination of money laundering plainly stated, this had been "an obvious reference to the Bank of Nova Scotia."24 There's no proof that the bank actively invited this sort of business. And the bank itself has never been charged with violating money laundering statutes. Yet there's no denying the numerous incidents in which it had been used in the 1970s and early eighties to wash dirty and black funds. By journalist McGrath's tally, defendants relied on Scotiabank branches in the Bahamas and the Caymans to launder their money in about a dozen major prosecutions in the U.S.

Take the case of Bruce "Peewee" Griffin, a Florida drug smuggler who the FBI estimates made profits of $100 million US a year between 1975 and 1981. According to testimony before the Bahamian commission, Griffin deposited $22 million US in cash at the Scotiabank in Nassau over a four-month period in 1979. As journalist William Marsden reported, the money was then transferred to the Cayman Islands, entering the Scotiabank account of a company called Cobalt Ltd. "From there, the money was wired back to the U.S. into Scotiabank's New York City branch. Griffin then dispersed it among numerous corporations he owned in the U.S."25

The bank was also used to wash some of the Sicilian Mafia's earnings from the so-called Pizza Connection operation, in which American pizzerias were used to conceal heroin trafficking. The financial conduit was a money launderer by the name of Salvatore Amendolito, a middle-aged New York fishmonger who typically dressed "in various shades of grey silk, nicely chosen to complement his abundant wavy silver-grey hair."[26] Two deposits stand out. On November 11, 1980, Amendolito deposited $233,387.20 US in small bills at the Bank of Nova Scotia in Nassau. The next day, he delivered $329,983.12 US "in money orders, travellers' cheques and cashiers' cheques all under $10,000" — apparently to evade American cash reporting requirements.[27]

In denying that it had deliberately attracted dirty money, bank chairman Cedric Ritchie stated: "Because of both the nature of our business in the Caribbean and the unique vulnerability of that region to drug traffickers, it was inevitable that criminals would attempt to use our bank for their nefarious purposes."[28] Moreover, maintained the bank, the known cases represented but a tiny fraction of its overall activities of this, the region's most important financial institution. As one official put it: "In the context of the business we do in the Caribbean, these cases wouldn't amount to one one-thousandth of one percent. . . . It's not surprising to find [some] bad apples in all of the activities that we carry on in the Caribbean."

The bank's explanations, however, proved little match for the horrendous publicity those "bad apples" generated. Most widely reported were two messy (and costly) court fights in the early 1980s over American subpoenas for offshore records. The first case involved a 1981 U.S. grand jury subpoena for the bank records of the previously mentioned Twist. The writ was served in a roundabout fashion — on the bank's Miami branch, not on the relevant Bahamian office. The Bank of Nova Scotia balked at obeying the order, saying to do so would violate Bahamas' bank secrecy laws. In June 1982, the bank was found guilty of contempt and fined $500 US a day until it turned over the documents. About a year later, the fine was boosted to $25,000 a day, at which point the bank capitulated. Said Gordon Bell, the bank's president at the time: "We resisted as long as we could. . . . The fine put us in a position where we were unable to avoid compliance." The case cost the bank more than $100,000 US in fines.

The second incident was similar, though it proved more ticklish — and expensive. It involved the bank records of another American marijuana smuggler, Frank Brady. This time, too, a U.S. subpoena to obtain the documents — issued in March 1983 — was served on the Miami branch, even though the relevant files were in Scotiabank branches in the Bahamas and the Cayman Islands. And once again, the bank refused to comply, citing bank secrecy laws in the two jurisdictions. Similarly, a fine of $25,000 US a day was subsequently levied. It went into effect on November 14, 1983. Within days, the Bahamian files were surrendered. Matters were much stickier in the Caymans, where officials were deeply worried that the release of bank records would hurt the tax haven's reputation for guarding client confidentiality. They took such a hard line on the matter that the Scotiabank documents were not turned over to American authorities until late January 1984 — and only after the personal intervention of its governor. By that time, however, the fine had swollen to $1.825 million US.

At the time, the bank's willingness to cooperate with drug investigations was questioned. There were even suggestions that it had been "stonewalling," that it had no qualms about accepting drug profits. In hindsight, the bank appears to have done everything it could to comply with the subpoenas while still respecting the letter of the law in the affected tax havens. And it seems to have been quite warranted in fearing criminal prosecution for violating the laws of the Caymans and the Bahamas. Yet despite its apparent good intentions, the bank found itself, as one source familiar with the cases put it, caught "between the dog and the lamp post" — between aggressive American prosecutors and officials in the two tax havens who were equally intent on guarding their sovereignty.

Some observers suggest that much of the "Brady" fine may have been unfairly levied. About $1.3 million US of the $1.8 million US penalty resulted from the late delivery of a few overlooked carbon copies of documents. Yet, says American dirty money expert Ingo Walter, they contained no information that was not in previously surrendered records. Moreover, he says, the omission had been rectified after being spotted by the bank itself — not by the prosecution.[29] Equally intriguing to Walter, who expressed some sympathy for the bank's predicament, is evidence that U.S. officials had at their disposal a much easier route for acquiring records from the Caymans. (Recall that the islands' resistance contributed mightily to the Brady fine's upward spiral.) According to Walter: "There was apparently in existence at the time a secret exchange-of-letters between the United States and the Caymans setting out an agreed procedure for securing bank records and other information pertinent to U.S. criminal investigation." In this light, it was not without some justification that Scotiabank chairman Ritchie later defended his institution's actions, stating: "We tried every legal means to obtain permission to release the documents. But ironically, it was the U.S. officials themselves who refused to take the steps necessary to obtain the co-operation of the Cayman government. Certainly the bank wasn't stonewalling."[30]

According to previously classified External Affairs memos released under the Access to Information Act, Ottawa repeatedly urged Washington to seek the required information through other means, like letters rogatory. Under such a procedure, a Canadian court could have obtained evidence required in an American legal action. But, as stated in a diplomatic note dated September 27, 1983, even though such alternatives could have provided information "more efficaciously than through a subpoena. . . . It is all the more regrettable, therefore, that agents for the Attorney General of the United States have not followed these mutually agreed procedures." Why not? A 1985 Senate report suggested it was part of a pugnacious brand of American diplomacy — aimed at sending a no-nonsense signal that "U.S. pressure could continually force international banks to comply with subpoenas."[31]

Even before "the Brady affair" ended, however, Ritchie moved to clean things up — and stem the bad publicity from that case and others. As he frankly admitted: "We failed to appreciate the extent to which banks would become an unwitting pipeline for drug profits. . . . In hindsight, there can be little doubt that some of our branches were used unwittingly to launder drug-related profits."[32] Lawyer Marshall was hired especially to deal with the bank's Caribbean headaches. Though all the instances involving "bad apples" had occurred prior to 1982, the legal fallout (and the bad publicity) would not settle until 1988 — when Lehder was convicted. By then, Marshall had already consulted experts in Canada and the United States on how to reduce the bank's vulnerability. And, as the 1990 federal study noted: "Partly in response to [the] allegations, the Bank of Nova Scotia has enacted strict policies to combat money laundering in both its domestic and its international branches."[33]

The Scotiabank's policies — based on the twin pillars of better knowing their customers and more dilligent probing and identifying of suspicious transactions — would influence financial institutions throughout North America. Its employee training programs and videos, in particular, were widely emulated. All of which helps explain drug smuggler Leigh Ritch's comment in 1988 to a U.S. Senate panel that the bank had become "the very hardest one" for drug money laundering.[34]

Beyond the world of banking, the Scotiabank's legal troubles in the United States had far-reaching implications for Canadian-American relations. Both the "Brady" and "Twist" cases had occurred mostly under Pierre Trudeau's Liberal administration, with its long-standing concerns about national independence. The government plainly did not like the way these legal actions had been handled south of the border and was especially rankled by Washington's indirect pressure tactics. In both instances, the heat was placed on the

Miami branch of the Scotiabank to get records from branches in third countries, although the Miami operation was not linked to the case. Clearly, said Ottawa, the United States was overstepping its authority and impinging on Canadian sovereignty. A "confidential" External Affairs memo dated July 8, 1983, and released under the Access to Information Act, put it this way: "Under principles of international law, one state normally may not order a person over whom it has jurisdiction to act outside its territory in ways that would violate the laws of the state where the conduct is to take place. In this regard, the government of the United States would no doubt be offended if a United States company operating abroad were ordered, on pain of penal sanction and attachment of its local assets, to commit an act in the United States that would violate United States law." The issue was so important that it was discussed at the Cabinet level at bilateral meetings. The finance minister, Marc Lalonde, for instance, took up the matter with his U.S. counterpart, Donald Regan, during a meeting in November 1983.

Out of such discussions came some fundamental changes, though only time will gauge their ultimate effectiveness. Most important was that the United States and Canada subsequently negotiated a mutual legal assistance treaty. Later each reached similar agreements with a number of Caribbean jurisdictions, including the Bahamas and the Caymans. As a result, there are now agreed-upon legal frameworks for obtaining subpoenaed documents from key foreign domains — without having to resort to coercion or directly intruding on anyone's sovereignty.

The Bank of Nova Scotia's legal problems had another consequence: they prompted Ottawa to be better prepared in case such situations recurred. The case is credited with leading to the passage of the Foreign Extraterritorial Measures Act of 1984, giving the federal government the power to order a Canadian company to disregard an American law. Ironically, the act was implemented not by the Liberals, but by their replacements in the 1984 election — the Tories of Brian

Mulroney, who are considered by many to be less diligent in guarding Canadian sovereignty. Whether the new powers would have made a difference in the "Brady" or "Twist" cases, however, is anybody's guess.

There is no doubt that the Scotiabank's travails in the Caribbean helped transform Canadian banking attitudes. The extent of that transformation is something the industry may not be willing to fully admit. But it has definitely made an impression on Michael Mackenzie, Canada's banking watch-dog. "There has been a change of culture," said a candid Mackenzie, who before his appointment as the federal Super-intendent of Financial Institutions had been Scotiabank's auditor. "I think in the 1970s and prior, there was a certain casual attitude to all of this." But, he said, if you examine the banking sector over a five-year span — say 1979 to 1984, or 1980 to 1985 — "one does see a lot of changes." Mackenzie says banks now recognize that they do "have an obligation to know [their] customers, to satisfy themselves . . . that they're not conniving in breaking laws. . . . They didn't pay attention to that in the late 1970s."

So what are the broad consequences of this "change of cul-ture" and of the banks' anti-money-laundering measures? It is difficult to determine precisely, though one result is beyond doubt: the more overt flows of tainted funds have probably been curtailed. It is therefore unlikely that anyone could now get away with lugging a scuba equipment bag full of dirty cash into one of the Big Six Canadian banks either at home or abroad. So there is now little prospect for a future in money-laundering-through-major-Canadian-institutions for glassy-eyed, scruffy-haired, military-uniformed, college dropouts like Steve Yakovac. Now he would more likely take his business to institutions that are far less active in the fight against dirty money laundering — less regulated storefront currency exchanges or smaller trust companies, for instance. In the Caribbean, there are more than enough other institu-tions — some consisting of nothing of more than a brass plaque on an office wall, a fax machine and a telephone — to handle his needs.

Beyond that, the effects of tighter Canadian banking policies are more difficult to gauge. Whether banks have also significantly hampered more sophisticated criminal financiers — or (more likely) simply made their task more arduous — is open to debate. Certainly, the know-your-client approach has its limitations. As bankers will admit privately, they cannot keep out shady clients who appear well-heeled and present suitable credentials and references. The Duvalier laundering scheme is a case in point. On a larger scale, so is the spectacular demise in 1991 of the empire of the late media baron, Robert Maxwell. Twenty years earlier, an official British inquiry had said he was unfit to run a public company. Nonetheless, major banks in Britain, France and the United States set that — and much else about the unsavoury Maxwell — aside to lend him and his two public companies upwards of $4 billion US. As the *Economist* put it, "Without them, Maxwell would have been unable to run what was, in effect, a massive international confidence game."[35] Yet, how much faith can be placed on the know-your-client judgment of institutions that, in the words of the *Economist,* were "at best, naive and, at worst, complicit."[36] Thus, while Canadian banks may have improved their methods of fending off dirty money laundering, they remain vulnerable, in part, because of other less vigilant institutions.

Since August 1991, for instance, Pakistan has allowed its banks to guarantee total secrecy for holders of accounts in foreign currencies. As a result nearly $1 billion US is estimated to have poured into Pakistan, no questions asked. [37] Such a development worries drug enforcement officials who fear that Pakistan may be becoming a haven for narcotics profits. Consider an ad placed in the March 16, 1992, edition of the *Wall Street Journal* by the central bank of Pakistan. In touting the benefits of its five-year bearer bonds, the State Bank of Pakistan pointed to some unusual features: "No questions asked about the source of the funds" and "No identity to be disclosed." Moreover, "no income tax" and "no wealth tax" would have to be paid on them. American officials took a dim view of the practice and ordered the Pakistani bank to stop selling the bonds in the United States. The offering, ruled U.S. officials, "suggested that the purchase of these bonds was a means of avoiding income taxes and allowed for the interpretation that money laundering was being solicited, thereby raising serious policy concerns, as well as concerns over compliance with U.S. law." The State Bank denied it intended to encourage tax evasion or money laundering. Nonetheless, it complied with the American order.[38]

International issues aside, consumers of Canadian banks at home and abroad have undoubtedly been affected by changing industry attitudes to dirty money laundering. Canadian banks have increasingly asked clients to explain unusual transactions, such as sizeable cash deposits, and this has not sat well with some people. After all, financial privacy remains a valued asset, as the hapless Scotiabank discovered on at least one occasion. In late 1986, Neil Connors, a client in Grand Falls, Newfoundland, angrily closed his account after being twice asked to explain where he got a $1,900 cash deposit. Connors, who buys and sells collectibles, was so incensed that he vented his indignation in a letter to his local paper. He wrote that when asked to justify the $1,900, "I told her [the teller] I didn't think it was any of the bank's business." The unfortunate local branch manager later replied, explaining in a letter in the same newspaper that "stepped-up vigilance has been required to respond to the increased sophistication of the methods used to launder illegitimate profits through financial institutions."

Canadian bankers must sometimes wonder if they can ever win.

A beaming Jean-Claude "Baby-Doc" Duvalier and
Michele Bennett, photographed in May 1980, one week before
their wedding, which cost an estimated $3 million US.

A page from Michele's notebook details a visit to Boucheron, the Paris jeweler, in
December 1987. Tonton, *or uncle, was Michele's pet name for Baby Doc.*

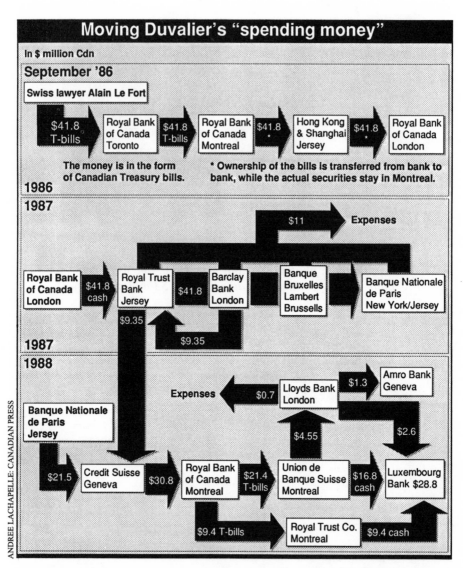

Moving Duvalier's "spending money"

In $ million Cdn

September '86

Swiss lawyer Alain Le Fort

$41.8 T-bills → Royal Bank of Canada Toronto → $41.8 T-bills → Royal Bank of Canada Montreal → $41.8 * → Hong Kong & Shanghai Jersey → $41.8 * → Royal Bank of Canada London

The money is in the form of Canadian Treasury bills.

* Ownership of the bills is transferred from bank to bank, while the actual securities stay in Montreal.

1986 / 1987

$11 → Expenses

Royal Bank of Canada London → $41.8 cash → Royal Trust Bank Jersey → $41.8 → Barclay Bank London → Banque Bruxelles Lambert Brussells → Banque Nationale de Paris New York/Jersey

$9.35

$9.35

1987 / 1988

Amro Bank Geneva

$1.3 ← Lloyds Bank London → Expenses ← $0.7

$4.55

$2.6

Banque Nationale de Paris Jersey

$21.5 → Credit Suisse Geneva → $30.8 → Royal Bank of Canada Montreal → $21.4 T-bills → Union de Banque Suisse Montreal → $16.8 cash → Luxembourg Bank $28.8

$9.4 T-bills → Royal Trust Co. Montreal → $9.4 cash

ANDREE LACHAPELLE: CANADIAN PRESS

"Essentially, Canada was used as a place to break paper trails and to make it difficult to trace [the $41.8 million] properly,"
said a source familiar with the Duvalier finances.

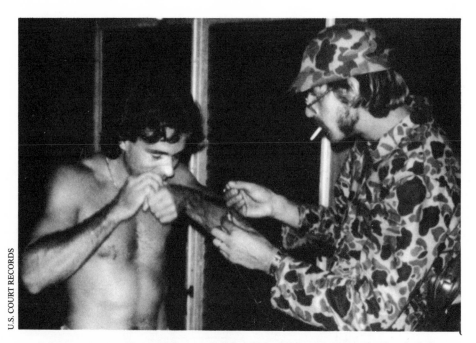

*Money courier Steve Yakovac (right) helps drug kingpin Carlos Lehder
sample some cocaine on Norman's Cay in the Bahamas in 1978.*

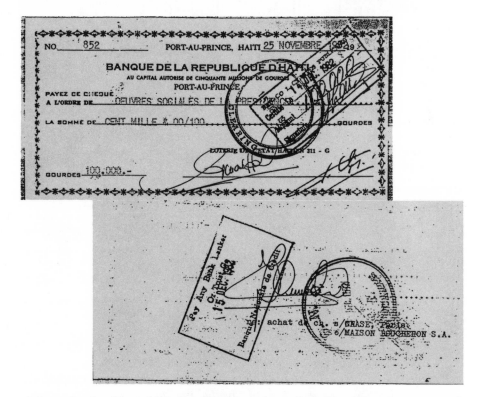

*Meant for the "Social Works of the Presidency," this Duvalier cheque, worth
about $20,000 US, ended up paying a bill at the Paris jeweler, Boucheron.*

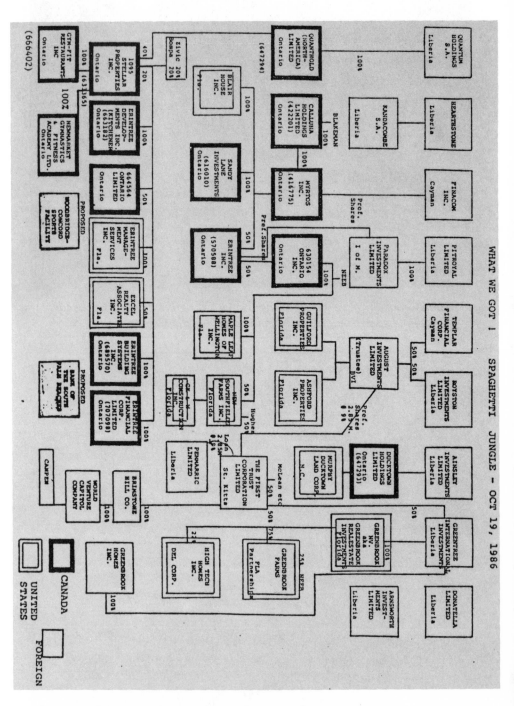

A diagram of the "Spaghetti Jungle," the most complex drug money-laundering scheme ever fully unravelled in Canada.

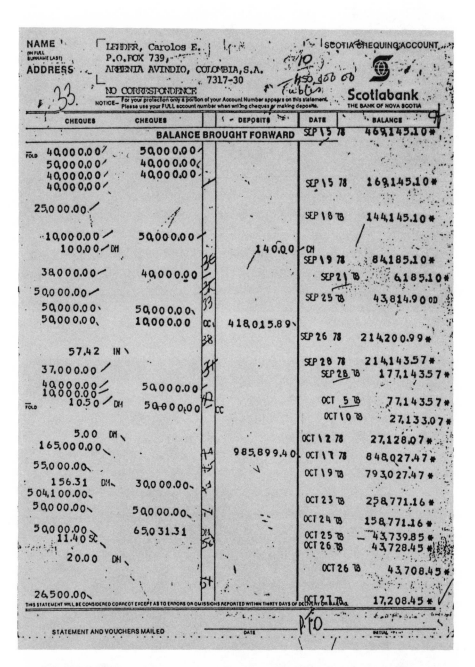

Between 1978 and 1980, more than $11.4 million US flowed through Carlos Lehder's accounts at the Bank of Nova Scotia in Nassau.

*This suitcase, containing slightly more than $1 million,
was seized by the RCMP in Montreal in 1989.*

The pride and joy of Elena and Nicolae Ceausescu — the garishly decorated Palatul Primaverii, or Spring Palace, in the heart of Bucharest.

Just before their arrest, Elena Ceausescu apparently took something hidden in this bed, located in a rarely used room in their Snagov villa.

Liviu Turcu (left), a top member of Romanian Intelligence, and other Romanian officials, meet in the 1980s in Bucharest with Yasushi Akashi (centre), deputy UN Secretary General. Traian Chebeleu (right), is now the spokesman for the Romanian Foreign Ministry.

Shooting "Evil's Fortune" in Romania. From left to right, host Linden MacIntyre, producer Susan Teskey, the author, cameraman Colin Allison. Missing: Wes Blanchard.

■6 USING AND ABUSING OFFSHORE TAX HAVENS

C all it Brother Eduardo's hallowed innovation. Some time in the mid-1980s, he found a way to marry altruism and avarice, creating a wondrous concept that he espoused across Canada and the United States. According to one typically pious pamphlet, his Circles of Light Church would "aid in the endless fight to feed the hungry, research health and treatment, as well as ensuring every donor's quest for financial enhancement." In practice, the man known in Philadelphia as Robert Graven had built a scam with a twist — the booty was sanitized offshore. "Donors," as they were politely called, were invited to contribute $105 to the church's chapter house in Montserrat, a tiny Caribbean tax haven. In return, they got access to a complex pyramid-selling swindle. That's a kind of pull-yourself-up-by-your-bootstraps fraud in which late arrivals pay off initial contributors until the charade collapses.

The good friar promised that faithful donors who did their bit — that is, roped in two other donors who, in turn, did the same — could (potentially, at least) realize a profit of

$46,720 US. And, as they pocketed their tax-free gains, they'd also have the warm feeling of knowing that their $105 was going to specially selected charities. Brother Eduardo assured them that his approach had none of the flaws usually found in what he euphemistically called the multilevel marketing field — "greed, bad management and flawed marketing plans." Among the plusses was Montserrat. Why use a Caribbean haven? Simple, really. "To ensure, safeguard, and guarantee the integrity of the Circles of Light Church's gift and donation program," explained a newsletter. "It avoids possible hijacking and disruption by misguided and overzealous people." He didn't explain what would motivate the misguided and the overzealous or who they might be.

Some 28,000 adherents in Ontario, Quebec, British Columbia and twenty-one American states took the bait and were bilked by Brother Eduardo of more than $1.4 million US. As Scotland Yard investigators sent to Montserrat, a British dependency, discovered, donations never went near any charity. Instead, they entered a sophisticated laundering operation with one goal — to benefit Robert Graven. Money was first funnelled into a local financial institution, the impressive-sounding First American Bank. From there, it was broken into small amounts to avoid suspicion and wired to the United States.[1] Graven was convicted in 1991 in his home town of Philadelphia.

Crooks and swindlers of many stripes — including relatively small-time con men like Brother Eduardo — are attracted by the camouflaging potential of tax havens. As the screws have tightened in the United States, home to the most potentially lucrative illicit markets, "criminals have simply moved their money laundering operations offshore where they anonymously deposit the cash in banks and then wire it from shell corporation to shell corporation," concluded a U.S. Senate report in 1990.[2] Noted swindlers have taken a similar tack. Take Robert Maxwell, the late British media magnate, for instance. In the spring of 1991, with his media empire crumbling, he made a desperate (and covert) bid to prop up the sagging price of shares in Maxwell Communication Corp., one of his public companies. He was forced to do this because he'd used MCC shares to secure more than £300 million in loans to his companies. If the value of those shares dropped, his creditors would demand higher collateral. To avoid being squeezed, Maxwell secretly (and illegally) bought MCC shares through a series of anonymous corporate fronts in havens like Switzerland and the British Virgin Islands. The ultimate cost was a staggering £200 million. Worse, those funds were, for the most part, clandestinely siphoned from his own companies' coffers and employee pension funds. Little is likely to be recovered.[3]

Some offshore sanctuaries are worse than others. For a time, Montserrat — which in the mid-1980s sold banking licences by the fistful for a mere $10,000 US apiece — was in disrepute for attracting "a golden horde of con-artists and scam-merchants, plus stacks of funny money belonging to, among others, General Manuel Noriega."[4] British authorities eventually stepped in to clean house. In March 1991, the island revoked 311 banking licences — including that of Brother Eduardo's favourite, the First American Bank.[5] Fertile ground was not far away. Many of the dirty money operators kicked out of Montserrat merely moved nearby to the even more destitute island of Grenada, best known for having been invaded by the U.S. in 1983.[6]

To be fair, Panama had a much worse reputation than either Montserrat or Grenada before the fall of Noriega. Starting in the 1970s, planeloads of profits earned in the U.S. drug trade would arrive at Panama's airport and be quickly absorbed into its banks. The scale of this money flow was nothing less than staggering. In June 1987, for example, some $29 billion US was on deposit in Panamanian offshore bank accounts. That's "six times the amount capable of being absorbed locally in the economy of Panama [which happens to use the U.S. dollar as its national currency] and ... the equivalent of nearly 10 percent of all U.S. currency in circulation worldwide."[7] Panama was also notorious as a scoundrel's refuge. In 1973, for example, it sheltered fugitive financier John C. Doyle, the tough-minded head of Canadian Javelin Ltd. He'd been charged in St. John's, Newfoundland, with defrauding Javelin of millions of dollars through some imaginative scams — resulting in an unfinished Canadian legal saga that dragged on into the 1990s. (He also faces a three-year prison term in the U.S. for a 1963 securities fraud conviction.)

Few are the tax havens that have not been touched by tainted funds. Rarer still are the big-time money laundering schemes that do not involve a haven or two. The now-defunct Bank of Credit and Commerce International, for instance, kept much of its dirty linen hidden by being based in Luxembourg and rinsing some of its grimiest transactions through its Cayman Islands operations. This helps partly to explain the mysterious disappearance of most of BCCI's capital. Touche Ross, the bank's liquidators, guesses that depositors can get back only 10 cents on the dollar from a bank supposedly valued at $20 billion. If that's the case, says the *Economist*, then BCCI may have lost, stolen, given away or hidden at least $15 billion. "Some of the money may have been sheer invention. For years to come, courts and fraud squads will be asking where the rest went."8 To find the (probably elusive) answer, they'll likely spend much of their time trolling through tax havens. Indeed, a veteran team from Touche Ross's Toronto office — some of whom had helped unravel the affairs of Italy's Banco Ambrosiano, which collapsed in 1982 — headed straight for the Caymans shortly after BCCI's fall in 1991.

Such frequent intertwinings of the shady and the offshore breed suspicion, skepticism and probing questions: What good are tax havens anyway? Does their legal usefulness make up for their role as escape hatches for the world's cleverer sorts of swindlers and pilferers? The answer from many quarters may surprise anyone uninitiated in the intricacies of high finance and global commerce: Yes, tax havens do play a vital role in the legitimate business world. Indeed, great chunks of international banking and trade would sputter to a halt without them. For instance, havens help complete deals involving investors from different countries. If such agreements were not signed on tax-neutral soil, they might crumble under the weight of the different fiscal regimes in each investor's country of residence.

Or look at major banks. As much as half the world's money is reckoned to either reside in or flow through sophisticated tax havens like the Cayman Islands, which also act as offshore financial centres.[9] They offer bankers attractive tax rates, looser regulations and a modern infrastructure. By operating in such a centre, a bank in, say London, can "book," or register, loans in a low-tax milieu like the Bahamas. Conversely, it can shift costs and expenses to high-tax London — and thereby whittle down recorded profits.[10] Thus, costs are trimmed and bottom lines bolstered, while customers get cheaper loans and higher rates of deposit. You only have to visit Georgetown, the capital of the Caymans, to see how attractive major banks find this. Georgetown's financial district is said to have "the highest density of banks and fax machines in the world."[11]

The most important kinds of offshore financial business involve Euromarkets. Basically, they're transactions in hard currencies held outside their countries of origin — that is, U.S. dollars on deposit in Luxembourg or Japanese yen in the Caymans. A bank operating in the Euromarkets, for instance, might take in $1 million in U.S. dollars from a Venezuelan oil man and then lend it to help a tea grower in Sri Lanka expand her operations. Why they're called Euromarkets is something of a mystery. One plausible explanation is that in their infancy in the mid-1950s, Euromarkets mostly involved Eurodollars — itinerant American dollars held in London. What prompted this sort of recycling is also open to debate. Some experts think the impetus came from the ex-Soviet Union. During the Cold War, it wanted to keep its holdings of American dollars safely outside the United States and its banks.

By definition, Euromarket business is unregulated. That is, the depositing and lending of Eurocurrencies is beyond the (usually costly) domestic controls of central banks and monetary authorities. For example, a bank accepting a Eurocurrency deposit would not have to pay deposit insurance on it, as it would have to on a domestic deposit account. Euromarket transactions are very profitable no matter where they occur — even in high-tax London, an important Euromarket centre. What makes Euromarket transactions even more lucrative, however, is if they are registered in a low-tax offshore financial centre like the Cayman Islands. While manifestly lucrative to bankers, this also opens the door to dirty money launderers. Concluded a U.S. Senate report in 1983: "The Euromarket is a critically important and legitimate feature of international commerce. But in the haven countries where money is laundered and operations hidden, it is unregulated. Thus, the same conditions which facilitate international commerce also create international [criminal] opportunities."[12]

For multinational corporations, havens are a legitimate means of remaining competitive and conserving profits by unsnarling the tangle of tax regulations that enmesh their various operations. All kinds of companies do this. In the 1960s, even Tussaud's Wax Museums Inc. tried to reduce its taxes in the U.S. by having a Netherlands Antilles firm hold the title to the world-famous wax figurines and lease them to Tussaud. But the bid was disallowed by American tax officials.[13]

These days, corporate treasurers scour the world, searching for the least tax resistance to flows of capital and profit. Amid the cutthroat rivalries of the international marketplace, this is prudent, especially since one's competitors are invariably doing the same thing. This process is broadly known as treaty shopping. A tax treaty is an agreement between two countries that ensures that citizens of both "get fair and equal treatment on the income they earn in each other's" jurisdiction. That is, it tries to avoid taxing the same income twice.[14] Treaty shopping involves examining such treaties in order to find the low-tax stepping-stones between the place where income was generated and where you want it to end up. It does not necessarily involve havens, but experts like to use them because of their light tax bite.

It's akin to letting "your fingers do the walking through the tax treaties," says researcher David Perry of the Canadian Tax Foundation. Or connecting the tax-pruning dots. Moving profits from Australia to Canada with the least turbulence may mean taking the funds through Hong Kong, the Netherlands Antilles and Malaysia — and then to Canada. At each border crossing, the profits might take a different form — entering Hong Kong as dividend payments or the Netherlands Antilles as royalty fees — depending on the tax treaty. The idea, he says, is "to make sure that the whole thing [complies with] the letter of the law."[15]

Smart bits of computer software are especially designed for this purpose — to pilot the wary through the world's fiscal shoals. One sophisticated program, known as Comptax, is available from the respected International Bureau of Fiscal Documentation in Amsterdam. Using up-to-date data on tax regulations in more than one hundred countries, it "calculates the tax effects of transferring funds [dividends, royalties and interest] from one country to another."[16] In some cases, suggests Perry, things can go too far. "Treaty shopping is a problem and it's an abuse if you're using treaty shopping solely to reduce tax payable. It's [then] an overzealous extension of the basic principle . . . that you examine the tax systems of the two countries you're dealing with to make sure that you don't get unintended [tax] consequences."

Besides creating a blacker bottom line, multinationals' use of tax havens helps minimize their subservience to national taxmen and bank regulators, and by extension, trims global firms' links to the countries in which they operate. On the flip side, it reduces a state's ability to implement pro-active economic policies. As such, the offshore contributes to the momentum of a much broader process, one that's well under way and is probably irreversible. According to *Business*

Week, "Though few companies are totally untethered from their home countries, the trend toward a form of 'stateless' corporation is unmistakable."[17]

This clever manoeuvring is profitable for individuals and businesses that are sufficiently wealthy or large enough to take advantage of tax haven benefits. It may also be seen as a good thing by those who believe that capital is most efficiently handled by private hands unfettered by governments or national frontiers — or by those who discount the value of the regulatory safeguards that exist in much of the Western banking world.

The benefits pale for those who, like most of us, are not rich enough to use such measures to escape the taxman's reach. Or who are worried that the tax-slimming use of havens by large firms and the wealthy may leave their less-mobile-and-well-off fellows holding the bag — and paying higher levies. (It is unclear to what extent this actually occurs.) Others who would see few benefits in the use of tax havens might include a harried finance minister worried about how to reconcile dropping revenues with the soaring cost of health and social benefits; a business critic who wonders if, at heart, multinational corporations simply do not want to pay any tax in the countries where they operate; or a consumer who lost money in the collapse of the regulation-shy and tax-haven-loving BCCI.

Many ostensibly legitimate uses of tax havens fall into a grey area. Anecdotes abound of Canadians hiding assets in a Bermuda or a Panama to put them out of reach of a spouse or an acrimonious business partner. Because of the attendant secrecy, there's no way of estimating how many people take such action, though most experts reckon the overall number is small. In litigation-mad America, the *Economist* reports that doctors and lawyers worried about the possibility of damaging lawsuits — and stung by sky-high insurance premiums — are doing much the same thing. A popular new financial instrument is the Asset-Protection Trust, which sharply restricts who gets access to disputed funds in a haven.

It might even replace pre-nuptial agreements, suggests the *Economist*: "A financially conscious Romeo can simply put his prize monetary assets out of Juliet's reach, and never tell her."[18]

Tax havens come in many flavours — from young upstarts like Vanuatu, a tiny South Pacific republic, to established Alpine monarchs like Liechtenstein (also, incidentally, the world's largest producer of sausage casings and false teeth). Liechtenstein's enticements drew the previously mentioned John C. Doyle, among many others. (Robert Maxwell was fond of it, too.) In 1968, Doyle allegedly raked in as much as $4 million by funnelling the purchase of a worthless timber concession in Labrador through a Liechtenstein ghost company, Société Transhipping.

Many lean on English roots. "Havens operating under English trust and common law are preferred, for English law is understood and respected worldwide," writes Richard Blum, the American authority on the offshore. "Thus, one will see that many havens are, or were, dependencies of the British Empire." Similarly, English — the universal business language of our age — also tends to be the lingua franca of many havens.[19] This is another plus for havens with British origins.

Tax havens must be politically stable if they are to keep attracting funds. In the 1970s Beirut declined rapidly as a haven for Middle East funds. The bedrock Swiss have always had a huge edge in this department, as demonstrated by the enormous influx of Mideast flight capital in the first few days after Iraq's invasion of Kuwait in 1990.

In all tax havens, the financial sector contributes mightily to the local economy — a factor often cited by their supporters. Montserrat, for instance, has few tourist-attracting facilities or natural resources. Even its beaches compare unfavourably with its neighbours'. But in recent years, the offshore sector has proved to be a boon, providing roughly 5 percent of government revenues — "a crucial element in balancing the budget."[20] The contribution is much higher in neighbouring Curacao, where the offshore's contributions make up 25 percent of the federal budget.[21] The same is true of thriving Luxembourg, which is home to some holding companies of such powerful Europeans as Italy's Agnelli family, owners of the automaker Fiat. The financial sector helped tide the European Grand Duchy over the rusting of its once powerful steel industry.[22]

Canada has even tried to benefit from a quasi-haven operating in Montreal and Vancouver. The provincial governments of Quebec and British Columbia offer tax breaks on some types of banking and securities transactions with foreigners if they are consummated in one of the two cities. These provincial benefits go beyond the slim advantages offered in 1986 by Ottawa. At the time, the federal government designated Montreal and Vancouver as international banking centres. But mindful of ruffling the feathers of Toronto, the country's financial centre, Ottawa kept the benefits for rival Montreal and Vancouver to a minimum. So far the pickings have been slim for those two cities, coming nowhere near the riches earned by a Luxembourg or Liechtenstein.[23]

Tax havens are run by a modest army of professionals — lawyers, accountants and bankers. Some become very wealthy in their work, small elites tending to be the great beneficiaries in Caribbean tax havens. In Montserrat, for example, most of the profits of its offshore sector were pocketed "by small numbers of very highly paid local lawyers . . . legal fees for new license applications were probably in excess of $500,000 US per year and annual retainers possibly amounted to a further $2 million US."[24] In some cases, expatriates take the lion's share of the bounty.

Successful havens also need a slew of specialized service-providing firms. Some sell off-the-shelf, ready-to-use shell companies, much as any retailer might sell a loaf of bread or a rug. A ready-made Panamian company, for instance, will set you back about $800 US; a Hong Kong one, a mere $350 US. Other firms establish and run trusts and ghost companies, right down to keeping orderly ledgers and recording the (quite predictable) results of annual meetings. They'll often provide tame shareholders and pliant nominees for the board of directors, too.

Visit many tax havens and you'll find a curiously amoral mindset and some unusual see-no-evil attitudes to things like drug money laundering. As recently as the summer of 1990, an official of the Netherlands Antilles warned, with a straight face, that Caribbean tax havens "will have difficulties in being too generous in defining the offence of drug money laundering. They have a legitimate concern with preserving bona fide business."[25]

A similar outlook was embraced by two middlemen I met on a snowy morning in December 1990 in Lugano in the Italian-speaking part of Switzerland. This elegant city — nestled among snow-capped mountains and graced with a majestic finger lake — has long had a checkered reputation. In the 1980s, for instance, it had been a favourite laundering spot for the Sicilian Mafia. So much shady money was pouring through the quiet town "that one prosecutor was seriously alarmed that it could undermine whole sections of the Swiss economy."[26] Lugano also had its share of intriguing Canadian connections. It was where the controversial Canadian Walter Wolf put down roots in 1972.[27] (Wolf was the jetsetting financier whose links to Pierre Trudeau did not stop him from warmly courting leading members of the rival Tories.) Lugano was also where Atomic Energy of Canada placed a suspicious payment of $2.5 million in April 1974, just after Argentina formally agreed to buy a Candu reactor. A day after being deposited, the money vanished into an account codenamed "Opera" in a Geneva bank.[28] The mystery wasn't solved until a decade later when an Argentine investigation found that the money had ended up in the hands of Jose Galbard, the economy minister and the man who had put the deal together. Although AECL lost money on the sale, Galbard ended up receiving a total of $4 million in bribes before emigrating to the United States, where he lived for the rest of his life.[29]

For the most part, Lugano's citizens earn their keep by servicing tax-shy Italians. One day, I watched a steel-grey limousine with Milan licence plates pull up in front of one of its discreet banks. Out came a polished, silver-haired man and his burly, chamois-gloved assistant lugging a heavy suitcase. They quickly stepped inside the bank and were promptly ushered into a specially guarded back room by an unctuous functionary.

When I mentioned the episode to my two contacts — brothers who requested anonymity — they merely shrugged. It happens all the time, they said. We met in a steamy café that smelled of rich espresso and fresh baking. The two men, sharp-eyed and with impeccable manners, were in a bubbly mood as they explained their burgeoning enterprise. "We're business consultants," they explained in refined Italian. The elder of the two pulled out a scrap of paper and began to sketch out a possible deal. Say an Italian investor has a complex proposition: she wants to use Spanish capital to build a fertilizer plant in Germany to supply an emerging market behind the former Iron Curtain. The two brothers will use clever bits of financial engineering to ensure that all the money movements — from inflows of Spanish investment capital to outflows of Eastern European profits — meet as few tax hitches as possible. This will involve a sturdy chain of offshore shell companies and anonymous bank accounts. In the process, they'll also ensure that everything — especially the identity of the tax-shy Italian investor — is kept secret.

"What if the resulting entity is involved in some sort of skullduggery?" I asked. "Or what if the aforementioned fertilizer plan has drastic environmental consequences?" The two men shrugged. They'd faced such questions before. In the mid-1980s, one of their clever business structures had been implicated in the murky international trade in toxic wastes. Any remorse? None. "If I sell you a gun legally and then you use it [illegally], it's your problem," one of them said. They finished their coffee. We shook hands. They went out into the pristine Alpine air. I could hear them chatting freely and laughing as they walked away. No scruples, no sleepless nights for this jovial pair.

Tax havens come from a long tradition, vying "in age with the world's oldest profession."[30] Merchants in ancient Athens so wanted to avoid a 2 percent tax on imports and exports that they apparently made a twenty-mile detour.[31] In the Middle Ages, on the other hand, the Hanseatic League cities in what is now Germany prospered by gently taxing commerce,[32] and in the eighteenth century, the American colonies funnelled trade through Latin America to avoid paying British-imposed duties.[33]

In the 1930s some enterprising Canadians caught the offshore, tax-avoiding bug. Among the first was Sir Harry Oakes, the gold mining tycoon who made his huge fortune in the muskeg of the Kirkland Lake region of northern Ontario. In 1933, he escaped what he considered the Canadian government's exorbitant tax bite and moved to the Bahamas, where he was mysteriously murdered a decade later. Some researchers have raised the possibility that Oakes may even have dabbled in a kind of money laundering scheme — funnelling funds through Mexican banks to get around wartime currency restrictions. But that was never conclusively proven.[34]

In the post-war era, many other Canadians followed the same path. The industrialist E.P. Taylor, best known for owning the farm where Kentucky Derby winner "Northern Dancer" was bred, became a citizen of the Bahamas in 1975. And more recently, Michael DeGroote, who built the giant waste-disposal firm, Laidlaw Inc., moved to Bermuda in 1990. But few Canadians better grasped the value of a tax haven than the billionaire Irvings of New Brunswick. In 1971, the family — routinely listed among the world's wealthiest — began making spectacular use of a subsidiary of their giant refiner and retailer, Irving Oil. Called Irving California Oil Co. Ltd., or Irvcal, its most important attribute was that it was located in a haven — Bermuda. Irvcal acted as an intermediary in a deal that family patriarch K.C. Irving signed with Standard Oil of California, now called Chevron. It was worth a staggering $1.2 billion US between 1971 and 1975. And, using a technique known as transfer pricing, a large chunk of the resulting profits were sheltered under Bermuda's protective umbrella.

Under the deal, Standard Oil did not directly sell its Saudi crude to Irving Oil in New Brunswick but went through Irvcal instead. It bought the crude from Standard Oil for $2.10 US a barrel and sold it to Irving Oil for $2.90. Irving Oil got the tax-free profits out of Bermuda in the form of a dividend, which was split between Standard Oil and the Irving family.35 The transaction came to light when the Canadian tax authorities rejected the arrangement, arguing that the Bermuda subsidiary had no legitimate business purpose. Irvcal, they said, was merely a "guise" to hide inflated earnings, a business structure whose sole purpose was to hive off profits in a tax-free atmosphere.

The Irving family appealed, arguing that everything was done openly and that the arrangement was above board because the price paid by Irving Oil was fair market value. New Brunswick consumers were not overcharged, they contended.36 Irving's case proved the most persuasive. In February 1991, the Federal Court of Appeals ruled in Irving's favour, conceding that Irvcal was "a tax avoidance scheme, pure and simple." Nevertheless, said the court, that was okay, since a fair market price was paid by Irving Oil. Said the court: "Be all that as it may, a transaction or arrangement does not fail effectively to avoid tax simply because it lacks a bona fide business purpose." Revenue Canada had to repay Irving Oil some $200 million in taxes and interest.

The Irving Oil case underscores the potential benefits of using a haven — and raises doubts about Revenue Canada's scope of action in dealing with such transactions. "Sure, it's a big problem," concedes a Revenue Canada official who asked not to be identified. Irving Oil is not alone. A large number of other Canadian-based multinationals have also benefited from going offshore. Mostly, says a federal tax expert who spoke off the record, they're trying to reduce foreign taxes — not Canadian ones. For example, Dutch companies are often used to hold the shares of Canadian firms' international subsidiaries and to finance overseas operations. What are the benefits? If a Canadian company had a large American subsidiary, for example, repatriating dividends or profits straight into Canada would trigger a 10 percent withholding tax in the U.S. Many countries levy that kind of tax on dividends and profits going outside their borders. By channelling investments through the Netherlands — and its benevolent tax treatment of holding companies — the U.S. levy can be cut in half. Better still, tax havens can prune borrowing costs significantly using the "double-dip" technique.

Typically, the double dip allows a Canadian company to fund its foreign operations from Canada while deducting the interest cost in Canada. Yet the income from that investment will not likely attract Canadian tax. Say a Canadian company wants to fund its American operation. It borrows in Canada, where the interest is tax deductible. It then invests the money in shares of a Dutch holding company, which, in turn, may be registered in the Netherlands Antilles. The Dutch company then reinvests the funds into its U.S. subsidiary, which also deducts the interest cost. The interest cost has been deducted twice — once in Canada and a second time by the U.S. branch.

The double-dip worries the Auditor General of Canada. This federal spending watchdog raised the issue in its report for the fiscal year that ended March 31, 1990, warning that "this could result in lost tax revenue for Canada and increased tax revenue for the foreign jurisdictions." A federal tax expert who spoke on condition of anonymity agrees: "What should be of concern to Canada is why should that interest be deducted in Canada. There's no nice answer to that question. If you conclude that it shouldn't be deducted, what would you do to fix it — recognizing that you're talking about a large multinational corporation." Probably not a great deal. Since multinationals and their jobs are increasingly fleet-footed, governments are wary of rocking the boat. Admits the federal official: "These problems have been known for a long time. To come up with a solution that strikes the appropriate balance is very difficult."

Canadian tax officials have now imposed tougher rules on transfer pricing and have tried to make it harder to siphon international profits into tax havens.[37] Regardless, tax havens continue to attract Canadian firms. No one really knows how many use them, what impact this has on federal coffers, or the extent to which this increases the burden borne by individual taxpayers. The federal tax expert reckons the revenue loss is "certainly in the tens of millions" of dollars every year. But he also cautions: "I'm not sure that the evidence is in that it's such a massive problem in terms of size that it's urgently screaming for a solution." Tax expert Donald Brean of the University of Toronto says it's difficult to accurately gauge tax-haven activity or "the implicit revenue costs to bona fide source and residence countries" for the very reasons "that tax havens are used in the first place. Even more difficult is the task of distinguishing funds channelled through tax havens consistent with proper international tax planning and sound [and legal] multinational corporate financial policy from less scrupulous manoeuvring under the general heading of tax evasion."[38]

While the impact of tax havens on government revenue-gathering is impossible to measure, it's clear that they do offer benefits available only to the select few. Does this breed inequities in the tax system? Yes, suggests federal tax expert David Dodge. In an article in 1988, he noted that sophisticated "tax avoidance schemes are used mostly by wealthy and well-advised taxpayers: the resulting higher rates of tax are unfair to the majority of taxpayers."[39] In response, the federal government is pinning its hopes on the general anti-avoidance rule, or GAAR (pronounced gah-rh), which has a spawned a new verb: tax-avoidance-scheme-constructing lawyers worry about getting GAAR-ed. Unveiled in the Commons in 1988, the rule tries to limit tax-planning strategies that have little or no business purpose other than limiting the tax bite. Would GAAR have checked schemes like the one used by the Irvings in the 1970s? Views differ. Says a federal tax official: "GAAR would allow Revenue Canada to take a fresh approach to this one. . . . [But] I don't think it's by any means assured that that same kind of case coming forward wouldn't be successful again."

The uncomfortable fact is that the legitimate ways of using tax havens to avoid taxes are easily parroted by drug-profit-laundering schemes. This is worrisome for above-board tax lawyers and accountants and their clients, who do not want to be tarred by the dirty money brush. But it's even worse for drug cops, for this can drastically amplify the scope of their problems. It is tricky enough, after all, to differentiate between tax avoidance and tax evasion when deals pass through a fiscal paradise. It is much more difficult to spot the chameleon-like doings of shady money launderers who are disguised as genuine tax-flinchers.

Actions by individual jurisdictions have done little to make the law enforcers' job easier. Whenever one country shuts some money laundering loopholes, shy capital merely moves elsewhere. In 1991 when Switzerland announced that it would no longer allow lawyers to hide the identities of clients when depositing funds into Swiss banks, neighbouring Liechtenstein continued to allow lawyers and trustees to provide such anonymous secrecy. The result: money quietly crossed the border into Liechtenstein.[40]

A broader approach is advocated by John Kerry, the U.S. senator whose pronouncements a few years ago caused heart palpitations in Ottawa. In 1988, he shepherded the so-called Kerry Amendment through Congress. It ordered the U.S. Treasury Department to reach agreements with foreign countries — and especially offshore havens — requiring them to, among other things, record all American dollar transactions worth more than $10,000. If they balked, the U.S. President had the power to cut off the jurisdiction from CHIPS and other U.S. systems for electronically clearing transactions and transferring funds. That is a hefty club, since those systems are the underpinning of world trade and finance.[41] A haven that was not plugged in would not survive long.

So far, however, Washington has been slow to put the Kerry Amendment into effect. This is hardly surprising since, historically, meddling with tax havens is fraught with danger — as a British admiral found out in the eighteenth century. During the American Revolutionary War, he invaded the Caribbean island haven of St. Eustatius, or Statia, which had been supplying arms and other goods to the rebellious colonies. He made the mistake of destroying its warehouses and seizing all kinds of merchandise. The problem was that they had been owned by British businessmen, who proceeded to sue the admiral. He was dogged by the ensuing legal problems for the rest of his life.[42]

The U.S. Treasury, charged with implementing the Kerry Amendment, had a similarly unpleasant experience in an incident that one newspaper headline dubbed "Blunder in Paradise." On June 29, 1987, the U.S. Treasury announced an end to Washington's income tax treaty with the Netherlands Antilles. Too large a share of potential American tax revenues were disappearing into that sunny group of islands off the coast of Venezuela. No one anticipated the repercussions, since no one took special notice of the $32 billion US worth of Eurobonds (securities denominated in Eurocurrencies) that annually passed through the islands.

Shortly after the announcement, however, U.S. officials got a taste of the important role played by tax havens in international finance: world markets went haywire. "Prices on the outstanding bonds fell by between 15 and 20 percent, for a total potential loss of between $900 million and $1.2 billion [US] to United States investors, and a total of between $3 billion and $4 billion [US] to foreign investors," wrote the *New York Times*.[43] Huge American issuers of Eurobonds like RJR Nabisco and J.C. Penney considered calling in their bonds.

Less than two weeks later, the U.S. Treasury relented and, with much egg on its face, drastically modified its decision.[44]

The underlying lesson of "Blunder in Paradise" is that it would be troublesome to fiddle with havens for any reason — even to meet the currently fashionable goal of stemming drug money laundering. For one thing, the harsh penalties of the Kerry Amendment might, if unilaterally imposed, have a quite different (and unintended) effect. Salvatore Martoche, the Assistant Secretary of the U.S. Treasury, warns that foreign banks and companies could simply pick up their marbles and go play elsewhere: "Competing payment mechanisms [could] develop and competing clearinghouse equivalents to CHIPS could be developed . . . a comparable system has already been developed in Japan." To refute those who maintain that this would never occur, Martoche draws a comparison between the United States and the Roman Empire, which also "thought it would last forever."[45] That is, not even the United States is powerful enough to single-handedly ban certain types of financial activity and to defy the forces of financial innovation such actions might unleash.

So, will anyone in the foreseeable future, including the wielders of the Kerry Amendment, have a tangible impact on the excesses of tax havens? Likely not. "You could shut them down, theoretically," says Stamler, the former RCMP assistant commissioner. But this, he says, is "a consensual type" of activity. "The public of the various countries of the world want this kind of facility. They want to be able to avoid taxes."

Ultimately, it's not likely that tax havens will be seriously tampered with — since they've become such an integral part of the world financial system. The world's crooks and criminals will be the richer for it.

■7 THE CANADIAN PIONEER

On September 21, 1966, an elderly man with a deep voice phoned a suite at the Royal York Hotel in Toronto. The conversation was brief, just long enough to set up a meeting with the suite's occupant. Then the caller said, "Carry on as you have been," and hung up.[1] The discussion did not go unnoticed, however. It was picked up by an RCMP bug, transcribed and passed on to American authorities. That such an apparently innocuous chat would get such treatment was partly due to the caller's identity. He was Meyer Lansky, a five-foot-four-inch, dapper gambler, then in his early sixties. At the time, mob-busting policemen thought he was the financial genius who had developed elaborate offshore banking systems for laundering the illicit profits of American organized crime.

Lansky was certainly a gangster of the first order and, at one time, a major force in organized-crime-tainted casino gambling in Nevada and the Caribbean. He was also, incidentally, the kind of larger-than-life crime figure much valued by Hollywood. (He was portrayed in the Warren Beatty film *Bugsy*, and as the thinly veiled Hyman Roth in *The Godfather, Part II*.) But a pioneer in laundering money through offshore banks? Not quite. According to the meticulous research of Lansky's biographer, Robert Lacey, and to other evidence, if anyone should be credited with being such a trail-blazer, it was not Lansky, but the occupant of the Toronto hotel suite.[2] He was about the same age as Lansky, slightly taller (by a scant two inches) and equally natty. His name was John Pullman, an affable Canadian who lived, for the most part, in Switzerland. And according to Lacey, it was Pullman who introduced Lansky to what many thought was a key Lansky innovation — "the possibilities of using offshore banks as channels and repositories for the cash generated by Meyer's Las Vegas skims."[3]

Lansky's reputation has suffered since his death in 1983. He was influential, yes, but not the head of what the FBI, among others, thought in the 1960s and 1970s was a criminal empire operating along the lines of General Motors.[4] The Lansky-era version of American organized crime seems to have been less a corporate monolith than loosely linked entrepreneurs cooperating on specific deals — allied more by profit making than by ethnic ties or clan loyalties.[5] Similarly, Lansky's fortune is now thought to have been far less than the $300 million US some Mafia-watchers once thought.[6] More to the point, he was not very sophisticated in covertly handling what wealth he had — until Pullman came along. Neither, for that matter, were other top American criminals of Lansky's generation.[7] One telling anecdote concerns a former bookmaker who recalls borrowing $150,000 US from the head of one of the five reputed crime families in New York and receiving "a shopping bag full of cash wrapped in newspapers 30 years old."[8] Not a sign of financial sophistication. And in sharp contrast to Pullman's methods. Says Lacey: "Those who dealt personally with Meyer [in the 1960s] agree that his guru was the loquacious and likeable John Pullman, who had a clever new way to do everything, and who had never met a problem that he could not fix."[9]

Pullman, who died in 1985, was part of what Rod Stamler, the retired RCMP assistant commissioner, considers a uniquely Canadian contribution to the development of money laundering. Historically, he says, "there has been a strong involvement by Canadian lawyers, accountants, etc., who have gone to offshore areas and have set up [money laundering] systems there." Stamler points to Robert Vesco, the American fugitive who allegedly pilfered millions of dollars from a mutual fund empire in the early 1970s. Vesco, who is said to have laundered the money through a maze of offshore "black holes," used a Canadian, Norman LeBlanc, as his accountant and trusted aide. Why Canadians? "We're very international in our outlook," says Stamler. "The U.S. criminals think of Canada as being very close to Britain and therefore being in close connection to the [British Commonwealth] tax haven areas in the Caribbean. . . . There's always been that connection with Canada. Our Canadian criminals and U.S. criminals connect naturally."

Born Wolhyn Pullmer in Russia on September 19, 1901, Pullman emigrated with his family to Canada in 1908. Strikingly similar were the early years of Meyer Suchowljansky, the future Meyer Lansky — which is perhaps one reason why they trusted each other. Lansky was also born in Russia in the early 1900s — no one knows the exact date — and his family arrived in the United States in 1911. Pullmer attended school in Toronto until the age of ten but did not stay in Canada long. After working as a bell hop in Penetanguishene, Ontario, he emigrated to the United States in 1918, changing his name to John Pullman and joining the American army. After being discharged, Pullman lived in Chicago and worked for a firm called Yankee Amusement Co.,[10] and at some point in the 1920s, he became a bootlegger and had his first encounters with Lansky.

On May 18, 1931, Pullman was convicted of a Prohibition offence in Grand Rapids, Michigan, near Chicago,[11] for which he served six months of a fifteen-month sentence. It was the only criminal blot on his record. There's no evidence that he was involved at that point in the financial end of the illicit liquor business. Neither is it certain that his Prohibition-era relations with Lansky — then in a major liquor smuggling operation with Charles "Lucky" Luciano among others — were as close as Pullman later privately boasted.[12] But at the very least, Prohibition allowed Pullman to brush up against big-time liquor smuggling and make what turned out to be some useful contacts.

During Pullman's formative years in the 1920s and 1930s, the field of confidential money handling was quite a primitive endeavour. A notable exception was the way some profits were handled by the founding family of the Seagram distilling empire, the Bronfmans. Their activities during Prohibition have long been a source of controversy, but while the American ban on alcohol certainly invigorated the Bronfmans' bottom line, what's usually left unsaid is that their actions were quite legal — and that other Canadian distillers were doing much the same thing. Moreover, most of the Bronfmans' vast fortune was made after Prohibition's repeal in the United States in 1933 — thanks to imaginative marketing strategies, some well-timed gambles and Sam Bronfman's business savvy. As historian Michael Marrus notes, many others who profited from Prohibition failed to capitalize on its repeal.[13] That being said, the Bronfmans nevertheless took great pains to conceal how millions of dollars came into their hands from Prohibition-skirting customers in the United States.

Some of the details are in RCMP files unsealed in May 1991 under an Access to Information request.[14] The files — compiled into a musty, 900-page bound volume — summarize the Crown's evidence in the 1935 trial of key Bronfman family members. They faced four charges of conspiring to defraud Ottawa of $5 million in customs duties on Canadian liquor — ostensibly meant for foreign markets — that was allegedly smuggled back into this country. The fifth charge was liquor smuggling into the United States.[15] The Crown did show that the Bronfmans exported large amounts of liquor — sometimes through such exotic locales as Bermuda and Belize. But it could not prove that the booze intended for foreign markets had actually been smuggled back into Canada and sold without taxes being paid. Neither could it demonstrate that it was up to Canadian courts to administer the Prohibition laws of the United States. In the end, the Montreal court ruled that the Bronfmans had done nothing wrong — for under Canadian law, vendors did not have to document where the liquor they sold was heading. Said the verdict: "The agencies sold liquor to all who would buy and these acts were legal in the countries in which they operated. They were not obliged to verify the destination of the goods they sold, nor was there any obligation upon them to inquire of the buyers what they intended to do with their goods."[16]

Though their substantial export activities were judged legal by a Canadian court, the Bronfmans did favour a decidely covert approach to handling their U.S. revenues. Why they did so has never been fully explained, though it seems likely that they wanted to outfox the Canadian tax system. One Bank of Montreal letter dated December 26, 1931, and seized by the RCMP referred to the Bronfmans' desire "not to sign letters personally as such action might subject the Company to income tax in the Dominion of Canada."[17] Presumably, the Bronfmans also wanted to protect their American customers from unwanted governmental attention — whether from the enforcers of Prohibition or the Internal Revenue Service.[18]

Hence the Bronfmans' laundering operation. It revolved around what RCMP investigators described as fabricated "trade names." One such fiction — "John Norton" — was used in conjunction with the Atlas Shipping Co., a trading firm controlled by Brintcan Investments, the Bronfman family holding company. No one called "J. Norton" actually existed. Yet "he" was the destination for all kinds of money. The "J. Norton" name acted as a filter for Atlas Shipping, cleansing U.S. revenues earned by other Bronfman-controlled export firms. The scheme was similar to more modern laundering systems. As one RCMP memo stated: "Late in the year 1930, a scheme was devised to prevent the names of either the Atlas Shipping Company or the Bronfmans' being exposed during transactions resulting in remittances from the United States, and the name of J. Norton, fictitious and non-existent, was used as the trade name. Customers would remit funds through the medium of telegraphic transfers, bank drafts or personal cheques made out to this name."19

"J. Norton" was an anonymous receptacle for receiving the funds. It acted as a secret sieve, breaking the paper trail between the origins of the money — customers in the United States who'd managed to circumvent the Prohibition statutes — and the Bronfmans themselves.

How did it work? According to another RCMP memo: "In some cases, money was wired directly to the name of J. Norton, Montreal, from various points in the United States. In other cases, American funds or cheques would be taken to the Bank of Montreal, Drummond and St. Catherine Streets [in Montreal], and a draft would be purchased in favour of J. Norton. This draft would then be deposited to the credit of one of the Atlas Shipping Company accounts [at the same bank]."20

Another popular trade name was "Joseph White Reg'd." It, too, was apparently used to anonymously receive payments. In 1933 alone, the RCMP documented that some $8 million was deposited into the Bank of Montreal account of "J. White Reg'd."21 Many of the deposit slips for this account were initialled by David Costley, Brintcan's secretary-treasurer. According to the RCMP files, large sums were then transferred from this account to those held at the same bank branch by Atlas Shipping Co. Again, many of the enabling documents were initialled by Costley.22

Other Canadians on the seamier side of the liquor trade in the 1920s could have taken a lesson from the Bronfmans. Consider Rocco Perri, a Hamilton mobster who revelled in his reputation as the "king of the bootleggers." He apparently relied on relatively transparent techniques for handling his earnings. A good portion of his wealth seems to have been kept in simple bank accounts. One of his few known attempts at subterfuge had limited effect — the money was put into accounts under the name of his mistress, Bessie Starkman. A brief investigation of their financial affairs in 1927 turned up eight accounts, which had total deposits of more than $860,000 between 1922 and 1927.[23]

No one knows what first drew Pullman to the world of covert offshore finance — or when he began to learn the tricks of the trade. This is no surprise. Pullman spent much of his life trying to keep a low profile. "If you saw him in an airport or a hotel, he was very unassuming," recalls George Wool, a Vancouver lawyer who investigated some of Pullman's activities in the 1970s while a member of the RCMP. "He was very amiable. I never knew him to be angered. He was very diplomatic." Don Docker, another retired RCMP officer who was familiar with Pullman's activities, has similar memories: "Nobody ever recognized him because he had such a low profile. He could walk down [Toronto's] Bay Street and I bet you there wouldn't be a dozen people who'd know who he was."

What is known is that Pullman lived in the United States for three decades, becoming a naturalized citizen in 1943 in Chicago. He returned to Canada in 1948 and got his citizenship six years later. Somehow, between Prohibition and the early 1960s, Pullman became quite wealthy, though it is unclear to what extent his fortune may have been illicitly acquired. He did profit from a number of legitimate ventures in the United States, including a chain of automotive parts stores in the American Midwest and forays into the food business. At one point, he owned a company called Federal System of Bakeries. Recalled Pullman: "We used to show how to bake bread without hands touching it."[24] He said he sold it for $2.5 million US.

Pullman continued to prosper after moving north of the forty-ninth parallel — thanks, he said, to a shrewd eye for real estate bargains and lucrative stock issues. Law enforcement officials greeted this with a measure of skepticism. Despite his extensive legitimate holdings and business ventures, there would always be questions about the origins of some of his assets. "He was independently wealthy," says Wool, the former RCMP investigator. "But I didn't know specifically where he got his money."

What caught the eye of law enforcement in the early 1960s was Pullman's emergence as a sophisticated offshore financier with a decidedly shady clientele. By the end of the decade, he was being described in U.S. law enforcement circles as "one of the Mafia's most influential associates and financial advisers [who] is frequently utilized by them for investing syndicate money."[25] An important clue to this role surfaced on March 19, 1965, at the Miami airport. It resulted from a gaffe by Sylvain Ferdmann, a then thirty-year-old, Harvard-educated, Swiss economist. While loading some satchels into a car, Ferdmann dropped a piece of paper, which an attendant turned over to U.S. authorities. It was a receipt, which stated: "This is to acknowledge this 20th day of December 1964, the receipt of Three Hundred and Fifty Thousand $350,000 dollars in American bank notes for deposit to the account of Maral 2812 with the International Credit Bank Geneva, the said sum being turned over to me in the presence of the named signed below." The witness was John Pullman. The bookish-looking Ferdmann, it turned out, was a money courier, carrying the tax-evading profits that Lansky and others had skimmed from various casinos in Las Vegas. And as the note indicated, he was helping Pullman shift those illicit funds out of the United States to safe haven in Switzerland.[26]

In the simplest form of casino skimming, a percentage of each night's take is diverted before it is officially tallied and recorded. The FBI has calculated that the sums filched this way in Las Vegas between 1960 and 1965 totalled $12 million US a year. According to the U.S. agency, the skims were collected in Miami and then sent offshore, often personally carried by the likes of Ferdmann. Pullman played a central role in these transactions. Investigators traced his money-gathering voyages from Miami to the Bahamas — where, for a time, he was president of the disreputable Bank of World Commerce — and on to Switzerland.[27]

Interestingly, Pullman also had an office at the International Credit Bank — the destination of the funds Ferdmann carried. It was later revealed that Pullman had "some financial interest" in it, as well.[28] In fact, he received a 1 percent commission on deposits he recruited for the bank, and for a time was close to its head, the mercurial Tibor Rosenbaum. Rosenbaum was something of a mentor to Pullman and is thought to have been the source of many of Pullman's ideas on offshore finance.[29]

The Ferdmann note dovetailed with other information that U.S. authorities were compiling on Pullman. By 1967, they were describing him as the Geneva bank's "contact for handling Mafia money" and "a very close associate of Meyer Lansky and it is reliably suspected that much of the Mafia money is transported to him through Lansky."[30] Thanks to a timely leak from the FBI, the activities of Pullman and Ferdmann were publicly trumpeted in the September 8, 1967, issue of *Life* magazine — complete with a grainy picture of Ferdmann carrying a bulging satchel to an airplane. The disclosures left Ferdmann shaken for a long time. Years later he told a *New York Times* reporter who'd tracked him down: "I'm scared since 1967. I'm bloody scared. Please leave me out of your story."[31]

Pullman took it all in stride. He did not sue *Life* magazine, but he transferred his personal accounts from the International Credit Bank to the much larger Crédit Suisse, where his account was called simply "John Pullman."[32] He explained that he'd simply "divorced" himself from Rosenbaum for business reasons. "Mr. Rosenbaum, who was the president of the bank, was investing too much money in one country and I didn't like it," Pullman said. "The country was Israel. He was very close to Israel and I thought that it was dangerous for a bank to invest most of their assets in one country. So I pulled out of there and I went to a big bank which was more stable."[33]

Despite Pullman's protests to the contrary, the divorce was less than final. Pullman may have been worried about Rosenbaum's business practices, but he continued to attract new clients to the International Credit Bank — and have an office there — long after he shifted his personal accounts elsewhere. A prized client was Lansky, whose account was code-named "Bear." Pullman also recruited other depositors of the same ilk, including Joseph "Doc" Stacher, another Las Vegas skimmer and former bootlegger.[34] As Pullman admitted years later: "When I went out after accounts I didn't go to reporters earning $10,000 a year. I went to millionaires that had money. I couldn't go to ditch diggers so I went to Las Vegas. I tried to get accounts from people that owned casinos. That's how I got to know a lot of people."[35]

Moreover, Pullman acted as a combination host and financial adviser when scores of American crime figures visited Switzerland. Pullman spoke French, a valued skill in Geneva, which had long been a furtive-money mecca for francophones from around the world. When Lansky and his wife, Teddy, visited Switzerland in 1965, for instance, Pullman met them at Geneva airport and then "accompanied the Lanskys to Lausanne and on a trip to West Germany."[36] Such trips were often monitored. By 1967, U.S. law enforcement officials had pegged Pullman "as a guide for the more prominent Mafia members and principal non-member associates while they are on European excursions."[37]

The Geneva bank collapsed in 1974 amid charges that it had engaged in fraud and other offences, but Pullman was never implicated in any wrongdoing. Other than whatever shares he may have owned, it appears that he lost no money in its failure — having shifted his own funds to Crédit Suisse. His friend Lansky, however, seems to have come out much worse. Rosenbaum's close ties to Israel — which had apparently so offended Pullman — had had the opposite effect on Lansky. He'd devoted much of his latter life to exploring his Jewish roots and so was eager to invest in Israel. Though some accounts suggest Lansky was miraculously able to spirit his funds out of the Swiss bank just before the collapse, it seems likelier that he was one of the depositors whose savings were wiped out.[38]

Pullman's expertise did not stop at Swiss banking. He also knew his way around tax havens such as Liechtenstein and Panama. In Liechtenstein, he had a trust called Delami Establishment, which, according to an affidavit given to the U.S. Securities and Exchange Commission in 1975, brought him profits of "millions of dollars."[39] Among other things, Delami had been a holding company for a hotel called the Delmonico in Miami. To his eternal regret, he sold the Delmonico for a mere $500,000 US in the early 1960s.[40] In Panama, Pullman had a company called Samson International S.A., which he had set up in the 1950s. For the most part, it held bonds, certificates of deposit and mortgages. Neither Delami nor Samson was ever linked with any improprieties.

For law enforcement agencies, understanding Pullman's stature in the underworld was a long and involved task. The Ferdmann note aside, they learned most about him from various eavesdropping operations. One bugged conversation, dated September 20, 1966, and picked up at his Royal York suite, underscores Pullman's close financial links with Lansky, who was very ill at the time. And it is at odds with Pullman's public statements that Lansky was nothing more than a casual acquaintance. RCMP snoops heard Pullman's somewhat cryptic comments to his wife, Yvonne: "He's in the hospital, very bad, you know. . . . If I could see Meyer, I would have right now 20,000 francs to deposit in the bank. If Meyer dies, it goes to his estate. But I have $200,000 that does not. The problem is that Meyer is the only one that they can rely on. With Meyer it will always come."[41] In fact, as noted earlier, Lansky did call Pullman one day later to arrange a meeting.

Another conversation which gives us some insight into Pullman's methods was recorded seven days later. It was between Pullman and Alvin Malnik, a Miami attorney who was investigated by gaming officials in Nevada and New Jersey in the 1970s.[42] According to an investigator's summary of the call: "Involved business dealings were discussed in great detail and an agreement was reached, item by item, as to how each was [to be] reported for tax purposes. . . . They next turned to a discussion of a gambling casino in Paris. 'Between Eiffel Tower and the Place Concorde.' Pullman made it clear that Lansky had given an okay." Later, the two men discussed Lansky's business acumen, and Pullman acknowledged the commission he received for handling Lansky's funds — 1 percent of the amount.[43]

On August 12, 1963, a bug in Malnik's office overheard a Lansky courier delivering a document containing information gleaned from a source at the U.S. Justice Department. Another copy, he said, was sent to Pullman.[44] Pullman's reaction to what the courier described as "counterintelligence information" was never recorded. But if he did indeed receive the document, it must have caught his eye. For it dealt with the Bank of World Commerce, the notorious Caribbean offshore institution of which he was president, that had been founded in June 1961 in Nassau, the Bahamas.

Pullman was no stranger to the Caribbean or to Latin America. Not only did he have a Panama-registered corporation, he also claimed to have owned a Colombian coffee plantation.[45] And in 1959 he'd had a brief soujourn in revolutionary Cuba, where Lansky was running a casino, the Riviera. Lansky was in some trouble at the time because Fidel Castro's new regime was looking particularly askance at Havana's Mafia-tarnished casinos. They were the visible focus of widespread anger over the excesses of the previous strongman, Fulgencio Batista, and if the casinos were nationalized, Lansky was in danger of taking a massive financial bath. Using his Canadian citizenship as leverage, Pullman repeatedly lobbied Castro to allow Lansky to take his huge casino investments out of the country. His efforts were to no avail, despite the fact that Pullman had got so close to Castro that he was once seen on the podium with the Cuban leader. Lansky ended up losing millions of dollars when Havana's casinos were nationalized in 1960.[46]

Pullman did better at the Bank of World Commerce, which proved to be a useful funnel for illicit profits. The list of its other officers and directors also alarmed U.S. authorities. Alvin Malnik was a director, and so were Edward Levinson, convicted of Las Vegas skimming in the 1960s, and Mike Singer, a controversial former Teamsters' union official who was close to Jimmy Hoffa. Hoffa — who embodied the Teamsters' corrupt practices and close links with organized crime — himself owned some shares. Concluded a U.S. Justice Department study, based on a 1962 investigation by the U.S. Internal Revenue Service into the bank and other similar institutions: " 'shell' banking institutions have been established in the Bahamas by individuals closely connected with gambling interests, international underworld couriers, James Hoffa, and the Teamsters Union. . . . It appears that the banks have been set up by underworld interests as repositories for skimmed gambling money from the United States in a location outside the jurisdiction of the Internal Revenue Service."[47] Not surprisingly, the Bank of World Commerce was shut down in 1965 under U.S. pressure.

In the late 1960s, when Pullman was in his sixties, allegations of his crime links began to be uttered publicly by Robert Morgenthau, a crusading prosecutor in New York City who would play a crucial role in the early 1990s in exposing the activities of the Bank of Credit and Commerce International. "John Pullman was for years a courier for the mob," Morgenthau, then U.S. attorney for the Southern District of New York, said in 1969. "Now he handles their investments for them through Swiss bank accounts."[48] Part of Morgenthau's information appeared to come from a source inside the International Credit Bank itself.[49] Morgenthau acknowledged in a recent interview that significant amounts of information also came from RCMP bugging operations — like the September 1966 ones on his Royal York Hotel suite — during Pullman's frequent Canadian visits.

Morgenthau and others were particularly interested in Pullman's investments in Canadian property. That he was flush with funds was obvious to anyone in the real estate business in Toronto in the postwar period. He made loans to all kinds of concerns, including construction companies, nursing homes and firms in the food business. In one documented instance, he helped finance the completion of one of the city's first shopping centres, the west-end Dufferin Plaza. (The current owners of the mall were never involved with Pullman.)[50]

Where did Pullman's investment capital come from? Was it all his own money? Yes, he maintained to his dying day. Police in Canada and the United States weren't so sure. They'd documented how Pullman had been involved, at one time or another, in most facets of laundering U.S. organized crime profits — from being a money courier to running a shady offshore bank to acting as an agent for a Swiss bank. They wondered if his investments in Canadian real estate and mortgages weren't just an added service, the icing on the cake for his American criminal clients looking for safe repositories for their laundered funds. Though this was a reasonable supposition, it was never proven in court. Pullman would inevitably stress during his rare interviews that the money he invested in Canadian real estate (which he claimed totalled $2.5 million in the early 1970s) was his own. He added that all the other allegations against him, and particularly Morgenthau's charges, were nonsense. He denied everything — that he had handled criminal funds, that he was ever a money courier and that he was close to Meyer Lansky. He claimed that his only contacts with Lansky were innocent and infrequent — that they'd only met for the odd card game in Florida.[51]

So why not go to the United States to clear up all those misconceptions? After all, Morgenthau and other U.S. officials, who had tried unsuccessfully for years to question him, had even offered him immunity. No way, said Pullman. As he told Peter Moon of the *Globe and Mail* in 1974: "They want me to tell them everything I know. And then if I happen to forget something they'll put me in jail for perjury." He ignored a subpoena to appear before a Detroit grand jury too, explaining to Moon: "The FBI would double-cross their own mother. I have no time for them."[52] He had no time for the RCMP either, whom he'd accused of harassing him. Certainly, he hated disclosing anything to them. After they raided his home in Switzerland in 1975, he phoned his wife and told her to "start a bonfire and just destroy everything in the house so that in case the police come again there's nothing to find."[53]

If there was so much supposed evidence against Pullman, why wasn't he nabbed? Part of the reason, say some of his former pursuers, was that what Pullman did in each phase of the laundering cycle was perfectly legal. There was nothing wrong, on the face of it, with attracting (albeit unsavoury) depositors to a bank in Geneva or with making loans (with albeit mysterious funds) to Toronto developers. Equally problematic was the fact that his activities in one laundering cycle could not be linked with those in any other. It was impossible to show, for example, that the funds invested in Canadian real estate had come from Las Vegas casino skimming. This was partly because Pullman and his activities were fragmented through too many jurisdictions and too many havens. He was a Canadian living in Switzerland handling funds that might have come from Las Vegas through the Bahamas. And, in turn, he was investing large sums — which may or may not have come from Las Vegas — from Switzerland and perhaps through companies in other havens, into Canadian real estate.

In hindsight, the search for the links to complete the circle was not very extensive either. After all, money laundering was not a crime in Canada at the time and did not become a crime until after Pullman's death. George Wool, the former RCMP investigator, recalls that when he looked into Pullman's affairs in the 1970s it was for a specific purpose — to examine his possible connection with a stock fraud in Toronto. "As a police officer, I was not looking for evidence of laundering," he says. "I knew that when I went to the United Kingdom, they would always ask us about currency violations. That meant nothing to me. . . . I would have said that it's nice to know where Pullman gets his money. But that was no legal concern to me. Canada, at the time, was looking for investment. Why would I even look where the money came from? We used to get repeated requests about currency violations. I wouldn't have any interest in it. Where Pullman got his money from, who cares? My purpose as an investigator was looking for crooked stock deals."

Pullman was acquitted of wrongdoing in 1977 in the stock fraud case that Wool investigated — a complicated scam involving shares in Toronto-based Aquablast Inc., a now-defunct industrial cleaning concern — but there is lingering suspicion that Pullman's extensive investments in Canadian securities were also a laundering vehicle. In this particular case, says Wool: "Pullman bought the [Aquablast] stock. Pullman kept the stock. Pullman ordered it sold. The money came from Switzerland, got cleaned out in Canada, through Toronto, and then went back into Switzerland." But was it money laundering? Perhaps, but there was no conclusive proof.

It was the taxman who expressed the deepest interest in the origins of Pullman's funds and in what authorities felt were his laundering activities. In the 1970s, the Department of National Revenue (now Revenue Canada) launched a major probe into Pullman's considerable money lending operation, an investigation that would not be completed until 1983. Focusing on his 1971 and 1972 tax assessments and some 708 transactions in Canada, they suspected that he was using his Swiss residency to evade taxes. The shortfall in unpaid taxes, they charged, was a staggering $2,051,403.10. Not so, argued Pullman, who been involved in an apparently minor income tax problem in 1958. (According to court records in Ottawa, Pullman lost that case.) In this much larger action, Pullman also filed an appeal. After all, he argued, he didn't live in Canada. He had no office here. He was not employed here.

And he negotiated no transactions here. Sure, his funds may
have ended up being invested in Canada, but only on an occa-
sional basis, and all the negotiations occurred outside Canada.
Besides, he argued in a 1976 statement of claim, he was "in a
state of virtual retirement."

Pullman resided with one of his three sisters in a Toronto
apartment during the time-consuming proceedings. (The
Aquablast prosecution was being put together during the same
period.) The strain showed during some of the cross-exami-
nations by federal lawyers. He was often chippy and petulant.
Yet, on occasion, he showed flashes of a mischievous humour
and a nimble mind. When asked during testimony in 1977 by
a lawyer for the Crown about Chillon, one of his companies,
the then seventy-six-year-old Pullman replied: "You will have
to ask a man by the name of Mr. McDonald, who at the time
was with McCarthy and McCarthy." Who was this McDonald
at the prestigious Toronto law firm? Why, the solicitor who
formed the company around 1960. As Pullman deadpanned:
"You cannot ask me things going back that far, I do not
remember, but I remember his forming the company." Pullman was apparently referring to Donald MacDonald (the court
stenographer had misspelled the name as McDonald), the then
federal Minister of National Revenue — and thus one of Pullman's opponents in the court case.[54]

As the case proceeded, it became clear that the Department
of National Revenue had come upon something very interesting indeed. Though Pullman had homes in Lausanne, Switzerland, and Monte Carlo, he maintained extensive ties with
Canada. As one government document asserted: "The Plaintiff is and was at all material times a Canadian citizen, and,
inter alia, has three sisters residing in Canada, sojourns at frequent intervals in Canada, maintains in Canada bank accounts,
a safety deposit box and trading accounts with Toronto securities dealers, owns or controls several Ontario corporations
and directly or indirectly holds various long-term investments
in Canada."[55] The evidence added up to one thing, argued
National Revenue: "a money-lending business carried on by

him in Canada." And a complicated one at that. It could only be understood as part of a larger business activity — one whose sole purpose was to launder money.

Even though this was not yet a crime, the Crown was trying to use the money laundering argument to show that his financial manoeuvres had no normal business purpose. As stated in a 1977 Crown affidavit, the statement of defence, it was alleged that his activities "included the transport, concealing and disguising 'or laundering' of certain monies for the purpose of reinvesting such monies in business."[56] That is, individually, Pullman's activities may have seemed above board, but put together, the Crown charged, you could see that they were links in a complicated money laundering chain and thus not a valid means of reducing the taxes he owed.

Pullman's lawyers demanded that the "money laundering" reference — which they described as "scandalous, frivolous and vexatious" — be removed.[57] They successfully argued that it was contrary to the rules of the court to make such a reference, and it was duly taken out of the government's statement of defence. Federal lawyers made one last bid, arguing that even though the laundering allegation was no longer in a key trial document, the concept of money laundering was essential. And they demanded that it remain in their formal pleading — stating that Pullman's transactions in Canada could only be understood as part and parcel of a "larger business of laundering money." This "could well be the decisive factor in determining the central issue in this appeal." The trial judge ruled otherwise and the laundering allegation was struck out of the Crown's formal pleading.

Perhaps the final nail in the coffin of the Crown's "money laundering" argument came in 1981 during the examination of Ralph Cox, a key investigator at the Department of National Revenue. After a series of heated exchanges, Pullman's lawyer posed the central question to Cox: "Did you find any evidence at all that there was laundering of funds in Canada?" His answer: "No, we did not." Pullman finally won his case, which wrapped up in 1983. He died two years later.

No one, in the end, was able to prove in a Canadian court-room that Pullman had been a money launderer. As former RCMP investigator Don Docker put it: "There was no mystery to what he was doing in a general sense. What he was doing specifically, I don't think anybody would ever know." And according to Stamler, the former RCMP assistant commissioner, the Pullman case emphasizes the difficulty of trying to prosecute someone who uses Canada to hide funds illicitly earned elsewhere: "It's very hard in Canada to deal with that kind of money laundering because you have to prove what offence was committed and by whom, and you have to identify that these are the proceeds of a criminal offence somewhere, where there was no offence in Canada."

Two recent cases provide an intriguing postscript.

The first suggests that Swiss couriers are still ferrying large amounts of cash across the Atlantic. A Canadian police investigator tells of a Swiss national who said he was employed by a Swiss bank to fly to Canada bearing suitcases full of cash. Once here, he'd exchange it into a different currency. For some reason, it was cost-effective to do this. Or so the Swiss courier was able to convince Canadian authorities — not an insurmountable task, since it's legal to carry cash across the Canadian border.

The second investigation suggests that an operation familiar to Pullman and his patron Lansky is still going on. It involved a major Las Vegas casino that was being skimmed of what one law enforcement source described as "phenomenal amounts of money." A Canadian, said the source, "in effect, was the bagman, the money launderer carrying cash. This individual was getting a commission somewhere in the vicinity of . . . 4 or 5 percent of whatever he laundered. He did it through Toronto." The Canadian launderer received some $5 million to $6 million in commission over an eighteen-month period. "You're talking about $100 million-plus in a year and a half that was skimmed off there," said the source. "This guy didn't do any of the skimming. All he'd do was carry the cash up.

There was one streetcorner in Toronto where there are four banks, one at each corner. He had accounts at each one. He just zigzagged back and forth across the street, then circulated through and then it was all hidden back down south of the border again as loans and different things to various corporations. . . . It was being laundered through Canadian banks and back out as loans through the equivalent of our numbered corporations all over the States."

John Pullman would have approved.

∎8 HEAVENLY BANKERS

Michele Sindona was an audacious Italian banker who amassed a personal fortune worth more than $500 million.[1] He also revered Machiavelli, handled some of the murkier finances of the Vatican and the Italian Mafia and liked to fold bits of paper into papal hats during meetings. (Thugs threatening his enemies used such paper papal hats as their calling card.)

Sindona's most famous protégé, Roberto Calvi, was cut from a different cloth. Where Sindona was charismatic, Calvi was coolly reserved; where Sindona boasted of wearing thousand-dollar pin-striped suits, Calvi quietly favoured dark, subdued clothing; and where Sindona liked to punctuate his conversations with quotes from the Italian poet Dante, Calvi's idea of a masterpiece was the American pulp novel *The Godfather*.[2]

Still, the two had much in common — in life and in death. They were born three weeks apart in the spring of 1920. They died under equally curious and unexplained circumstances: Calvi was found hanging under London's Blackfriars Bridge in June 1982; Sindona was poisoned in a high-security Italian prison in March 1986. (Calvi and Sindona were said to have made similarly murderous enemies — including some Mafia figures. But whether the Mafia or other adversaries figured in their deaths remains a mystery.)

Their worldly affairs had followed similar paths. Both, for instance, were closely linked with the Vatican. Sindona was known as "the pope's banker"; Calvi had the loftier title of "God's banker." Both piloted banks that went spectacularly bust amid massive fraud — Sindona's Franklin National Bank in the U.S. in 1974 and Calvi's Banco Ambrosiano in Italy in 1982. And they supervised the illegal manipulation of hundreds of millions of dollars — money laundering on a gargantuan scale. Both also shared a deep interest in Canada, thereby joining the long list of holders of shady funds drawn to the true north.

If there was a fanciful way to get rich in Canada in the 1950s, it was by finding uranium. At the height of the Cold War, the grey metallic element seemed the magic key to unlimited future prosperity. After all, it was needed for everything from atomic weapons to the embryonic nuclear power industry, and at the time it was scarce in most places. Canada seemed to have so much of it, however, that even small-timers could strike it rich. As the historian Michael Bliss put it: "Huge uranium strikes were made, complete with the usual miners' tales of romance or adventure or intrigue. . . . It was better to have a uranium than a gold mine in the 1950s. . . . "[3]

Word of the uranium boom spread across Europe and into Italy, which sent many of its citizens to work in the mining operations in Elliott Lake, Ontario. Sindona took notice too. In 1954, an article on the uranium craze in an Italian newspaper piqued his interest. At the time he was a rising tax lawyer in Milan known for his wizardry with tax shelters — and a freshly minted millionaire. With a partner, accountant Raul Baisi, he flew to Canada and bought a 530-acre farm near Blind River, Ontario, for $12,500. Though uranium prospectors had been active in the area, Sindona never struck it rich.[4] He did use the farm, however, as a haven for some fifty refugees who'd fled from Hungary during the failed revolt in

1956. (Sindona was an avowed anti-Communist, so he would be sympathetic toward such refugees.) He eventually helped them find work in — where else? — the Canadian uranium industry.[5]

The trip in 1954 whetted Sindona's appetite for Canada. Recalls Charles Albert Poissant, a now-retired Montreal accountant who did some work for a Sindona-related firm in Canada, "When I knew him [Sindona], he was very honest, very active and very dynamic. Canada interested him." What particularly intrigued Sindona was the ease with which property in Quebec could be anonymously held. As journalist Robert Hutchison discovered, real estate operations in Quebec using a nominee name could avoid "the land-transfer duty act and, as a further guarantee of anonymity . . . could avoid registering a deed of land sale altogether."[6] That suited Sindona's needs perfectly.

He was soon investing in Canadian real estate through his *"homme de confiance"* Amadeo Gatti, an Italian accountant who emigrated to Montreal in 1961. By 1971, Sindona's Canadian investments had grown to some $100 million, according to his own estimate.[7] Much of it was in real estate in the Montreal area, including the Montreal Stock Exchange building.[8] And it was handled, for the most part, through Societa Generale Immobiliare, a giant real estate conglomerate he'd secretly acquired from the Vatican. Sindona's operations in Canada were quite opaque. Gatti would get his orders and execute them discreetly. Says Poissant: "All that we knew was that Mr. Gatti represented him here. . . . But we never knew Sindona's actual role."

Why so much secrecy? It probably had everything to do with the origins of the funds he invested. At the time, the power of Italian banks to export lire or lend abroad was severely restricted by the government in Rome. Such regulations, however, were routinely circumvented by Sindona, and during his career, he laundered huge sums siphoned from his banks in Italy — a service he performed for other clients as well. After clandestinely funnelling the money abroad, he would complete the wash cycle by injecting the sanitized funds into legitimate ventures. Some of Sindona's investments in Canadian property were rinsed this way, says Luigi Di Fonzo, Sindona's biographer. In one instance in the 1960s, Sindona purchased millions of dollars' worth of land in Canada for himself and for his top client, the Vatican. He did this through a series of Liechtenstein corporations, including a couple which belonged to the Vatican — Tuxanr, A.G., and Ravoxr, A.G. The land was then split into building lots and sold. The profits ended up in Swiss bank accounts controlled by Fasco, A.G., Sindona's holding company.

For much of the post-war period, Italy had tight currency controls. While largely effective against people of ordinary means, they were easily skirted by the many tax-shy members of Italy's upper strata and helped Sindona hone his money laundering skills. As he once freely admitted: "It was not for nothing that I had the most successful tax-law firm in Italy."[9]

All kinds of people seem to have used his boltholes, including run-of-the-mill evaders of currency and tax laws. Two other groups of clients, however, were far murkier. There were elements of the Italian Mafia. And there were Sindona's fellow members in the conspiratorial "Propaganda Due," or P-2 Masonic lodge, a secret cabal of influential Italians whose membership list included seventeen army generals, the heads of all three Italian secret services, fourteen magistrates, three Cabinet ministers and thirty-eight deputies and senators. "Financial support for P-2 activities allegedly came from the Mafia's narcotics trafficking as well, and was laundered through fiduciary accounts in Switzerland by Sindona," said the U.S. President's Commission on Organized Crime in 1984.[10] One apparent conduit was Finabank, a Geneva-based financial institution which Sindona (whose personal account at the bank was code-named MANI 1125) jointly owned with the Vatican. "The laundrymat of Mafia and masonic dirty money" was how Carlo Bordoni, a former close associate of Sindona, described it.

Finabank collapsed in 1974 just after Sindona's Franklin

National Bank went under in the U.S. Finabank seems to have had a Canadian connection, too. In a 158-page detailed affidavit filed with a Milan judge in 1977, Bordoni said that illicit funds belonging to the Mafia and P-2 members were funnelled from Finabank into the United States through Canada and Mexico, using three firms linked to Sindona, including a now-defunct Montreal company.[11] Another conduit was Milan-based Moneyrex, a Sindona-controlled firm that in the 1960s pioneered the international currency brokerage business.

An Italian Parliamentary commission discovered that while Sindona's laundering methods had many variations, the Vatican bank, the Instituto per le Opere di Religione, or IOR, figured in many of them. Using the Vatican's status as a sovereign state, the IOR has the status of a foreign offshore bank in the heart of Rome. So for an Italian, moving funds to the IOR is as good as sending them to Liechtenstein or the Cayman Islands. Sindona loved this loophole. Typically, an Italian client wanting to shift money outside the country would start by depositing the funds at Sindona's Banca Privata Finanziaria in Milan. The money would then be shifted to an IOR account at the Banca Privata. This transaction would be explained to the authorities as a normal interbank transaction involving the Banca Privata's own funds. The IOR would then transfer the money, in the currency of the client's choice but minus a commission, to an account it held at Finabank in Geneva. From there, the money would be further washed through a series of Sindona-controlled, tax-haven-based companies.

One of the most frequently used companies was the Monrovia Financial Corp. Registered in the African haven of Liberia, it figured prominently, as we're about to see, in a shadowy Canadian deal in 1971.[12] At the end of the process, the money would be clean, bearing no trace of its origins and no sign that it had been accumulated abroad by skirting Italian currency and tax laws. And it would be freely available to invest internationally or back into Italy as a loan from anonymous foreign investors.[13]

Sindona used such a scheme to perfection in 1971 to launder money into Canada — and thereby rejuvenate a faltering cog in his American corporate empire. He had first ventured into the United States in the mid-1960s and had built up sizeable holdings through aggressive takeovers. (At one point, he even owned the famed Watergate complex in Washington, D.C.) Not all his deals went well, however, as the balance sheet of one U.S. firm, Argus Inc., indicated. In 1970, he had used Argus in a bid to acquire a Toronto-based company known as Seaway Multicorp. The attempt failed. But, in the process, Argus was hobbled by a debt of $5.896 million which had been used to purchase Seaway shares.[14] To clear up the mess, a deal was worked out with Seaway Multicorp.: the Seaway shares that Sindona had bought were exchanged for its hotel division. It consisted of seven motor inns in the Montreal-to-Windsor corridor. That much was known publicly. What wasn't learned until much later was that Argus's coffers would be replenished with money siphoned from Sindona's banks and laundered through some tax havens — all behind the veil of a legal transaction in Canada.

The Argus operation was a classic example of Sindona's facility with offshore financial shell-games. The hubs were a couple of obscure entities — Interlakes Canada Holding S.A. of Luxembourg and its wholly owned subsidiary, Interlakes Canada Realty Corp., set up in Delaware, Maryland. So complex was the scheme that the liquidators in Luxembourg of Interlakes Canada Holding didn't complete their work — begun after the collapse of Sindona's international empire in the 1970s — until late in the next decade. Based on documents and information they and Italian officials compiled, here is how it worked:

On June 28, 1971, Interlakes was set up in Luxembourg. The Delaware subsidiary was established a few days later. Both were controlled by the Liberian-based Monrovia Financial Corp., also known by the initials MOFI.

On August 11, 1971, Argus acquired the hotel division from Seaway Multicorp. in exchange for Seaway shares bought one year earlier.

The next day, Argus sold this division for $6 million to Courier Hotels International Ltd., whose president was none other than Sindona's Canadian confidant, Amadeo Gatti. Argus's treasury, depleted in the failed takeover a year earlier, was thus refilled — at least on paper. But no money was actually transferred, since Courier, renamed Seaway Hotels, had not yet received the $6 million. That occurred about two months later. But first, it had to be covertly moved out of Italy.

On October 22, 1971, Sindona's Banca Privata Finanziaria deposited $3.35 million US in Luxbank, a financial institution in Luxembourg. Luxbank had a fiduciary agreement with Banca Privata. That's a special service offered by banks in places like Switzerland and Luxembourg. They take in deposits and then lend them entirely at the depositors' direction and risk.[15] Under such an agreement, Luxbank lent the $3.35 million — at slightly more than the interest rate paid for Banca Privata's deposit — to Monrovia Financial, which injected it into the Luxembourg entity, Interlakes Canada Holding.

Luxbank charged the borrower, Sindona, a rate set by the depositor — in this case, also Sindona. The bank was paid separately and so did not have to rely on its usual source of profit — the spread between the rate paid on deposits and that charged on loans. Hence, the paper-slim interest-rate difference between the deposit in the Luxembourg bank and the subsequent "loan" to Monrovia Financial.

At about the same time, another Sindona bank, Banca Unione, deposited $2.706 million US with yet another Luxembourg bank, Crédit Industriel d'Alsace et de Lorraine. This second Luxembourg bank, in turn, lent this amount under a separate fiduciary agreement and, again, at a slightly higher rate than it paid for the deposit. The recipient was another of Sindona's "anonymous bridges," Romitex Corp. of Panama. Romitex mimicked Monrovia Financial and also injected the

$2.706 million into Interlakes Canada Holding. Then Interlakes Canada Holding transferred the accumulated $6.056 million — through other offshore intermediaries, thereby further blurring the trail — to its subsidiary, the similar sounding (and confusing) Interlakes Canada Realty Corp.

That same day, October 22, 1971, Seaway sold the land under four of the hotels to Interlakes Canada Realty Corp. for $6.056 million. In return, Seaway agreed to a leasing arrangement under which it could operate the hotels on land belonging to Interlakes Canada Realty. The cost: a monthly payment of $62,500 for twenty years to Interlakes Canada Realty for the use of the land. By selling the land, Seaway obtained the funds to pay off its debt to Argus, which was rejuvenated with fresh capital.[16]

Had an Italian bank regulator or fiscal cop snooped around, the transfers by Banca Privata and Banca Unione would have looked quite normal — as funds deposited and earning interest in two Luxembourg banks. Italian banks routinely used such transactions to round out their balance sheets. The real purpose was hidden by the fiduciary deposits. (In October 1971, Banca Privata Finanziaria and Banca Unione had placed two such deposits — totalling $6.056 million — into two banks in Luxembourg.) Moreover, bank secrecy in Luxembourg, Liberia and Panama prevented regulators in the depositor's home country from knowing that the funds were simply moving out of those institutions for altogether different purposes. There was nothing out of the ordinary to Canadian eyes either. The Argus sale of the hotels would have looked like a smart divestiture of assets, the kind of deal reported daily in the business press. And the money, by all appearances, would have come from a source quite familiar to Canadians — foreign investors. There would have been no apparent sign of impropriety.

The deals, in fact, were merely ruses to allow Sindona to illegally funnel $6.056 million US of his depositors' money out of Italy, hide their origins and use them for his own ends.[17] Sindona was very concerned about keeping these transactions secret. At one point, he apparently learned that Giorgio Ambrosoli, the Italian liquidator of the "Gruppo Sindona," was nosing around the Interlakes deal. In the files of one of his lawyers, investigators discovered a reference to a demand that "Ambrosoli be road-blocked."[18] In the end, Ambrosoli got too close to too many Sindona deals. He was executed by three men outside his home in 1979. Sindona was later convicted of having sent the assassins.

Though Sindona had great hopes for long-term investments (and perhaps long-term repositories) in Quebec, few projects apart from his real estate holdings were ever realized. Gatti, on his behalf, incorporated a Montreal firm called Technique-bec Ltée., on March 16, 1961. Techniquebec never lived up to its promise, holding, at its height, only a few properties and a small aggregrate producer. Techniquebec saw so little activity that when it was wound up in 1985, no annual corporate filing had been submitted to the Quebec government for years. The lack of business was not for lack of trying, however. Sindona proposed various ventures to Quebec authorities that would have involved Techniquebec, including a steel mill and a chemical pulp plant. The province wasn't interested. It seems Sindona was too secretive about the source of his funds and his anonymous backers.[19]

Quebec officials had cause for concern. Dealing with Sindona-related firms was hazardous. When Celanese Corp. of America bought an 80 percent stake in a Sicilian board mill, Siace, in the 1960s, it ended up losing some $75 million US. Sindona, a Siace director, had helped find the buyer. The case came to the attention of Philip Mathias, a Canadian reporter who was among the first to catch on to Sindona's scams in the 1960s. According to Mathias, Italian investigators stated that Sindona's associates in Siace were siphoning money out of the firm "by paying astronomically high prices to supplier companies owned by their wives."[20] Something similar seems to have happened with a New Brunswick pulp mill in the 1960s, which had been financed with provincial funds. Mathias wrote: "Sindona brought in a well-known Italian paper manufacturer for respectability, and a secretive Panamanian shell company as a siphon for funds."[21]

Some also saw Sindona's hand in a huge fraud involving a forestry complex at The Pas in northern Manitoba in the late sixties that ended up costing the province an estimated $70 million. Though the scam had many eyebrow-raising parallels with the Siace debacle, the evidence was never conclusive. Don Docker, a former RCMP chief superintendent who investigated the case, says: "I spoke to Sindona on two occasions and he denied any involvement at all in the project. And on no occasion did I find him involved." Nevertheless, there was sufficient concern among some Manitoba officials to have Dun and Bradstreet International investigate Sindona in 1967 — well before the scandal broke at The Pas. One Dun and Bradstreet study, now gathering dust in the Manitoba provincial archives, paints a glowing, if in hindsight naive, picture of Sindona: "He is described as a wealthy individual of high moral and commercial standing."[22] This "highly moral" individual would spend the last years of his life in prison in the United States and Italy, convicted of fraud and embezzlement and of the murder of Giorgio Ambrosoli.

In the turbulent 1970s, many wealthy Italians turned their thoughts to Canada. Among them was Roberto Calvi. At a time when Red Brigade terrorism and a rising tide of Mafia-style abductions seemed unstoppable, Italian executives like Calvi lived under often stifling security. Going to work was a military operation, consisting of a drive in a heavily guarded motorcade to the equally well-guarded Milan headquarters of his Banco Ambrosiano.[23] Personal safety was not the only concern causing well-heeled Italians to look abroad. It was also widely feared that the once robust Italian economy was being irreversibly depleted by industrial strife and soaring inflation. Ads began appearing in leading Italian newspapers touting the benefits of investing in property in Toronto and Montreal. Not even the October Crisis of 1970 could dim Canada's prospects as an attractive alternative.

In the early 1970s investigative journalist Philip Mathias began spotting some strange movements of capital into Canada from Lugano, the banking centre of the Italian-speaking Swiss canton of Ticino. A Lugano company like Fidinam S.A., for example, controlled some $70 million in Toronto real estate in July 1972. Yet it was loath to discuss the origins of its investment capital. A few months later, Fidinam's Canadian subsidiary made headlines for another reason, figuring prominently in a major political funding scandal in Ontario.[24] Recalls Mathias: "At that time it was illegal to export money from Italy. The money used to come across the border in suitcases. It would be deposited in a bank in the Ticino and would then be invested in real estate in Canada." Calvi, for his part, did not consider Toronto or Montreal fit for his Canadian refuge. He looked further west. As his son, Carlo, put it: "The plan was that he would retire to Alberta. . . . I think my father was very much oriented toward land and agriculture, natural resources, that sort of thing. . . . Then on the other hand, he was just one of the many [Italians] that invested there at the time."[25]

Calvi — whose gloomy eyes, high forehead and thick moustache seemed tailor-made for Italy's editorial cartoonists — joined the Banco Ambrosiano in 1946. It was then a sleepy Milanese bank much favoured by Roman Catholics. Calvi rose steadily through the ranks, impressing his superiors with his work ethic and quiet resolve. In the late 1960s came a turning point — he met Sindona. The shrewd Sindona noticed that "beneath the skin of the lowly functionary, there lurked in Calvi a man clearly set on winning wealth and power."[26]

Calvi became Sindona's acolyte — which goes a long way to explaining why Calvi's baffling financial dealings so resembled his mentor's. Money was frequently laundered through offshore ghost companies controlled by other ghost companies and which, in turn, oversaw still more ghost companies. With Sindona's influence, Calvi reached the number two position in the Ambrosiano in 1971, becoming its managing director and undisputed taskmaster. According to the liquidators: "At all material times from December 1971 until his death in June

1982, Calvi controlled the Ambrosiano Group."[27]

Calvi proceeded to turn Banco Ambrosiano into Italy's largest private banking group and a rising star in international finance. Yet Ambrosiano was strangely different from its rivals. It had no offices in the prominent banking centres of London and New York. Instead, its most important operations were concentrated in havens like Luxembourg and the Bahamas and in out-of-the-way locales like Nicaragua and Peru.[28] There was much to hide. For it was through a number of secret accounts and ghost companies in such places that the Ambrosiano group lost an estimated $1.3 billion US.

Liquidators contend that artificial stock transactions were a favoured method of siphoning huge sums out of the Banco Ambrosiano. Calvi would sell Italian shares to an offshore company that he secretly controlled before buying the stock back at an inflated price. In the process, the artificially gener-ated profit would be sent to a Calvi-controlled shell company in a tax haven — and Italy's currency control laws would have been circumvented through a seemingly normal deal.[29] Authorities eventually cottoned on to some of those scams. He was convicted in 1981 of illegally exporting currency through suspicious share transactions. Ironically, his appeal was to be heard around the time of his death in 1982.

As liquidators discovered, illegal currency transfers were not all that stank in Ambrosiano's affairs. Strange loans were made to "worthless companies" and were never repaid. An example occurred on June 29, 1979, when Ambrosiano's Nicaraguan entity forwarded $9 million US to Nordeurop, a Liechtenstein ghost company. The telex requesting the trans-fer uses the word "gives" to describe the money movement, though it is listed in the Nicaraguan subsidiary's books as a loan. Nordeurop, in turn, "gives" the $9 million to another Ambrosiano subsidiary in Panama, which records the sum as a fee. Yet there was no sign that any work had been performed to earn this fee, and no clear explanation of why the money needed to twice cross the Atlantic to travel from Nicaragua to nearby Panama.[30]

Just as curious were the huge sums — more than $100 million US by one count — that Ambrosiano-related firms forwarded to people like Licio Gelli, head of the P-2 Masonic lodge, and Umberto Ortolani, Gelli's ambitious lieutenant, who had accounts at the Bank of Montreal in Montreal. Funds were sent to Gelli and Ortolani "without any commercial justification," said the liquidators. All these multi-million-dollar shady deals were laundered through an extensive network of ghost companies. Their sole purpose: "to carry out dubious transactions in a manner designed to conceal their true nature and purpose," concluded the liquidators.[31]

So much secrecy. So much laundering. To what end? First, to enable Calvi to secretly take over Ambrosiano itself. In many cases, ghost companies, clandestinely controlled by Calvi, would acquire shares in Ambrosiano paid through loans from Ambrosiano's offshore entities. Elaborate systems and complicated transactions were set up to keep the phoney loans from being discovered. But not all the money went in this direction. Calvi deeply believed in the need to be protected by "occult powers." By this he meant the P-2 Masonic lodge and the Roman Catholic Church. From his P-2 protectors, Gelli and Ortolani, Calvi received a measure of shelter from the prying of Italian authorities.[32] It was as payment for protection, the liquidators charge, that the two had received the previously mentioned unauthorized loans and payments.[33]

The Vatican bank also helped Calvi. Late in 1981, questions were raised among international bankers about the complex network of ghost companies that had purchased Ambrosiano shares. To bolster Calvi's position, the Vatican bank provided letters of comfort, indicating that the IOR stood behind eleven ghost companies. In return, Calvi gave the IOR a secret letter absolving it from any responsibility for meeting the ghost companies' financial obligations. (The letter turned up after Calvi's death and was used by the Vatican to bolster its claim that it had no financial obligation to the victims of the banking crash.)

Amid all this fraud and embezzlement, the liquidators allege that Calvi also helped himself to funds looted from the Ambrosiano and subsequently laundered them. Some of those funds, they charge, were used to buy assets in Alberta. Not so, counters son Carlo Calvi who currently lives in Montreal. He says the Canadian properties were purchased with the family's own capital.

The liquidators of the non-Italian bits of Calvi's empire stumbled onto his Alberta assets in the most private of his document caches: two safes at the RoyWest Trust Corp. in the Bahamas. So important and so secret were these safes that not even RoyWest officials knew the codes. Only three people had had access to them: Calvi, and since his death, his son and his widow. With a court order in hand, the liquidators broke into the safes in March 1987. Inside they found some $600,000 US worth of jewellery and details of three secret RoyWest accounts holding cash balances of $9.5 million. All kinds of other documents were uncovered as well, including sensitive records of Calvi and his personal ghost companies. Among these were registers and bank receipts confirming details of shady multi-million-dollar deals with Sindona, Gelli and Ortolani. The liquidators also found documentary links to other tangible assets: a ranch worth $4 million US in Nicaragua dating from the period when Calvi had been close to that country's dissolute former strongman, Anastasio Somoza, and some vacation properties in the Bahamas. Such finds had been anticipated. What surprised the financial gumshoes was what they called Calvi's "Canadian connection." It consisted of a ranch bought in 1974 for $830,823 from Don Cormie, the controversial founder of the now-defunct Principal Group of Edmonton; and the Rocky Mountain Plaza, a Calgary office building bought for $7.6 million in 1974 and sold for $24.9 million in 1982.[34] There's no suggestion of impropriety against anyone that Calvi dealt with in Canada, but no one had expected Calvi assets — let alone what appeared to be his retirement nest-egg — to be located in Alberta, so far away from his usual haunts.

Roberto Calvi's Canadian assets are now at the heart of a protracted dispute, which began in 1987 when liquidators went to court in Alberta and got permission to freeze them. The resulting legal battle reached the Supreme Court of Canada. In the process, the original airtight court order was significantly cut back. And the two sides are now trying, through a slow and intermittent procedure, to reach a settlement.

According to the liquidators, the properties were acquired in 1974 through two Alberta nominee corporations, Alix and Dunkeld, which were set up shortly before the purchases by Don Cormie's law firm, Cormie, Kennedy. Calvi's name never appears on the incorporation papers or annual returns of the two firms. What liquidators have not been able to fully explain is how the funds used to purchase the ranch and the office building reached Canada. According to their probe, the money seems to have come anonymously through Swiss banks to Alix and Dunkeld in return for demand promissory notes — a kind of legally binding IOU.

Strangely, the promissory notes do not appear to have been secured by any mortgages on the real estate,[35] which at the very least indicates an especially trusting relationship between Alix-Dunkeld and whoever provided the funds. Swiss bank secrecy prevented the liquidators from finding the true owner of the notes, though they think the Swiss banks "were in fact acting on behalf of Calvi."[36] They believe that the money came through some sort of loan-back laundering scheme — illicit funds invested in Canadian real estate through loans rinsed by a secret sieve in Switzerland. For one thing, the liquidators point out, some documents related to these promissory notes were in Calvi's RoyWest safes. Further, it appears that some of the promissory notes were shifted from one Crédit Suisse branch to another in 1974 — at roughly the same time as Sindona's downfall. Similarly, in 1977, the promissory notes were transferred to another Swiss institution, Lombard Financial. This occurred just after a nasty campaign to discredit Calvi in Milan orchestrated by Sindona, who had, by this time, fallen out with Calvi. The inference: the promissory

notes were moved in 1974 and 1977 just when Calvi was taking evasive action to safeguard his private affairs. At the other
end, liquidators looked at the flow of funds into Calvi's Swiss
accounts in the 1971–74 period — until just before his Alberta
acquisitions. By their reckoning, the totals reached $10 mil-
lion US, though they concede: "It has not yet proved possible
to analyze each and every movement of funds into and out of
the relevant accounts."[37]

One infusion of capital is particularly interesting, however.
In December 1972 a Calvi account at Crédit Suisse, under the
name Ehrenkreuz, received $3,278,688 US. It was transferred
directly from Sindona's account — code-named MANI 1125
— at his Finabank. According to Italian authorities, those
funds were part of "unjust profits" earned by Calvi in a scam
with Sindona.

As in many similar cases, the liquidators' investigations
were hampered by complex transactions running through myriad tax havens. And they were based on the weight of (sometimes limited) circumstantial evidence. The result was that in
the end, they were unable to discover a smoking gun — that
is, a direct link between embezzled funds and the Canadian
assets. It is on this shortcoming of the investigation that the
Calvi family's case rests. It notes that the liquidators "cannot
trace a single dollar of the funds allegedly improperly received
from them into Alberta."[38] That was certainly the admission
of a key liquidator, Gerald Paisley, under cross-examination
by Calvi family lawyer Brad Nemetz in June 1987:

Question: Sir, are you able to trace a single dollar
which was taken, which you say was received by Roberto
Calvi in his capacity as a fiduciary of your companies,
can you trace a single dollar of that from its receipt point
into Alberta?

Answer: I believe it's probable that's what's happened,
but at the present with the incomplete information I'm
not able to actually do that in detail.[39]

The issue of the ultimate source of the funds will eventually be decided either by the courts or through an out-of-court settlement. Whatever the outcome, it is clear that Roberto Calvi went to great lengths to hide his financial tracks into Canada. As one source close to the investigation charged: "This is pretty classic laundering." Whether it was illegal or improper has yet to be determined. Like much else, the origins of the funds may turn out to be one of the secrets that Calvi took to his grave.

■9 OF BAGMEN AND SLUSH FUNDS

On April 19, 1970, a handful of Canada's most powerful businessmen — ram-rod federalists, every last one — met privately at the elegant Montreal home of financier Paul Desmarais.[1] What brought them together was the worrying rise of the Parti Quebecois, a growing force in the Quebec provincial elections that were about to be held. While Norris Roy Crump, then head of the huge conglomerate the Canadian Pacific Railway, was certainly on hand, the identities of the other visitors were never confirmed. Years later, Desmarais thought that Earle McLaughlin, the then chairman of the Royal Bank of Canada, might have attended. But McLaughlin, for his part, couldn't remember the gathering, though he said it was "possible" that he had been there. Regardless, it is safe to say that collectively, Desmarais and his guests managed billions of dollars in assets and employed thousands of Canadians.

"I remember calling a few businessmen together to talk about the situation in the province of Quebec at that time," Desmarais recalled years later. "I asked them to go over the situation because the Liberal and Union Nationale parties were making requests. We had a meeting to discuss it."

Within days of the gathering, a secret (and quite legal) anti-separatism fund was up and running. It was controlled by a trusted Liberal Party bagman. And it was underwritten by business leaders identified as having been at the meeting and others. The fund came to light more by accident than design — as a result of theft charges laid against the bagman. The court case had another ramification. It briefly illuminated a usually murky side of Canadian politics — how confidential pools of money are (often legally) raised, laundered and spent.

One day after the meeting, Crump, McLaughlin, Fred McNeil, then chairman of the Bank of Montreal, and Charles Bronfman, head of the Seagram spirits empire, contributed $10,000 apiece to the fund. Sam Steinberg, founder of the huge food retailer that bore his name, chipped in $5,000. Twenty-four hours later, Desmarais — whose vast holdings ranged from pulp and paper plants to the influential Montreal daily, *La Presse* — sent $10,000. The $55,000, all of which had come from special company accounts, was a hefty sum in the days before the inflationary ravages of the late seventies and early eighties.

Most of the payments and their destinations were recorded only vaguely in the companies' books. Significantly, too, they were personally made by the heads of the corporations themselves and handled "in a special way" by company accountants, recalls Rod Stamler, the then RCMP inspector who investigated the case in the 1970s. The payments, for instance, were entered in the ledgers of the Bronfman company, Distillers Corp., as "special expense, private and confidential"; at the Royal Bank as a "special payment"; and at Desmarais's Power Corp., as "miscellaneous payments." The more accurate notation, "political donation," appeared only in Steinberg's records. In a departure from the norm, the payments by the CPR, Royal Bank, Bank of Montreal and Distillers were made by anonymous bank draft rather than official company cheque. Curious, too, was the fact that the money did not go directly to the separatist-fighting Liberal Party or into its regular account at Montreal Trust. Instead, the money went to veteran Liberal bagman Louis de Gonzague Giguère, Pierre Trudeau's first Senate appointment in 1968. He deposited it into a special "in trust" account at a downtown branch of the Bank of Nova Scotia in Montreal. He was to use the funds as he saw fit; they were under his total control. Nor would any of the six businessmen subsequently ask what the money had been used for. As Steinberg later stated: "When we make a political donation, we just make it out. Then whatever happens after that, we never know."[2]

According to Giguère, the contributions stocked a secret fund to "fight separatism in all its forms." Within days of getting the money, he quickly began dispensing it. On April 27, 1970, a cheque for $3,000.50 went to Jean Chrétien, then a federal Cabinet minister and now the national Liberal Party leader. A day later, a cheque for $4,505 was issued to a Liberal organizer in the Saguenay region of Quebec. In mid-May, a further $1,000.50 was paid to an assistant to the late Jean Marchand, then another federal Liberal Cabinet minister. So went the fund's quite legal and proper disbursements until November 1970. At that point, Giguère shifted the remaining $20,000 into a personal bank account — which is where it quietly resided for years.[3]

As time passed, the threat of separatism seemed to recede. In 1973 the PQ elected just six candidates, one fewer than in 1970. Not surprisingly, the anti-separatism pool of money in Giguère's hands was soon forgotten, and it would have remained so except for an in-depth RCMP probe of influence-peddling allegations against him. (He was eventually acquitted of all charges.) During the inquiry, Stamler's investigators accidentally stumbled across the remnants of the special anti-separatism fund, which by 1976 had dwindled to $16,536. Giguère, they alleged, had put the funds into his own account so he could pilfer them. In May 1976, the Senator was charged with theft.

When the case went to trial three years later, Giguère used an unusual but ultimately successful defence. He argued that what seemed like larceny had been, in effect, a money laundering scheme (though he didn't use the term). They were confidential transactions and manoeuvres whose sole aim was to shield the origins of the fund. The point was to guard the donors' privacy, as Giguère had been instructed to do from the start. As *Globe and Mail* reporter Richard Cleroux wrote: "He said there was a need for secrecy because the businessmen had clients and shareholders who might not share their view, and offered as proof the fact that four of the six had sent bank drafts, which are harder to trace than cheques."[4] Though unstated, personal safety might have been another reason for the secrecy. Some of the six donors were identified in manifestos of the terrorist Front de libération du Québec (FLQ), whose politically motivated kidnappings and slaying of a provincial Cabinet minister triggered a national crisis in October 1970, just months after the fund was established.[5]

Throughout the trial, the Crown faced an uphill battle. The testimony of the fund's donors did little to support its case. In fact, the judge, Jean Goulet, would later sharply criticize some of their statements, saying "rarely have we had occasion to read so intelligently evasive testimony. They abounded in circumlocutions."[6] In cross-examination, Giguère stood by his guns — and his "money laundering" defence. Had there not been better options for resolving the issue than for Giguère to secretly retain the funds in November 1970? Would it not have been easier simply to turn them over to the Liberal Party? That would have gone against the donors' wishes, he replied. "If they had wanted to give to the Liberal Party they could have given the money directly . . . as they often did."[7] Besides, he said, he kept the money to bolster the federalist cause. If that was the case, countered the cross examiner, why had he not expended any funds in the 1973 provincial election? Because the Liberal victory was so clearly assured, he replied.[8]

In July 1979, Giguère was cleared, though the victory was a hollow one. Judge Goulet ruled: "Just because I acquit him does not mean I find him innocent."[9] Goulet explained his decision by saying he wasn't sure who, if anyone, had been defrauded — the Liberal Party or the six donors[10] — and he blamed the verdict partly on the lacklustre testimony of some witnesses. Goulet said they provided "evasive responses as if they were afraid of getting their feet wet."[11]

Historically, secret funds have been part and parcel of Canadian politics. Indeed, political finance as a whole "has always been enveloped in an aura of mystery," wrote Carleton University professor Khayyam Zev Paltiel, an authority on the subject, in 1966.[12] The situation has changed somewhat in recent years — especially since 1974 when the Election Expenses Act decreed, among other things, that all federal political party donations over $100 must be made public. In earlier times, however, secrecy more easily accommodated wealthy patrons who did not want anyone to know how they spent their money. To guard the confidentiality of such donors, party functionaries relied on simple forms of laundering. In some cases, this was done to conceal illegal political payments — money disbursed in the expectation of receiving some favour in kind. This might take the form of kickbacks, lump sums paid to achieve a specific result — like ensuring that an industrial project could be built on land zoned residential. Or it might involve a tollgating scheme, a kind of ongoing duty exacted on private-sector providers of government services — such as levying a fixed percentage of the value of highway-paving contracts. In other cases, contributions were laundered not to mask unlawful transactions, but to avoid embarrassment and public humiliation, damaging in the worlds of both politics and business.

On the flip side, politicians and political parties found this equally convenient. As always, they had an immense need for money — to pay for everything from renting meeting halls to printing brochures and posters. More often than not, the invoices outstripped the amounts that could be earned from party memberships, bake sales and gala dinners. In earlier times, fund-raising systems imbued with confidentiality prevented anyone from readily discerning how party coffers were filled or how much they contained. Thus, no one could raise disturbing questions when a large party contributor benefited from a governmental decision. As historian Michael Bliss put it: "The use of cash in political donations paralleled intimate personal contacts between businessmen and politicians. Details of the relations are, not surprisingly, hard to come by."13 What this spawned was a secretive system that favoured powerful donors and the politicians who cozied up to them — not ordinary citizens.

Senator Bill Kelly, the legendary fund raiser for the provincial Tories in Ontario in the 1970s, says secrecy was not of paramount importance to him. "I wanted disclosure," he said, "but a lot of businessmen didn't, and some of the party people thought donations would fall off. . . . A political party has no God-given right to run up bills and not pay for them. Since somebody has to pay, somebody has to collect. Canvassing for bucks is the same type of responsibility as canvassing for votes. You can't win without them both."14

It was up to the bagman to make the system work. His ability to attract contributions was enhanced by the fact that benefactors saw him as a significant influence on the leadership of the party. Also important was the fact that the bagman (it was a mostly male preserve) would often act as a "secret sieve," performing a kind of money laundering operation, removing traces of the origins of contributions so that politicians and parties could spend the money freely without fear of public disclosure.

The techniques were usually rudimentary — and effective. Giguère's method was a popular one. Donors would deliver personal cheques, bank drafts or even cash to the bagman who would then set up a special "in trust" bank account. Anyone trying to uncover the money's origins would only get as far as the personal bank account of a known party official who was holding funds in trust. The buck stopped there. Ditto for anyone on the other side of the "sieve" who was trying to investigate where a particular contribution had ended up.

An alternative method involved direct cash payments — probably the easiest way to keep matters confidential. In the 1950s, the Montreal industrialist J.W. McConnell used that approach to help Maurice Duplessis, the strident leader of the Union Nationale, win the 1952 and 1956 Quebec elections. Conrad Black, the Toronto financier who penned a biography of the late premier, calls the contributions "unique." And for good reason. Wrote Black: "They arrived within 48 hours of the dissolution of the Legislative Assembly in 1952 and 1956 and consisted of $50,000 to $100,000 in wads of fresh bank notes delivered in cartons for the Prime Minister's own attention."[15]

Cash seems to have been similarly used by Liberal Louis-Alexandre Taschereau, the Quebec premier whom Duplessis forced from office in 1936. Chubby Power, the legendary federal Liberal, discovered this on one occasion when he asked Taschereau to help fight a federal by-election. Power later recalled watching "the premier open a safe in his office and hand over twenty-five thousand dollars with a suggestion to return if more were needed."[16] In the 1980s, cash also seems to have been the preferred form of payment from the ex-Communist party apparatus in Moscow to the tame and compliant Communist Party of Canada.[17]

Political pools of money are not necessarily unlawful just because they're secret. Witness the Giguère case. However, this can make it difficult to discern which contributions are legal and which are illegal. "Some of them were illegal," says Stamler. "Some of them could be quasi-legal, but actually if you had all the facts, illegal in the sense that payments . . . into a political party for government action is definitely illegal." Illegal or not, one thing was clear: it would have been embarrassing (and strategically useful to opponents) if the existence of such funds and the identities of their contributors were revealed.

This happened in 1972 in an Ontario scandal over a $50,000 political contribution by Fidinam (Ontario) Ltd., the Canadian subsidiary of a Swiss firm that was becoming a major player in Toronto real estate. In July 1971, Fidinam issued a $50,000 personal cheque to provincial Tory bagman Bill Kelly — not to the party. About a month earlier, the Cabinet of Conservative premier Bill Davis had approved a controversial property deal with the company. It included a $15 million loan from the provincial Workmen's Compensation Board for a large Fidinam complex, known as Upper Canada Place, in downtown Toronto. Word of the secret contribution leaked out in November 1972 and raised some eyebrows — especially when investigators unearthed a telex that Fidinam's then treasurer, Betty McDonald, had sent to the Swiss parent in November 1971. When asked by head office to explain the $50,000 personal cheque issued to Kelly, McDonald said it was a "political donation, related to UCP/WCB." UCP apparently meant Upper Canada Place; WCB, Workmen's Compensation Board. The company admitted making the donation, but said that McDonald had made a mistake — there was no link between the $50,000 and the Cabinet approval.

Davis made a similar denial, but the issue would not go away. For months it kept the government in such hot water that even some Tory backbenchers called for the deal to be cancelled. It wasn't. An investigation by a Crown counsel found no evidence to indicate that there had been a breach of the Criminal Code. Yet, concluded Davis's biographer, Claire Hoy: "Technically the Tories were clean, but the political odors lingered on."[18] Indeed, the Fidinam scandal is credited by some observers, including Hoy, with prompting the Davis government to bring in provincial laws governing political contribution disclosure.[19]

Some secret political payments by businesspeople were part of elaborate tollgating schemes — under which they were awarded government contracts by paying a set proportion of the cost of the contract to the ruling party. The roots of such systems go back millennia, at least as far back as the Roman Empire, which experienced some of the worst known manifestations of such corrupt practices and paid a stiff price. Suggests one scholar, the empire's decline after 250 A.D. was due, in large part, to "public and private power [coming] to be treated as a source of profit. . . . The results were seriously dysfunctional."[20] In Canada, of course, contribution for gain is of considerably less magnitude. In the 1940s, the federal "Liberal party partly financed itself by insisting that individuals or entities in receipt of a government contract make a contribution to the party based on a fixed percentage of the contract's worth."[21] Some party bagmen in 1945, for instance, set a target of collecting 2.5 percent on $16 million in government contracts received from three Montreal railcar companies — a total of $400,000.[22] Such approaches were widespread. Notes historian Bliss: "Through the 1950s politicians toll-gated on government contracts, or expected systematic kickbacks, in most provinces."[23]

Similar systems have cropped up more recently. In New Brunswick in the late 1970s, reporter Philip Mathias found that, in general, a kickback was a prerequisite for doing business with government departments and agencies. The result, he said, was that provincial Conservative party coffers were full to the brim — topped up with millions of dollars in contributions that were put in "numbered accounts in Saint John, Moncton and elsewhere. A large portion of the contributions has been in the form of kickbacks. . . ."[24]

During the "golden era" of the Ontario Tories' Big Blue Machine in the late 1960s and early 1970s, some Tory bagmen allegedly ran an elaborate tollgating system. Journalist Jonathan Manthorpe describes a political contribution ledger shown to him by a junior Tory bagman: "Down the left-hand side of the lists were the names of the companies. Down the centre of the page was a column headed 'Business Record,' and there were entries after about 15 percent of the names. The fund-raiser explained that this referred to the amount of government business the companies had received. . . . On the right-hand side of the pages was another column headed 'donation record,' and there were entries for nearly all the companies."[25]

Aside from regular donations, businesspeople would sometimes make a kickback payment simply to grease the skids — to ensure that some particular action was taken. Rod Stamler, the former RCMP assistant commissioner, recalls that in the early 1970s he investigated a Hamilton businessman, Harold McNamara, who had been fed up with waiting for a late payment on a government contract. McNamara, who was convicted in 1979 in the Hamilton dredging bribery scandal, ended up personally delivering a $25,000 cash contribution to a political party bagman in Montreal. A government cheque was sent soon afterwards to McNamara. "Historically, it was common for political parties to have a Mr. Fix-It who would provide the facilities" for accepting secret payments, says Stamler. Yet, he suggests, it's usually difficult to see a cause and effect between secret payment and political favour. In this case, it was impossible to find the "smoking gun" tying the $25,000 to the subsequent release of the payment.

Some politicians go to great lengths to justify such a system. Stamler recalls a conversation with a prominent federal Liberal politician in the 1970s who voiced an unusual justification for a party receiving kickbacks and bribes — arguing that it was, in effect, preserving the integrity of the public service. "If the party does not accept that kind of contribution . . . ," the politician claimed, "then the government officials will accept it. And it's better that the party accept it and that the minister is aware of the fact that the person has been generous to the party and does something for them or takes his cause in mind." In other words, better to have a corrupt politician than a corrupt public servant. Stamler shakes his head. Yes, he suggests, that was actually put forward as a rationalization.

"I think it's stricter now in terms of what are party funds and what are not. But certainly a party, like any business entity, needs cash and needs money and needs to get things done. Historically, political parties are prone to this kind of money flow or are subjected to receiving it.

"I don't know that Canada is unusual in that sense. As far as bribery and kickbacks are concerned, in most other countries the politician receives them directly. Here, at least in some cases, they put it into the political party fund, which seems to legitimize it, but, in fact, doesn't really."

Individual politicians can also receive funds in questionable circumstances. Stamler recalls an unusual discussion in the 1970s with the late Jean Marchand, then a high-ranking Liberal Cabinet minister — and Quebec lieutenant for former prime minister Pierre Trudeau. Marchand stated, in a matter-of-fact tone, that people routinely gave him cash. He claimed not to know who they were or why they were giving him such gifts. At most functions in Quebec, said Marchand, somebody would inevitably and routinely "come along and stuff cash in my hands . . . I'd put the money in my pockets. I wouldn't even know who paid me the money. . . . I get all kinds of money from all kinds of people. So on one particular day a man stuffs a lot of cash in my hand, I don't even know what it's for."

The techniques used to launder political funds carry risks. As in the Giguère case, pools of money can be so well hidden that they simply disappear. "There have been a number of situations where there's a windfall all of a sudden because nobody knows that you have this special 'in trust' account," says Stamler. "I suppose it happens regularly. An organization disintegrates. Or people go on and only one or two people know that you have this fund."

The first such "lost" secret political fund dates back to the early days of Canadian Confederation. In the 1860s, Canada's first prime minister, Sir John A. Macdonald, was worried about the Fenian Brotherhood, American-based Irish revolutionaries who dreamed of an independent homeland and sought to invade what is now Canada in order to establish "a base from which to liberate Ireland."[26] To counter the threat, a fairly effective secret service was set up under the direction of Macdonald's trusted lieutenant, Gilbert McMicken, whose agents were the forerunners of the RCMP and the Canadian Security Intelligence Service. All kinds of covert ruses were employed to penetrate the Fenians and discover their plans. McMicken even raised the possibility of using of "one or two clever women" whose task would be to entrap some Fenian leaders "and thus as Delilah with Samson possess themselves of their secrets."[27]

All of this cost money — money that had to be kept as secret as the activities of McMicken and his operatives.

In the late 1860s, a special account was opened with the Bank of Montreal in Ottawa for "secret service" funds. Since there was little accountability for the public purse in the young Dominion of Canada, the money was spent solely at the discretion of four Cabinet ministers, most notably Macdonald. Remarkably, the ministers' word was enough to verify that the money had been properly used.[28] Trying to figure out how much was disbursed and where it had gone would later prove to be a frustrating task for the House of Commons' Public Accounts Committee. So would attempting to reconcile what had been legally allocated by Parliament for the secret service and what had, in fact, ended up in the special account. There were great gaps, for instance, between expenditures reported to Parliament and withdrawals from the bank account. In June 1868, for example, $50,000 of the funds allocated by Parliament "for Secret and Detective Service" was put into the bank account. A few weeks later, according to bank records, $21,991.41 was withdrawn. Yet, as recorded in the Public Accounts, only $15,081.41 had been removed. How had this occurred? Convenient bouts of amnesia held up the probe. The committee found that "this entry was made by the Auditor-General under verbal instructions from some Minister, but whom he does not remember."[29]

Little changed until just before Macdonald resigned from office in 1873. There remained about $32,000 in the "secret service" fund. Besides Macdonald, no one knew that this money even existed, since "the relevant public accounts showed that all the sums of which Parliament had knowledge had been actually expended."[30] That no one else was aware of this sum indicates Macdonald's iron grip over the "secret service" fund. When he asked the Auditor General, John Langton, what to do with the $32,000, Langton suggested a simple solution — that it be paid into general revenues.[31]

Macdonald did nothing of the kind. He kept control of the money and did not even disclose it to his successor,

Alexander Mackenzie. Langton forgot about the matter, too, assuming it had been properly taken care of. Macdonald also appears to have covered his tracks. In 1873, he had the Bank of Montreal send him "all the cheques and other vouchers" connected to the secret service fund. The Public Accounts Committee would later discover that these records had disappeared. According to the committee's report: "Sir John A. Macdonald presumes they were destroyed, or ought to have been, for fear of compromising parties employed for Secret Service."[32] In November 1875, the matter came to a head and Macdonald paid back $25,579.04. But he kept $6,600 — for, as he explained, "expenses incurred" before he had resigned as prime minister in 1873.[33] Two years later, the Public Accounts Committee gave Macdonald a slap on the wrist — that is, in parliamentary terminology, it censured him without naming him.[34] But he was never forced to repay the $6,600 or to fully account for it. At day's end, Macdonald emerged relatively unscathed, even though he'd left office in 1873 "with a sum of public money at his disposal over which he had kept control by devious devices, and some of which had never been appropriated by Parliament for secret service at all."[35]

A portion of the "secret service" fund seems to have been roughly put to the kinds of uses that Parliament intended. Thousands of dollars, for example, were expended in the investigation of the 1868 murder of Thomas D'Arcy McGee, Macdonald's Irish lieutenant. It was widely thought that a Fenian conspiracy had been behind the slaying.[36]

Yet this was a period when political party leaders took a hands-on approach to party financing and Macdonald was no exception. He apparently saw the secret service account as a flexible (and quite discreet) political slush fund. According to an insightful Master's thesis by W.A. Crockett: "A far larger portion of the funds set aside for secret service work was redirected to political activities. . . . [There's] strong circumstantial evidence to support the idea that secret service money was employed to bolster the fortunes of the Conservative Party."[37] In one instance, Crockett discovered some intriguing clues suggesting that $10,000 transferred from the secret service account in 1872 went to prop up the Conservative Party's electoral machine in eastern Ontario.[38]

To be sure, the initial covert establishment of the secret service fund was done lawfully by Parliament in response to the Fenian threat. Where it entered the realm of money laundering was after everyone forgot about the remaining money — everyone except Macdonald, of course. At that point, in 1873, not only did he not tell his successor about the fund — ensuring that it was indeed "lost" — but he seems to have sealed its fate by making sure that the paper trail of pertinent bank records was eliminated. Thus, the laundered money could have been used for partisan purposes, as Crockett indicates, without anyone knowing its origins.

Secrecy often surrounded trust funds set up to supplement the incomes of politicians. While today's politicians are reasonably well paid (too well, some might argue), until recently, the financial demands of public life were a heavy burden for all but the well-off. This was certainly the case for someone of modest means like Sir Wilfrid Laurier, the Liberal prime minister from 1896 to 1911. His biographer, Joseph Schull, described Laurier's predicament in the 1880s: "Trailed by debts and . . . entertained in lavish homes he could not aspire to himself . . . [he] was in reality the half-hearted servant of men who could buy and sell him twenty times over."[39] Laurier was therefore in a difficult position to refuse when, in May 1902, supporters purchased an annuity for him and his wife, which would give them $250 a month for life.[40]

Such trust funds were once a familiar feature of Canadian politics, usually providing not just a retirement nest-egg, but also covering some of the current expenses of party leaders. Though usually legal, the funds were often kept secret for fear of public embarrassment or of dampening other party fundraising activities. To maintain such confidentiality a form of money laundering was often required. Says Stamler: "In my experience, when you talk to the politician, he never knows where the money is coming from and doesn't know the connection." Paltiel agrees. Although "each leader usually names the finance chairman of his party . . . leaders tend to disclaim knowledge about the sources and amounts of party funds."[41] To this day, says Stamler, "the political party uses a lot of funds to support the leader. They get extra money. They get better accommodations, better travel arrangements. So the money goes fairly directly."

What motivates the donors of trust funds? In some cases, they view their donation as an act of public service. Others hope to receive a benefit in kind. Proving that benefits have indeed been given is difficult. In one celebrated case, Peter Larkin, the Salada Tea magnate, helped establish a huge trust fund for Mackenzie King, Canada's longest-serving prime minister, in the 1920s. Opinion is divided as to how pure his motives were. The historian J.L. Granatstein views Larkin "as a wealthy friend who was interested in making Mr. King financially secure. This was the reason for his gifts, so far as we know."[42] Journalist Jeffrey Simpson is less charitable. Referring to such trust funds as forms "of potential influence," Simpson writes that "at least King provided a clear quid pro quo: He appointed Larkin Canadian high commissioner in London, the same post later occupied by another King friend and benefactor, Vincent Massey."[43]

King is usually remembered as an eccentric much taken to spiritualism and communing at seances with his dead mother, but in matters financial, he was completely practical. And tight-lipped. By 1930, he estimated his personal worth at "over $500,000, exclusive of property which he estimated at a further quarter of a million dollars."[44] Yet he went out of his way to hide his considerable means, continually griping to Liberal Party officials that he was in dire financial straits. So convincing were his protestations that close collaborators were stunned by the size of his estate after his death in 1950.[45]

A cornerstone of his fortune was the personal endowment that Larkin set up in the 1920s just after King first became prime minister. As Larkin explained in a 1922 letter to a prospective donor, the fund's purpose was to remove from King's "shoulders a large share of the worries connected with the 'butcher, the baker and the candle stick-maker' and be able to devote his energies in full to the service of the Dominion."[46]

When it came to handling special funds, Larkin proved adept. In one instance, he planned to use a cheque sent by a donor to purchase Government of Canada bonds, then changed his mind. Instead of a cheque, he suggested in a letter to the contributor, it would be better to send impossible-to-trace cash. "It might be as well not to see my name on the cheque," he wrote, "as inferences are drawn from this sort of thing. Now would you mind cashing the cheque and placing the fruits of it with [an official] of the Royal Bank and ask him to forward it to me."[47]

The Larkin trust fund is a special case, both for its size and the elaborate secrecy that surrounded it. Some of the juiciest National Archives documents on the fund will not be unsealed until the next century but we do know that the Larkin fund's balance originally stood at $225,000 and subsequently grew with interest.[48] Much was done to keep its existence and that of its contributors secret. For one thing, it was held in an account at the Old Colony Trust Company in Boston, a predictable choice, since King seems to have been partial to bank accounts in the U.S. In the 1930s and 1940s, he also had some at the Bank of New York in New York City and at the First National Bank of Boston in Boston. Why was the Larkin fund held in Boston and not in a Canadian bank? "My only assumption is that King didn't want it talked about," says his biographer, Blair Neatby. Why? Because it might affect party fund raising? "No, I think his reputation," said Neatby. "The idea that businessmen had given him money — he would rather that it not be known."

In spite of King's scrupulousness, two contributions caused him great anxiety in 1931 during the Beauharnois Scandal, a troubling period that he described as "a real Gethsemane."[49] In March 1929, King's Cabinet approved key sections of the huge Beauharnois hydro-electric power development in

Quebec. The scandal broke two years later when it was disclosed that the project's backers had contributed hundreds of thousands of dollars to the Liberal party. Particularly worrying for King were the donations of Senator Wilfrid Laurier McDougald, a close friend and the chairman of the board of the Beauharnois Power Corp.

McDougald had put two deposits — a total of $25,000 — into the Old Colony Trust account. Suspiciously, both deposits — $10,000 on December 29, 1927, and $15,000 on October 1, 1928 — were made before the King Cabinet's Beauharnois decision. Though the funds were certainly questionable, there is no direct evidence that the money influenced the King Cabinet's decision, says historian T.D. Regehr, the leading expert on the Beauharnois debacle.[50] Yet King was so worried about how the payments might appear if they were disclosed that he later reimbursed McDougald. To King's relief, the Larkin fund was never mentioned during McDougald's testimony to a Parliamentary committee in 1931.[51] King himself weathered the scandal, successfully asserting that he was ignorant of the details of party finances.[52]

The issue of whether King was bribed will likely occupy Canadian historians for some time to come,[53] but the danger of "potential influence" seems to have been more troubling to other trust fund recipients. Louis St. Laurent, the Liberal prime minister from 1948 to 1957, was a case in point. He accepted a trust fund only on the condition that a kind of "Chinese wall" be erected between himself and his benefactors. Not only were the donors not to be made public; he did not even want to know their names himself. That, he felt, would ensure he wasn't beholden to them.[54]

There has been speculation that Lester B. Pearson, Liberal prime minister from 1963 to 1968, might have received similar help. Certainly, it was clear that Pearson was worried about his personal financial security when he decided to enter politics. In response, Walter Gordon, the economic nationalist, apparently raised "the funds for a modest annuity which would temper this source of hesitation," according to Denis

Smith, Gordon's biographer.[55] Pearson told the editors of his memoirs that the fund was in Mrs. Pearson's name "to provide a minimum of financial security for her. . . . Furthermore, Mr. Pearson made it a condition of accepting the annuity that he would not know who had contributed, thus protecting himself from ever being in the position of being asked to repay with favors the good deed done."[56] Geoff Pearson, the late prime minister's son, does not recall discussing such a fund with either of his parents: "There was certainly some arrangement. Just what it was I just don't know. . . . I doubt whether it was ever active. It was probably a paper promise of some kind. . . . As far as I know, it never actually happened."

Even the insinuation that confidential funds might exist can be damaging — as the Liberals discovered in September 1988. During that month news reports suggested that then federal Liberal leader John Turner might have personally benefited from such funds. Turner and senior Liberals, including Senator Leo Kolber, the party's former chief fund raiser, strongly denied the assertions. Nonetheless, the incident added to Turner's leadership woes in the crucial weeks leading up to that fall's federal election campaign.[57]

Prime Minister Brian Mulroney has faced similar kinds of allegations. During his first term, journalist Stevie Cameron of the *Globe and Mail*, revealed that Conservative party funds had been used to decorate and renovate the prime minister's official residence at 24 Sussex Drive. Though Mulroney was said to have repaid the loans, the political impact of Cameron's stories, including the much-repeated tales of Mulroney's fondness for Gucci shoes, was felt for years. Perhaps mindful of this incident, a Tory official, who confirmed in 1991 that Mulroney was receiving party funds to cover extra expenses, went out of his way to stress that everything was above board and that "the payments did not amount to a supplementary income for the prime minister."[58]

Revelations of secret political payments jarred Nova Scotia politics in the early 1990s, affecting both the provincial

Liberals and Conservatives. First came word that Liberal leader Vince MacLean was receiving $46,000 a year from a secret trust fund called Hawco, which had been set up in the 1950s. The resulting controversy dominated the provincial party's annual meeting in the fall of 1990. In the end, a chastened MacLean was forced to concede that he'd made a mistake — and promised to accept no more payments. As he told delegates: "There can be no secrets, perceived or otherwise."[59] Yet this quite legal practice had gone on for a long time. Gerald Regan, an earlier provincial Liberal leader and premier, admitted in 1980 that he accepted $142,000 from a party trust fund over fourteen years, explaining that "the trust fund had been kept secret because of anticipated pressure to use the money for election expenses."[60]

Though no impropriety was ever linked to the Hawco trust fund, what made the issue so contentious were persistent questions about the source of the contributions. One of Hawco's trustees, for instance, was former Senator Irvine Barrow. He had been convicted of conspiring to peddle influence in 1983, though he was acquitted in 1989 after a new trial was ordered. The source of Hawco's funding was never established, but evidence at Barrow's trials seemed to point to a possible origin. Elaborate tollgating schemes were described, in which "Liberal fund raisers demanded contributions from liquor companies and contractors in return for doing business with the government."[61] Another Liberal party trust fund, Howmur, was created in the 1970s as a "repository for both legitimate contributions and kickbacks from government contractors during the 1970s." Yet, noted one party official, the fund's origins are deeply buried. Said Liberal justice critic John MacEachern: "You could hire the best investigative firm in the country and you wouldn't be able to track those funds."[62] The trust fund issue continued to dog MacLean even after he stopped receiving payments, and it contributed to his decision in early 1992 to step down.

Another secret payments scandal touched the province's former Conservative premier, Senator John Buchanan. In this case, there had been no confidential trust fund, but between 1978 and 1990 the provincial party had itself secretly paid a total of $588,059 to Buchanan. The payments were quite legal. Yet they were concealed in two innocuous-sounding party accounts. One was called "leader's travel, office and other"; the second, "promotions, advertising and research."

Former party treasurer Roy Busche explained that the payments were listed as promotion "because that's what John Buchanan did for the party, he was one of the best promoters that it ever had." Of course, Busche admitted, he didn't know what exactly Buchanan had spent the money on. After the revelation, party officials tried to argue that the payments had not been secret at all. In the words of president Irene Swindells: "If party members weren't aware of the payments, it is because they didn't bother to ask."[63] The disbursements, nonetheless, caused an uproar in the province. The Halifax *Chronicle-Herald*, which headlined a critical editorial "Sweet Sound of a Whistle," welcomed the disclosure of the funding as "a virtuoso demonstration of blowing the whistle on the shadowy world of party finance."[64]

No politician was more damaged by the disclosure of secret payments, however, than the late Claude Wagner, the prominent Quebecer who placed second to Joe Clark in the 1976 Conservative leadership race. He entered the federal scene in the early 1970s at a time when the Tories were looking for a Quebec messiah — someone to play the role of George Etienne Cartier, Sir John A. Macdonald's Quebec lieutenant, and break the Liberal stranglehold in the province. Wagner appeared to be just the ticket. He had been a provincial Liberal justice minister in the mid-1960s and was widely admired in Quebec for his tough law-and-order stands. He caught the eye of many influential Conservatives — including Brian Mulroney. Hampered by a unilingual leader in Robert Stanfield, they argued, the party was doomed to electoral frustration unless it had Wagner.

After some assiduous courting, Wagner decided to answer the call. But he had deep uneasiness over his personal financial security. He'd take the plunge but, as he asserted repeatedly, he needed a safety net in case things didn't work out. That would be no problem, leading Tories assured him. Sometime in the summer of 1972 — with the likelihood of a federal election later that year — Wagner and Tory insider Finlay Macdonald met over lunch. Writes John Sawatsky, Mulroney's biographer: "After some friendly sparring they settled on $300,000. The Tories had purchased their star. . . . The George Etienne Cartier Trust Fund, as it was called, would give Wagner an estimated income of $30,000 a year before taxes. Contrary to the original notion of a safety net, even if he won a seat, he would collect it on top of his MP's salary."[65]

There was nothing illegal about the fund, though it was decidedly secret. Wagner's woes had a separate cause and were mostly of his own making. When rumours of a fund first surfaced in 1972, he sharply denied its existence. On September 5, 1972, the day he said he'd run for the Tories, he stated firmly: "I have no need of, I have never asked for, nor have I ever been offered any pension fund or financial compensation." The words would come back to haunt him. Little by little, Wagner was forced to recant. In November 1975, he admitted receiving $1,000 a month to boost the Quebec Tory organization. Moreover, he said, the money was from a fund set up after the October 30, 1972, election.

Things heated up in the weeks leading up to the February 1976 leadership convention. At the time, Wagner was seen as the "odds-on favourite" to succeed Stanfield. Then came a series of revelations about the fund.[66] Most damaging was the disclosure that "a large sum in cash was delivered to . . . Wagner four days before the 1972 federal election."[67] Wagner tried to lash back, but his counterattacks were unfocused and largely inconsequential, Then, as political scientist John Saywell concluded, "The Wagner campaign began to splutter."[68] Wagner's political career would never recover. He died in 1979.

Mulroney himself had to contend with allegations of a secret fund during his 1983 leadership campaign. Six months before the June 1983 convention, Dalton Camp, the former party president, fired what he later described as "a shot across the bow." Camp did not like the way the covert campaign to get rid of then Conservative leader Joe Clark was being secretly financed, and during a televised interview, he let the cat out of the bag, charging that the dump-Clark forces were being "lavishly financed by person or persons unknown. I have a good idea where some of that money came from, and some of it came from offshore."

One year later, Camp pointed the finger at Walter Wolf, a flamboyant entrepreneur with close ties to some key Mulroney insiders. Wolf had devoted much time in the early 1980s to honing a macho image — right down to boasting of keeping an Uzi submachine-gun in the heavily mirrored bedroom of his secluded Mexican villa. The label "offshore" also fit Wolf to a T. In 1972, Wolf — who once stated "I am in no tax zone" — established a base in Switzerland. Sometime later, he bought a home in Bermuda, another financial haven. But Wolf dismissed Camp's charge, saying: "I never contributed a cent." He did, however, admit to indirectly paying $12,500 apiece in directors' fees to two close Mulroney associates and members of the anti-Clark forces: Senator Michel Cogger and Frank Moores, the former Newfoundland premier. Said Wolf: "That is absolutely the only money I gave to anyone associated with the anti-Clark movement. And my view is that the money was paid for the professional services [to Wolf], not political activities." Moores, at the time, denied receiving any money from Wolf.[69] The allegations failed to derail Mulroney's leadership bid. Yet he did not escape wholly unscathed. As journalist Jeffrey Simpson suggests, the "misty stories . . . about offshore contributions to Mulroney from financier Walter Wolf" helped to tarnish Mulroney's triumph.[70]

Political finance is not necessarily murky or illegal, nor does it always involve schemes more typically associated with money laundering. Yet history has tossed up more than enough such cases — instances in which laundering-type methods

were used to hide possibly unlawful and invariably questionable financial links and manoeuvres that should have been
publicly revealed. Secrecy has no place in political finance. It
breeds distrust in already mistrusted public institutions. It
reinforces the advantages of those with the most money to
spend for political purposes — since their largesse is never
disclosed and thus made publicly accountable. To be sure, in
recent years, political finance has been made less opaque —
through such things as new federal and provincial fund-raising
and election spending laws, and changes in public attitudes.
But more needs to be done. For invariably, corruption thrives
in the shadows.

■ 10 NICOLAE CEAUSESCU AND THE LOOTING OF ROMANIA*

Near the heart of bleak and shoddy Bucharest stands something of an anomaly — a tiny district trimmed with braces
of ionic columns, wrought-iron gates and intricate façades
and domes. No endless rows of standard-issue, buff-coloured
apartment blocks here. Few encroachments, either, of that
other staple of Romania's urban landscape — Stalinesque
office buildings. The area is fittingly sprinkled with the kinds
of neo-Baroque architecture you find near the Paris Bourse or
in London's banking-and-brokerage quarter near St. Paul's
Cathedral. This is Bucharest's once thriving financial district.
Like Romania itself, the buildings are a little the worse for
wear. Rusting roofs, peeling paint and decaying plaster are
common, though the tilt of some edifices suggests worse
structural maladies. That the buildings survived at all is a

---

* This chapter grew out of research for the documentary "Evil's
  Fortune," produced by CBC Television's "the 5th estate," and
  broadcast on Tuesday, November 8, 1991.

minor miracle. Somehow they escaped the mad scheme of Nicolae Ceausescu, Romania's late dictator, to replace such "decadent" structures with his own soul-numbing concoctions. Then again, he had good reason to deal gently with at least part of the financial district.

For near its centre, in a sprawling complex at no. 22 Calea Victorici, were contained some of his deepest secrets. This is the address of the Romanian Bank for Foreign Trade — the financial conduit for the country's imports and exports. With its dimly lit offices and mounds of dusty ledgers, it appears backward to Western eyes — more reminiscent of a nineteenth-century Ottoman bank than of a modern enterprise. (There were hardly any computers in sight as recently as June 1991.) But appearances can be deceiving. Deep inside the bank was the highly efficient nerve centre of Ceausescu's multi-billion-dollar laundering operation. Known by the initials AVS, or Actiuni Valutare Speciale, which translates as "the special hard-currency compartment," it was run by a handful of bankers who were part of Ceausescu's labyrinthine secret police and espionage apparatus. In the 1980s, this clandestine unit — a carefully nurtured secret nestled in the heart of other secrets — rinsed huge sums from kickbacks, skims, tollgating schemes, bribes and extortion payments. For when it came to amassing and hiding money, Ceausescu — otherwise a plodding and completely unscrupulous party hack — displayed a deft touch.

"Ceausescu was Romania," says David Funderburk, the U.S. ambassador in Bucharest from 1981 to 1985. "The state treasury was his."

Nicolae Ceausescu was born in January 1918 in poverty in the tiny farming community of Scornicesti, about 160 kilometres west of Bucharest.[1] A dour, truculent boy, he grew up to become a sullen, bellicose dictator, and a vain one, too. At less than five feet six inches, he hated being photographed with anyone taller. His fawning corps of historians indulged his many conceits, extolling his milestones and his supposed talents: that as a stripling he would spend his nights poring over borrowed political tomes; that as a young man he had led a workers' revolt; and that as an orator and thinker he was unsurpassed (the Genius of the Carpathians, ran one of his more ludicrous titles). Such was the stuff of the multivolume biographies that his obsequious chroniclers routinely churned out and that his minions paid handsomely to have translated and reprinted abroad. This may now seem laughable, but to Ceausescu and his churlish wife, Elena, it was all vitally important. A two-page update on these foreign publishing conceits was on Elena's desk the day they were overthrown in December 1989.

In truth, Ceausescu excelled at little. His schooling was brief and undistinguished. When speaking, he tended to stutter and sputter; when angered, he sometimes became incomprehensible. (His teeth would click, too, recalls Funderburk, a long-time thorn in his side and often the focus of his rants.) Ceausescu was prone to bizarre behaviour and bizarre ideas. He was so fearful of disease that he is said to have washed in alcohol after shaking hands. At one point, for no apparent reason, he ordered that corn seeds in one region be planted closer together than was traditionally done (or was agronomically sound). The crop failed. He did read some Marx and Lenin while in jail in the late 1930s and early 1940s, but all he seemed to retain was a knack for stringing together Communist maxims, regardless of their meaning or pertinence. (By the late 1980s, platoons of ghost writers were kept busy penning another staple of Romanian bookstores: lumbering dissertations on scientific socialism issued under Ceausescu's name.) Neither was Ceausescu much of a cobbler, the trade to which he apprenticed in his youth. Nor was he a political activist. And, yet, he was a standout in one area. More than any rival, he possessed that thuggish blend of shameless subservience and ruthless ambition that ensured success in Communist nomenklaturas. It would serve him well.

He reached the top in 1965, winning election as First Secretary of the Romanian Communist Party. Ceausescu wasted little time in solidifying control. Rivals were eased out of important postings; toadies were rewarded. By masterful bits of plotting, conniving and back-stabbing, the party apparatus coalesced behind him. By and large, so did the Romanian people, for in the late 1960s Ceausescu seemed to represent a liberalizing trend and the hope of nationalist self-determination. Of course, this was well before he had reduced Romania to Third World penury, with the grimmest food rationing in Eastern Europe and the continent's highest infant mortality rate.[2] For a time, even the West doted on him for criticizing the Soviet invasion of Czechoslovakia in 1968.

As his power grew, so did his need for money — not for the increasingly worthless leis his government printed, but for the hard currencies of the West. In this, Ceausescu was not alone. If there is a common thread linking tinpot dictators of all stripes and all regions, it is an insatiable need for huge amounts of money. Loyalty, after all, is an expensive commodity. Supporters need a steady stream of well-paying jobs, pompous titles and gifts of scarce goods. So do their children and relations. So do potential enemies. Some observers reckon that this (self-serving) largesse may be the single largest drain on the fortune of Zaire's Mobutu Seko, who, like Ceausescu, belonged to the dictators' class of '65. Mobutu is estimated to have siphoned off at least $2.5 billion US from the treasury of his mineral-rich African nation.[3] Despots also invariably develop lavish tastes. The most obvious manifestation: an obsession for opulent quarters. Some like Mobutu build extravagant complexes in their hometowns, as if they need to prove something to kith and kin. So sumptuous is his, in the remote family seat of Gbadolite, that it has been dubbed "Versailles in the Jungle."[4] In a variation on the theme, members of the former East Germany's Politburo were ensconced in 247 acres of tightly guarded pine-and-birch grove near Berlin, complete with greenhouses that provided fresh vegetables and flowers year-round.[5]

Ceausescu preferred more variety. Scattered around Romania were at least thirty villas and hunting lodges (some estimates reach as high as eighty). All were ostentatiously (and garishly) decorated at great expense. Every Ceausescu residence was stocked with closets of plastic-wrapped towels and bedding, which had to be destroyed after a single use. And all official homes were kept at a steady seventy-six-degree temperature, summer and winter, just in case he dropped by. His crowning glory was the gleaming white (and still unfinished) People's Palace — since renamed the House of the Republic — which dominates central Bucharest. It is among the largest buildings in the world, and with its mish-mash of Greek and Roman architectural elements it evokes Albert Speer's visions of an urban Nazi utopia. So much marble was used in its construction in the late 1980s that a shortage of tombstones is said to have developed.[6] Since Ceausescu's downfall, no one has been able to find a practical use for this monstrous building. Razing it would be too expensive, while turning it into a hotel-cum-convention-centre-cum-trade fair has been dismissed as impractical.

In most things, Ceausescu's ego knew no bounds. Art galleries and public buildings featured flattering portraits of a benevolent, age-defying Ceausescu, often in the company of children or surrounded by flowers. Scores of such depictions now languish under lock and key in Room 44 of the National History Museum in Bucharest.[7] And his court poets and writers never faltered in lauding his supposed international prominence — right down to fabricating gushy messages from such Western luminaries as the Queen of England. To further massage his ego, advertisements filled with effusive praise and made to look like actual news reports were taken out in the foreign press. By all accounts, he thought the paid announcements were genuine. He also imagined himself a superb hunter and loved to spend hours merrily shooting away at all forms of wild game. Bears were a favourite target. It was widely believed that hidden sharpshooters picked off the prey that he missed. But for pure narcissism, little could rival the museum he bestowed on his hometown of Scornicesti. It was dedicated to honouring his reign — which he dubbed "the Era of Light." (An incongruous label, since power shortages and electricity rationing were endemic during the last part of his regime.) The museum's pride and joy was the purported remains of Europe's first human, who — surprise! — had also resided in Scornicesti. The bones, it turns out, were bits of elephant tusk.[8]

In spite of his lavish lifestyle, for the politically ambitious Ceausescu, world stature was far more important than earthly comfort. "Don't picture Ceausescu entirely as a greedy man, like other dictators, hoarding a lot of money for himself," says Liviu Turcu, an urbane former top member of the Romanian intelligence who defected to the United States in January 1989. "It was much more complicated."

Ironically, the dictator long coveted the Nobel Peace Prize and considered it a nagging affront that he had been overlooked for his role in the lead-up to the 1979 Camp David peace accords between Israel and Egypt. In Ceausescu's paranoid view, there could only have been one explanation for this omission — a plot by foreign enemies. So he put his intelligence service on the case to ensure that he won the Nobel. (He never did.)

Neither (in his mind) was he adequately recognized for other diplomatic initiatives: for supporting Third World issues, for trying to lead the Non-Aligned nations and for championing the Palestinian cause. This last included sheltering and aiding prominent terrorists such as Venezuelan-born Ilich Ramirez Sanchez, known variously as "Carlos" or "The Jackal." "Carlos" was a frequent visitor to Bucharest in the early 1980s.

To be fair, Ceausescu did have some diplomatic successes — such as his decision to participate in the 1984 Los Angeles Olympics and thereby weaken the East Bloc's boycott of the games. But ultimately, most diplomatic ventures failed to reap either prestige or power, because no one fully trusted him: not his Balkan neighbours, not the former Soviets, not the West, and not even the Italian Mafia. Ceausescu's approaches to the

Italian criminal entrepreneurs were brushed off, says Turcu, because they thought he was too unreliable a partner.

Despite his many failures, Ceausescu was undaunted: He continued to pursue his expensive dreams of attaining world stature. This, in part, accounted for his insatiable need for large amounts of hard currency — and for his extensive reliance on secret laundering schemes. He feared that disclosure of the source of his funds might compromise his aspirations. It was difficult, after all, to justify pocketing arms trade profits when one was fostering a reputation as a peacemaker. It was harder still to explain to the Israelis (whom he also courted) why Romanian funds were covertly supporting the Palestine Liberation Organization. Says Turcu, now a university lecturer in Boston: "He would have traded anything that would have allowed him to take another step towards being . . . the biggest and greatest in the world." An example of this ambition, he suggests, was Romania's diversion in 1986 of 12.5 tons of Norwegian heavy water to India, a country that has not signed the nuclear weapon non-proliferation treaty. The heavy water had been ordered for the Canadian-designed Candu nuclear station at Cernavoda, but the facility has not yet been completed. Instead, the water was shipped through a shadowy Liechtenstein-registered firm, Ridgenet, to India, the payments being laundered through the Romanian Bank for Foreign Trade. Though Romania made a small profit on the deal, Turcu said Ceausescu had a more important goal: "to get political favour" with India, which he was assiduously courting at the time. Says Turcu: "No one in Romania would do even a smaller operation without Ceausescu's knowledge, let alone such a difficult and delicate operation."

The vast security apparatus; the immoderation of his lifestyle in Marxist-Leninist terms; the diplomatic initiatives. All this cost money — hard currency, to be more precise. How to pay the piper? And how to do so secretly, without his enemies finding out? And, of course, how to stash some loot abroad for a rainy day? Such were the dictator's day-to-day financial concerns.

Nicolae Ceausescu started small. In the late sixties and early seventies, his secret policemen sought out Romanians with claims to foreign inheritances or insurance policies. In return for giving the hard currency benefits to the state, they were offered much less valuable lei but at a higher exchange rate than the official one. Many accepted — often under duress. Romanians who worked abroad — usually as teachers, doctors or scientists — also had to transfer a large chunk of their hard-currency earnings to the regime. Failure to do so was severely punished.

Sorin Dumitrescu, a Paris-based United Nations official, was arrested during a visit home in 1977. "I owed the Romanian state a sum of about 70,000 [French] francs — every Romanian citizen working abroad must, by law, turn over to the state the greater part of his earnings," he wrote years later. "In my case, it was a question of arrears since I had already paid over 120,000 francs." Dumitrescu, a world-renowned hydrologist, promptly paid the arrears. But he had to endure two years of detention and intimidation in Bucharest before mounting international pressure forced Ceausescu to relent. Said Dumitrescu: "I had won, but I shall remain marked for life by this ordeal."9

Such sources of funds were not enough, however. Larger ones were needed, and they were found.

On May 26, 1984, a beaming Ceausescu, standing aboard a specially built boat, cut a ribbon inaugurating a cherished project: the Danube–Black Sea canal. The 64-kilometre waterway was supposed to trim two days off the Danube River route to the Black Sea — or so Romania's tame media would have had you believe. In fact, the canal was a white elephant — so poorly constructed that it has never come close to meeting any traffic targets. Three years after opening, it was still operating at only 10 percent capacity. That much is widely known. Less obvious was Ceausescu's other reason for taking a keen interest in this project: it provided a ready source of hard currency — pilfered from a $100-million US canal-construction loan from the World Bank. According to former Romanian officials, a good portion of this credit, announced in January 1980, never went anywhere near the canal.

"We tricked the World Bank without their knowledge," says Mircea Raceanu, a former top diplomat who helped negotiate Romania's entry into the World Bank in 1972. "Ceausescu did [this] as a policy matter." In the late 1980s, Raceanu was imprisoned and sentenced to death by Ceausescu for his dissident activities. Raceanu moved to the United States in 1990 after attempts were made on his life in Bucharest.

The scam took advantage of the World Bank's worthy goal of injecting as much aid as possible into the local economy. Under its rules, suppliers of goods and services must compete for the contracts. Where possible, however, local firms get the nod — if they meet bank criteria for quality, cost and reliability. As it so happened, Romanian state companies won the bulk of the World Bank–financed contracts. But according to Raceanu and Turcu, they did so fraudulently — through false documents that purported to prove that Romania could provide the required goods and services. Says Raceanu: "They said they could make quality products in that area, which, in fact, they could not produce." Which is why the canal is such a shoddy structure, built of inferior steel and cement — deficiencies that go a long way to explaining its continuing woes.

Ceausescu acquired the hard currency in a roundabout way. When Romanian firms presented invoices to the World Bank, they were paid in lei, not in Western funds. But to buy those lei, the World Bank had to use hard currency. And it had to go to the only official purveyor of Romanian currency: the Romanian Bank for Foreign Trade. Unbeknownst to the Washington-based lender, the Romanian institution, in turn, put this hard currency at the dictator's disposal. Since his printing presses could churn out a limitless supply of lei, the cost of the goods and services used in the canal was borne internally — freeing up the hard currency for other purposes. The scam was cleverly disguised, says Raceanu. In his words: "Because it's done by Romanians and [the goods and services were] not bought from abroad, he could have used the hard currency for anything else. It was basically a fraud. But it's done in a way that if someone would look into it, an investigation would not lead anywhere."

Yet the deal was examined by a top fraud investigator. He was Rod Stamler, the former RCMP assistant commissioner, hired in March 1990 to find the funds that Ceausescu had pilfered. Stamler quickly concluded there had been a scam. "Documents prepared had no relationship to the project as it was developing," he said. That is, the submitted invoices were out of sequence with the usual stages of construction — cement, say, was apparently poured before the steel framework was in place. Nonetheless, Romania was adept enough at seeming to meet World Bank criteria that the agency never suspected. Officially, at least, it remains satisfied to this day, since Ceausescu subsequently repaid the $100 million US loan, a portion of the $2 billion US debt that Romania settled with the international institution in the late 1980s. In the end, says Raceanu, Romania was twice cheated. First, when the hard currency of the World Bank loan was diverted and a substandard facility was constructed. And second, when the loan was repaid with money that could have been better spent elsewhere — at a time when Romanians were suffering great privations.

Similar diversions of public funds — and equally disastrous projects — are found throughout the Third World, suggests the Canadian economist Patricia Adams.[10] In her view, such megaprojects help explain why Third World nations have so little to show for the huge foreign debt they amassed in the 1970s and 1980s, which totalled more than $1 trillion US in 1990. As Adams argues, this debt was built on a foundation of large-scale embezzling by public officials and wasteful spending. Many of the resulting megaprojects were ill-conceived and environmentally harmful; most experienced hair-raising cost overruns. Consider: a Brazilian steel plant built with more than $2.5 billion US in foreign loans, which sits idle; a sugar mill and plantation in the Ivory Coast erected with more than $1 billion US in foreign credit and whose cost of production was three times the world price of sugar; and a hydro-electric project in Colombia that cost more than $2 billion US in foreign loans, or the equivalent of half the country's social spending.

The citizens of such Third World nations are saddled with paying off horrendous debts for ventures they don't need — and that may, in fact, add to their woes. In the West, taxpayers are being asked to alleviate Third World debts — by forgiving obligations or by providing private lenders with tax breaks so they too can absorb these losses. Adams suggests the current approach is wrongheaded, since it rewards debtors who treat the public purse as a private asset. Her solution is at once radical and intriguing. As part of a move to democracy, Adams suggests Third World countries should reject their foreign liabilities. To do this, she urges them to invoke the doctrine of odious debts — "debt repudiation caused not because the debts imposed an excessive burden . . . but because they were contracted for illegitimate purposes by illegitimate parties."[11] Adams contends that if the world's poorer nations did this, lenders would be forced "to seek redress by suing, pursuing and where possible seizing the booty of the unrepresentative Third World elite which borrowed so recklessly in the name of their people. In so doing the lenders will be discouraging future elites from similar behavior."[12]

That option is not open to Romania. In 1981, Ceausescu himself began to put the brakes on foreign borrowings and started briskly settling all Romania's international debts — a folly that beggared his country. His reasons were at once xenophobic and megalomaniacal. He wished both to sever his reliance on foreigners and to demonstrate his peerless leadership in economic matters by pulling off what even the most fiscally conversative Western politician paid only lip service to. His attitude, says Liviu Turcu, was of "a very severe father to his children — you have to suffer now for the future." And so, imports were slashed, exports fanatically promoted. Electricity was so severely rationed that sometimes it was available for only a few hours a day. At night, Bucharest — once variously described as the Little Paris or the Paris of the East — fell into darkness. In winter, cars were sometimes banned to save fuel. Food became increasingly scarce. Perversely, Ceausescu thought his citizens ate too much. He devised a grotesque special diet and banned the baking of some traditional breads, one of the few remaining sources of nutrition.

In 1989, Ceausescu announced that all $10 billion US owed to foreign creditors had been paid off. Some Western observers, however, reckoned that about $1 billion US was still outstanding.[13] All in all, it was a pyrrhic victory: the economy was in tatters and ordinary Romanians had been brought to their knees. Factories were idled by a lack of foreign parts. Huge swaths of land were contaminated by excessive use of pesticides and herbicides — disastrously short-sighted ways of boosting farm production. To compound the tragedy, little of this food had reached Romanian dinner tables. So much was exported (the Soviet Union was a major market) that by 1989 the shelves of Bucharest grocery shops were mostly bare. At best, they offered meagre amounts of oily sausages, fatty pigs' knuckles and tinned sardines. The higher-than-average salaries paid to prominent party officials and top members of the Securitate provided little solace either. They, too, were savaged by Romania's unrelenting inflation — a case of far too many lei chasing far too few (usually shoddy) goods. By the late 1980s, for instance, Romanians of even Liviu Turcu's rank had to spend about 70 percent of their salaries on black-market food.

The dictator — living a princely existence in gaudy villas and trapped in what the *Economist* called "an island of the Orwellian past" — didn't seem to notice or care.[14] When some Western diplomats tried to alert him to the plight of his people, he grew angry and bolstered his disavowals with bogus statistics. Ceausescu, however, was not wholly immune to the consequences of his debt-repaying obsession. By turning his back on fresh infusions of foreign capital, he dried up useful sources of covert funding such as the World Bank loan diversion. Fortunately for him (and unfortunately for Romania), there were others. Like a capricious feudal king, he viewed its resources and people as his personal property. Says Liviu Turcu: "Ceausescu treated the whole country as his own yard."

"Better to breed Germans than pigs" went a popular adage in the Ceausescu era. The dictator himself is said to have uttered a similar remark: "Oil, Jews and Germans are our most important commodities."15 He was deadly serious. To get hard currency, Ceausescu sold ethnic Germans and Jews to West Germany and Israel. A tough bargainer, he shrewdly controlled the supply to prop up prices, squeezing out the most money for the least number of emigrants.

For the most part, he also maintained iron-clad secrecy. The fact that the money ended up in his confidential accounts first came to the attention of former U.S. ambassador, David Funderburk in the early 1980s: "The reports we got showed that they had secret Swiss bank accounts that were filled, in part, with money from his sale of Jews and Germans to Israel and West Germany." Some of those reports were from Ion Pacepa, Romania's former deputy chief of foreign intelligence who defected in July 1978 into the arms of the American CIA. In a book penned with the help of his new masters, Pacepa claimed that this trade had yielded some $400 million US by the time he'd fled.16 Yet, said Funderburk, no one in the West (including Canada) batted an eye because Ceausescu was seen as a valuable commodity — a maverick among Eastern Europe's communist regimes. Funderburk says the attitude was mired in Cold War realpolitik and went along the lines of: "He's our bastard. We've got to take care of him."

More than 300,000 Jews left Romania between 1945 and 1989. Initially, at least, most departed without the payment of fees to the ruling regime, though other, non-monetary, benefits did accrue to Romania. But starting in 1967, Ceausescu began charging a per capita amount, to cover transportation and education costs, he claimed. The fee was for nothing of the sort: the dictator was simply hawking his citizens. Once a year, an operative of the Mossad, the Israeli intelligence service, flew to Bucharest with a suitcase full of cash to make the payment. Israel officially denies any knowledge of this operation, though the disavowals are carefully crafted. They're quite accurate, so far as they go, since the hard currency was provided by American Jewish organizations, not Israel. To grease the wheels, however, Israel did purchase Romanian goods it didn't need (like prune jam) and provide some technical military aid.[17]

Thanks to the cash payments, at least 20,000 Jews were permitted to leave Romania — often taking the direct flight from Bucharest to Israel, then Israel's only air link with Eastern Europe. These 20,000 tended to be intellectuals or to hold important positions in Romania. Says Turcu: "Ceausescu saw it as a leakage of secret information. . . . So Ceausescu, in a way, traded his own secrets." Since the operation is still cloaked in secrecy, little precise information on the amounts paid is available. However, the Israeli journalist Yossi Melman, an authority on the Mossad, reckons it averaged $3,000 US per emigrant, for a total of $60 million US. From his sources, he supposes that about half the money ended up in Ceausescu's pocket.

The trade in ethnic Germans, who settled eastern Romania 850 years ago at the invitation of a Hungarian king, was much larger and more profitable. Starting in 1967, more than 200,000 ethnic Germans left Romania over a twenty-two-year period. Figures on the precise fees paid are unavailable, but some estimates of the cost to the German treasury go as high as $1.3 billion US. Turcu says some cash instalments were delivered by diplomatic pouch. Most, however, were officially transferred to the Romanian Bank for Foreign Trade. Yet after the revolution, no record was found of any of these payments. They, too, had been sucked into the black hole better known as the "special hard-currency compartment."

Equally well hidden were profits from Romania's huge arms export industry, which, according to U.S. government figures, earned at least $3.4 billion US between 1980 and 1987. Ceausescu was not choosy about his customers, and since he was useful in Eastern European geopolitics, the West turned a blind eye to the fact that he sold freely to many of the world's pariahs. Admits Funderburk: "We were aware of major arms shipments to Libya and Iraq."

Picture the Securitate's "special hard-currency compartment," or Actiuni Valutare Speciale, as a giant financial receptacle — in other words, as the ultimate laundering vehicle. Into it flowed all kinds of confidential, ready-to-be-washed funds. Coursing out were as many equally sensitive streams of money, already rinsed and rushing to meet myriad demands. Overseeing it all with an iron hand was Ceausescu himself. Says Turcu: "Many people knew a small part of the puzzle. Only Ceausescu could put it all together."

Of paramount importance for the secret money handlers' personal well-being, if for nothing else, was taking care of the expenses of Ceausescu family members during foreign travel. Before their arrival, Bucharest would cable the local Romanian embassy's intelligence chief — known as the resident — telling him to pay any normal expenditures out of his own budget. He would be reimbursed by the next diplomatic pouch with funds from the secret accounts of the "special compartment." In charge of this expense money was an intelligence officer who always accompanied each family member abroad. This was as much for their protection as to allow Ceausescu to keep an eye on his relatives.

In the 1980s, Ceausescu's alcoholic son, Nicu, for example, was routinely escorted by a counter-intelligence officer who had once been posted to Canada. Turcu identified the officer as Vasile Trandafir, who had served under cover as a Third Secretary at the Romanian embassy in Ottawa from 1978 to 1981. By all accounts, Trandafir was a busy man. Nicu's profligate trips to the gambling mecca of Atlantic City — made during his official visits to the United Nations in New York — were legendary.

In the greater scheme of things, however, such expenses were the least of the "special compartment's" worries. More significant and challenging was ensuring that adequate funding was available for the Securitate's own *caisse noire,* its covert finances. This was no simple matter. Ceausescu saw the organization as his most effective external policy tool. (Indeed, it was probably the most competent institution in Romania at the time.) Which is why he asked so much of it, demanding everything from the personal foibles of foreign leaders he wanted to exploit to ways of swaying world events (including, as mentioned earlier, the Nobel selection process). Yet the Securitate had to fend for itself. "Romanian intelligence needed a great deal of money for very expensive operations abroad," says Turcu. "Ceausescu gave the orders. He didn't provide the resources."

By necessity, the agency was more than just a collection of secret police. The Securitate's domestic operations kept a harsh grip on every facet of life (right down to having a special unit to ferret out purveyors of anti-Ceausescu jokes). The ranks of its external service, on the other hand, were peopled by far fewer bullies and thugs. More evident were capable financiers, business experts and analysts — some of Romania's best and brightest minds, including the tiny money-handling cell at the foreign trade bank. Yet even the self-financing Securitate occasionally had trouble hanging onto its funds. During the height of Ceausescu's mania for paying off foreign debts, he would even raid its treasury. No one dared object.

The task of keeping Ceausescu's finances secret was entrusted to two men who administered the "special compartment" for much of the 1980s. There was Colonel Stelian Andronic and, after 1986, his successor, Lieutenant-Colonel Constantin Angahelache. Both were highly capable people who had secret covers that allowed them to surreptitiously visit bank accounts in places like Switzerland and Liechtenstein — without raising any suspicion. Andronic, for instance, travelled as Nicolae Arnautu, a representative of Prodexport, the state food exporter. In that capacity, he often visited

Switzerland and had an account at the Union Bank of Switzerland in Basle. He was linked to a number of shadowy offshore
entities, including one called Danamia NV, which was incorporated in the Netherlands Antilles. Danamia, in turn, was
the locus for a cluster of other commercial fronts which
are thought to have hidden covert money movements.
Angahelache, on the other hand, went abroad as a member of
the Romanian soccer federation. According to Turcu,
Angahelache often visited the sport's world governing body,
which was conveniently located in the Swiss banking centre
of Zurich.

Andronic and Angahelache ran an extraordinarily complex
operation, constructed to meet a wide variety of situations.
Hard-currency cash payments, for example, would usually
be picked up by a two-man team, says Turcu. They would
carefully count the money and register the serial numbers,
recording the whole procedure on a tape recorder. Cash was
especially valued because it was difficult to obtain large
quantities of it in secret. It was therefore often sent abroad by
diplomatic pouch to covert safety deposit boxes, ready to fund
the next foreign operation — spying on expatriates or trying
to ferret out ways to improve Ceausecu's image in the Third
World, for instance.

Other payments that required the appearance of governmental legitimacy, such as Bonn's ransom for German
emigrants, flowed into accounts at the Romanian Bank for
Foreign Trade. To the curious, such funds would appear to
enter legitimate government coffers. Superficially, that was
true. But subsequently the payoffs would shift and effectively
disappear into the "special compartment's" own accounts at
the trade bank, which made them easy to launder. Three of its
secret accounts were especially important. An insider could
spot them right away: their identifying numbers shared the
same last four digits, 300-2. Turcu says the most important
(since it handled U.S. dollars) was no. 47–21–42–7–300–2. It
began operating in 1975 and his defection — "the act of
treachery of Liviu Turcu," as it was called in Bucharest —

led to its closure in 1989. Another account which received British pounds and hard currencies other than the U.S. dollar was no. 47-21-500-300-2.

"Usually, these accounts were established for situations in which you didn't have any other choice in receiving the money," says Turcu. "These accounts would be justified as being located in Bucharest and not in Switzerland. Otherwise some of the people making the payments would get suspicious or ask questions. That's why they were hosted by a Romanian bank. The most important operations of these three accounts was transferring the money to other secret accounts abroad. At the same time, no one [would] stop you from using some money from these accounts for buying a number of goods and services for the [Ceausescu] family or clan."

The trade bank was Romania's official monetary window on the commercial world. As such, it featured prominently in a preferred technique for shifting covert funds from Romania to secret accounts in Switzerland, Austria or Liechtenstein. Using a variation of the over-invoicing laundering technique, the money was blended with payments for legitimate business transactions. Say Romania needed to make a $1 million US payment for some French heavy machinery. The money would flow from the state trade bank in Bucharest to an apparently legitimate intermediary located in Switzerland. But instead of sending only the $1 million US earmarked for the French supplier, an additional sum would be tacked on. Though ostensibly also part of the transaction, this latter amount would never reach France. Instead, it would be diverted while in the hands of the Swiss intermediary and safely secreted offshore.

For the Securitate, it was a small step from hiding furtive money among commercial transactions to running such deals themselves. In the late 1970s, Ceausescu became increasingly disillusioned with the results of state trading companies and put them under heightened surveillance. Fearful of retribution if they made mistakes, Romanian trade officials grew reluctant to take chances and their results therefore suffered. Hence the stage was set for a robust new player — the Securitate.

"Never was a deal done in Romania . . . even medium-sized, in which Securitate was not involved," says Raceanu, the former diplomat.

At first, its role was to skim off "special commissions," or tollgating fees, worth anywhere from 3 to 6 percent of the trade deal. In 1988, for instance, Turcu reckons that about $65 million US was earned in this manner, a full $15 million US more than the previous year. Foreign businesspeople were fed many phoney lines to explain the rakeoffs. They were told that the money was for a special fund to hasten the clearing of Romania's foreign debts. Or to allow the Romanian firm in question to expand, at a time when its foreign earnings were being commandeered by Ceausescu. Or for a personal bribe. To anyone who knew Romania in those years the latter option was most unlikely, since the Securitate was ruthless about rooting out internal corruption, even though it was involved in shady practices itself, supposedly for the good of Romania.

Transactions were carefully structured to hide the rakeoffs, often involving two sets of contracts. The first would reflect the deal's actual cost. The second would be a secret addendum stating that the Western firm would pay a fixed percentage of the contract directly into, say, the Swiss bank account of an offshore shell company. Romanian law forbade its citizens to have hard currency, let alone foreign bank accounts — but these rules could be ignored by one man: Nicolae Ceausescu.

Many Western companies, suggests Turcu, had an aversion to paying an out-and-out bribe or a kickback — a reluctance born of home-country regulations or corporate ethical codes. But, he says, they were still willing to find creative alternate solutions that both sides could live with. One Western firm, for instance, apparently became an irrepressible booster of Romanian products. To that end, it provided Romania with more than $150,000 to promote exports. For some reason, however, the funds did not end up in the regular bank accounts of the Romanian Trade Ministry. They were deposited on June 30, 1989, into one of the three special accounts. "There's no

legislation forbidding you to pay a certain amount of money
. . . to advertising," says Turcu. "Different situations, different solutions, different approaches. Many solutions came from
the free-market experience."

In time, the Securitate went even further. In the early 1980s,
it established its own foreign trading companies, thereby
filling the void left by the less and less capable state import-
export concerns. Romanian exports were supposed to be handled by these official state trading companies. The trading firm
for steel and other metals, Metal Import-Export, for instance,
would receive set monthly quotas of products like rolled steel
and aluminum ingots, and it would try to sell them to foreign
buyers. On a routine basis, monthly quotas which should have
gone to companies like Metal Import-Export were diverted to
the Securitate's trading companies.

Western businessmen had no trouble recognizing the Securitate's entrepreneurs. Run-of-the-mill Romanian trade
officials were shabbily (and often loudly) dressed, constantly
fearful of being caught alone with a Westerner, and grateful
for even a pack of American-made Kent cigarettes (a prized
black market commodity). Their Securitate counterparts, on
the other hand, had a vastly different bearing. Self-assured to
the point of arrogance, they typically wore expensive suits,
entertained lavishly, and freely offered Kent cigarettes to visitors. Not surprisingly, the intelligence service profited mightily from importing Kents. It often repackaged the shipments
and illegally re-exported them to higher-value markets, often
in the Middle East. In so doing, it took advantage of the fact
that multinationals do not price their goods uniformly, based
on production cost, but on what the local market will bear.
Kents sold directly to, say, Japan, for instance, would be
priced higher than those sent to Romania. Hence, the profit
potential of selling Romanian-bound Kents in Tokyo.

Throughout his years in power, Ceausescu kept a tight rein
on all the Securitate's shadowy ventures — and their substantial profits. "All this money was at [Ceausescu's] disposal,"
says Turcu. "Every cent was spent with his knowledge.

He was the type of man who liked to know absolutely every move — no matter if it was unimportant."

The Securitate's most important captive trading firm was Dunarea, or Danube. Operating from a Bucharest mansion, it was an outstanding success, posting hard-currency revenues of $4.4 billion US from its founding in 1982 until 1989. To put that into perspective, realize that Romania earned roughly $4 billion US a year in hard currency in the late 1980s. What makes these revenues so astounding is that Dunarea did not produce a thing. It only acted as a brokerage — with a relatively small staff and low overhead — selling quotas of export goods to the highest foreign bidder. It was as if a Canadian aluminum smelter were to sell its goods — at roughly the cost of production — to an intermediary that skimmed off the full profit. "Dunarea took the cream," explains Turcu. Unlike regular state trading firms, Dunarea was able to guarantee prompt delivery and quality — features that helped attract foreign buyers and further undermined state trading companies.

"With Dunarea, Ceausescu created the means to avoid legal channels, to do things which were obviously behind the rules, which were kept very secret," adds Raceanu, the former diplomat. He says special subterfuges hid much of Dunarea's activities. Among other things, the trading firm had two sets of financial records: an incomplete and misleading one for circulating among top officials and a real one for Ceausescu's eyes only.

Another trading firm, Carpati, was named after Romania's famous range of mountains. It was supervised by the Romanian Communist Party through an agency euphemistically called the "Housekeeping" unit. In Romania's centrally planned economy, Ceausescu controlled the taps on the most important source of hard currency — the flow of export goods. To reward his party minions, monthly allocations of export goods — say aluminum or cement — would go to Carpati. Carpati, in turn, would use the resulting hard currency to import luxury goods. For instance, says Raceanu, Carpati purchased expensive foreign furniture for Ceausescu's extended family, but sold it — in lei — to family members as if it were ordinary, Romanian-made stuff. This was a ruse to conceal the dictator's opulence, he suggests. "It was a sort of game to show he lived by modest means."

Setting up a secret network of commercial entities has appealed to many dictators besides Ceausescu. In former East Germany, the foreign-exchange procurement agency, popularly known as Ko-Ko, had a hand in many murky (and very profitable) endeavours. Ranging from the sale of dissidents to the West for cash to secret arms deals, these transactions racked up estimated revenues of at least $29 billion US. Yet after the fall of the Communist regime, barely more than half that amount could be accounted for. Authorities suspect that at least $13 billion might have been fraudulently hidden in some of Ko-Ko's estimated 1,000 secret bank accounts in such places as Switzerland and Liechtenstein.[18]

Saddam Hussein did much the same thing. During the 1980s, he apparently skimmed 5 percent of Iraq's billions of dollars in annual oil revenues. Additional sums came from kickbacks paid by foreign firms wanting to do business with Baghdad. As much as $15 billion US in assets might have been diverted in this way, suggests Kroll Associates, the New York investigators once retained by Haiti and then subsequently hired by Kuwait to discover Hussein's secret funds. The money was secretly funnelled and laundered through an extensive network of dozens of trading firms. Many operated in Switzerland and Jordan under the watchful eye of trusted Hussein retainers drawn from the five secret services he controlled. Part of the money was secretly invested in prosperous, publicly traded firms — or set aside for the private use of Hussein's clan. Some of it was apparently used by his son to buy a $300,000 Aston Martin, just like the one Sean Connery drove in the James Bond movies. Other amounts covertly built up Iraq's military, allowing Hussein to acquire the kinds of weapons technologies that no one wanted him to have.[19]

This secret financial network served Hussein especially well after his defeat in the Gulf War in 1991. Part of the intricate system was dismantled following probes by Kroll and some Western governments. Enough apparently survived, however, to shelter billions of dollars — helping Hussein survive under the United Nations embargo imposed after the war.[20]

In December 1989, the regime of Nicolae Ceausescu was overthrown. The dictator and his wife made a pathetic attempt to escape, hiding, at one point, in a seed distribution centre. Their attempts were to no avail. They were easily captured and, on Christmas Day, tried before a military tribunal. The hearing left much to be desired, betraying the haste with which it was convened. The prosecutor briefly tried to pin down some details of the Ceausescus's secret fortune. He asked: "In whose name is the $400 million account in Switzerland?" Elena Ceausescu replied: "What account?" Prosecutor: "$400 million was deposited in Switzerland." Elena Ceausescu: "Prove it, prove it." But the line of inquiry was not pursued. The court seemed more determined to reach a verdict than to ferret out such details. The judgment was never in doubt; even the defence counsel joined in pressing for a conviction. Shortly after it was rendered, Nicolae and Elena Ceausescu — looking haggard and bewildered — were executed.

In the streets of Bucharest, the end of the Ceausescu era was greeted with the kind of rejoicing that followed the fall of Duvalier. And like the people of Haiti, Romanians urged the provisional government — an odd (and fractious) cluster of former dissidents, idealists and ex-communists — to find the hidden funds alluded to during the dictator's trial. The new leadership seemed to listen. The most outspoken on the issue was Dumitru Mazilu, vice-president in the first provisional government and a former dissident, who repeatedly pressed for quick action. As a result, in January 1990, Romanian officials began trying to find the secret funds. Two months later, two Canadians were hired to oversee the search. One was

Stamler, the retired assistant commissioner of the RCMP. His associate was Bob Lindquist, a forensic accountant in Toronto. They were attached to a special team drawn from a variety of Romanian government departments.

Though it began on a hopeful note, the investigation ran headlong into a series of roadblocks. Ominously, its difficulties seemed to parallel a waning commitment inside the government to enact meaningful reforms. One by one, former dissidents like Mazilu were eased out. (He now lives in exile in Switzerland. A still unexplained attempt was made on his life in Geneva in the spring of 1991 by two razor-wielding, Romanian-speaking men.) More and more former communists, including some closely linked to Ceausescu himself, took centre stage. Even pledges to disband the Securitate — made in the euphoria of the immediate post-revolutionary period — proved hollow. The provisional government promised that it would be succeeded by a new agency totally unlike its nasty predecessor. Things turned out differently. The replacement was the oddly named Romanian Information Service, whose ranks are chock full of former Securitate operatives. There's little evidence that it embodies the promised principles of an open democratic society. Phones continue to be tapped, informers recruited, and opponents of the government threatened and (in some cases) beaten.

In Romania, old habits die hard, as Stamler discovered. He was prevented from examining key documents, including the Ceausescu family's private papers and travel records. He was particularly interested in whatever personal effects were seized when the dictator and his wife were arrested by the army. Just before their arrest, the couple had made a brief visit to their villa in Snagov, a resort area near Bucharest. Elena Ceausescu ran to a rarely used bedroom and apparently took something from under a mattress. The army never disclosed what she might have found and jealously guarded all Ceausescu-related documents.

Stamler's efforts to examine the records of the Romanian Bank for Foreign Trade were no more successful. As for

Angahelache and Andronic, who had run the Securitate's "secret compartment" at the bank — they had simply disappeared. No one knew whether they were alive or dead. (When filming "the 5th estate" documentary "Evil's Fortune," we made inquiries in Bucharest about the two men's whereabouts, and were told this was a matter better dropped — and fast.) Likewise with Dunarea and Carpati. The two companies were wound up early in 1990, but no full public accounting of their affairs ever took place — and more importantly, no comprehensive information was discovered on what had happened to their once-bulging secret coffers.

In the face of these difficulties, Stamler began to dissect Ceausescu's laundering system, focusing on finding the dictator's personal nest-egg. He reasoned that the path to it would have two key features. The first, and the easiest to detect, would be the source of the money. Besides emigration fees for Jews and Germans, Ceausescu had few options beyond diverting profits from Romanian exports. Hence, thought Stamler, Ceausescu's chosen vehicle might have received the kind of preferential treatment accorded to a Dunarea or a Carpati. The second attribute would be far trickier to spot: a foolproof conduit for secretly channelling the money into a safe haven. It would have to dupe not only his domestic enemies, but also those outside Romania, including his resentful foes in Moscow, whom he'd routinely vexed. (They were most annoyed, for instance, that he had sent a team to the 1984 Olympics in Los Angeles.) To complicate matters, Ceausescu was far more restricted than dictators like Jean-Claude Duvalier of Haiti or Ferdinand Marcos of the Philippines. Unlike Ceausescu, who as a communist, could not own land outside the country, they could readily own private property outside their home countries, and personally establish foreign bank accounts and corporate fronts.

One possibility involved his elder brother Marin Ceausescu. In Stamler's view, the dictator was traumatized in 1978 when his former trusted aide, Ion Pacepa, defected. From then on, suggests Stamler, the increasingly cranky despot remained wary of the reconstituted (and much purged) Securitate. Thus, went the theory, Ceausescu turned to Marin to bypass the Securitate and to salt away a personal nest-egg. It is true that in the mid-1970s, Marin Ceausescu was appointed head of the Romanian trade mission in Vienna. This was an unusual posting, says Raceanu, the former diplomat. As the dictator's brother, Marin Ceausescu could have had much more prestigious assignments. Yet he remained in this relatively obscure job, suggests Raceanu, because Nicolae Ceausescu needed a trusted money handler abroad with a perfect cover for visiting various Western capitals. Certainly, one Western intelligence source concurs. Over a thick coffee in a quiet Austrian café, he told me that "Vienna was important" in handling Ceausescu's personal funds, noting that some payments had been traced through key Austrian banks. But, he cautioned, Marin had broken no Austrian law — the funds were not visibly tainted. He said "it was not illegal money" — because it had been countenanced by Romania's then legal head of state.

Marin's possible role in handling Ceausescu's most secret funds remains murky, clouded by his death. His body was found hanging in the basement of the trade mission in Vienna on December 28, 1989, just days after his brother's death. There were rumours that he had been executed after being tortured and that unusual visitors had arrived from Bucharest just before his death. Austrian authorities maintain it was a suicide, plain and simple. Yet, inexplicably, the secret safe in his office had been cleared out and his personal papers had disappeared. To this day, no one is sure who took them — or why.

A more fruitful lead for Stamler was an indication that part of Ceausescu's money-hiding machinery had outlived him. Indeed, Stamler maintains there was sufficient evidence of its continuing existence that "I [could] have presented an affidavit in a court outside of Romania." In July 1990, Stamler and Lindquist delivered a preliminary report to the Romanian government. It set out a blueprint for action — including establishing a special commission to search for Ceausescu's secret funds and starting legal proceedings against the surviving elements of the Ceausescu money laundering apparatus. Then, nothing happened. Communications broke down. Romanian officials repeatedly failed to return phone calls from Toronto. The Canadians were ignored. Why? Stamler's suspicions are twofold. Either he'd come too close to the truth, and powerful figures in Romania were blocking the probe. Or, from a more cynical point of view, perhaps the whole investigation had been intended, from the start, to be just a whitewash to assuage Romanian public opinion.

Officials in Bucharest would later explain that the Canadians were not retained because they were too expensive — since they would have charged a whopping $1 million a month for their services. Stamler dismisses this fee as grossly exaggerated. In fact, international financial investigations of this sort usually cost between $50,000 and $100,000 a month. Moreover, if Stamler's contention was accurate, Romania could rapidly have seized enough assets to fund such a probe and have plenty left over: "There was every indication that we could have successfully concluded this investigation by bringing millions of dollars in assets before various courts to be, in my view, returned to the people of Romania."

The claim that the Canadians were too costly would have made more sense if the Romanians themselves had steadfastly continued the search. A commission was set up, but there is little evidence that it accomplished a great deal. In Switzerland, for instance, federal officials in Bern made initial inquiries on Romania's behalf and prepared a report in April 1990. They sought additional information so the Swiss inquiry could proceed. Strangely, the Swiss received no further communication after the report was submitted. In the same vein, defectors and exiles who tried to help were given the cold shoulder. Turcu, for one, offered to share his vast knowledge of the former Securitate's finances. Inexplicably, his expertise was never tapped, and as time passed, the more proficient members of the commission were moved into other positions.

Romanian journalists — trying to follow up on the new government's promise to recover funds illegally diverted under

Ceausescu — were stymied. In February 1991, one enterprising reporter, Virgil Mihailovici, tried to track down supposed members of the commission and was plunged into a Kafkaesque routine, going from faceless bureaucrat to political hack, and back. All had cryptic remarks. No one had definitive answers. Most were evasive at best. Did the commission actually exist? he asked repeatedly. No one could say for sure.

Perhaps, some Romanians began to wonder, there had been no secret caches of money in the first place. Perhaps it had all been a myth. Or, said others, perhaps Ceausescu had spent all the money paying off the foreign debt. The evidence indicates otherwise. In July 1989, when the foreign debt had supposedly been settled, Carpati had had $54.26 million US in just one of its special accounts (no. 134) at the Romanian Bank for Foreign Trade. Moreover, Petre Bacanu, the respected editor of the crusading newspaper *Romania Libera,* reckons that Romanian hard-currency earnings from the 1980s exceeded the sums required to pay off the foreign debt by as much as $15 billion US. This surplus has still not been accounted for.[21] Even Virgil Magureanu, head of the new intelligence service, believes that as much as $1.5 billion US may be hidden somewhere. Nevertheless, he conceded in an interview in June 1991, the investigation had stopped before any money was retrieved. Why had this occurred "when most people believe that there's a lot of wealth to be recovered"? inquired Linden MacIntyre, host of CBC Television's "the 5th estate." Magureanu replied cryptically: "It's not the only odd thing that's going on right now."

Elsewhere in Eastern Europe, investigations were much better supported. The Ko-Ko inquiry in East Germany, for instance, was widely seen as a means of laying the past to rest in a unified Germany. There was a similar mood in the new Russian Republic, where the government of Boris Yeltsin in 1992 launched a full-scale effort to find funds pilfered by the former communists. According to one Russian official: "Party funds to the tune of $15 billion to $20 billion [US] have been deposited in foreign bank safes."[22]

To be sure, the Romanian commission's work did appear to pick up steam in late 1991. This might have been a mere coincidence, but the renewed efforts occurred shortly after the broadcast of "the 5th estate" documentary, "Evil's Fortune," which raised questions about the government's indolence on the issue. Just before Christmas 1991, the head of the commission, Mugur Isarescu, announced that the inquiry was completed. His main finding: no secret Ceausescu funds were discovered. The results were greeted skeptically in Romania and Isarescu's investigation does seem to have been less than rigorous. An informed Western European official describes the 1991 enquiries as ineffectual: "They have no detailed information. They are in the darkness, sailing in the mist."

And so disturbing questions linger in Romania, despite Isarescu's announcement. What happened to all the diverted money? Why were the Canadian investigators not retained? Why was the investigation not vigorously pursued? As American journalist William McPherson put it: "The question of the money . . . ought to be a simple question to resolve — if there is any real interest in resolving it."[23] The growing suspicion is that Stamler was right: powerful figures in Romania were able to dip into at least some of the secret funds and prevent a full investigation.

Concludes Turcu: "Nothing has changed."

■ 11 THE WILD WEST IN THE EAST

Where should the alert and enterprising money launderer look for virgin territory? Why, in Eastern Europe, suggests one polished Viennese banker. We met in his office in December 1990. Outside, amid the brightly decorated shops and cafés, the Viennese were preparing for Christmas as only the Viennese can. Inside, I was surrounded by quiet expanses of deep green marble and dark wood. Near an oversized desk were four matte-black Reuters trading screens, recording the ebbs and flows of world financial markets. The security was taut: bulletproof glass, surveillance cameras, well-groomed guards. His business is similarly hermetically sealed, thanks to Austria's rigid bank confidentiality laws.

This banker knows Eastern Europe well. During the Cold War, his institution brokered many deals behind the Iron Curtain. Some (though he denies it) were rumoured to involve the movement of funds on behalf of the Mossad, the Israeli intelligence service. These days, he suggests, money launderers will find few impediments in Eastern Europe, since the region's hard-pressed governments are too busy attracting capital and entrepreneurs to worry about such matters. Moreover, the newly liberated countries have remarkably little of the legal and regulatory infrastructure one takes for granted in the West. Banks are largely unsupervised. Commercial law and tax codes — as well as the legal systems to enforce them — are embryonic at best. There's little recourse for the swindled, and hence much scope for the swindler. And, of course, for handlers of illicit funds.

Some criminals recognized Eastern Europe's potential even before the Berlin Wall fell in 1989. Western intelligence agencies reckoned that the Bulgaria of former dictator Todor Zhivkov ran a giant money laundromat. According to an estimate in *Forbes* magazine, it rinsed more than $2 billion US in illicit profits in 1988 alone. Indeed, said *Forbes*, money laundering was "one of the few hard-currency earners for Bulgaria's broken-down Marxist economy."[1] Other astute criminals turned to neighbouring Romania, using it to wash part of their earnings from an elaborate international fraud.

Understanding this scam requires a grasp of how foreign goods are bought by many Third World states with centrally planned economies. Theirs is a delicate balancing act. On the one hand, such countries try to stretch their limited supply of hard currency by limiting the imports purchased with that currency. (In this way, assert the cynical, enough will be left over to keep the military and the secret police operating *and* to line the pockets of corrupt leaders.) On the other hand, imports cannot be so curtailed that shortages ensue, leading perhaps to food riots or the advent of rebel movements. This massive task is handled by the state apparatus. (In Canada, the system would be akin to civil servants overseeing the import needs of both the federal government and of the economy at large — buying everything from wheat and edible oil, to farm machinery and pharmaceuticals.) In the countries in question, bureaucrats venture into the world marketplace by relying on the expertise of middlemen. The resulting system is cumbersome, inefficient — and open to being defrauded.

In December 1988, the Algerian state food importer, or ENAPAL (l'Entreprise nationale d'approvisionnement des produits alimentaires), needed to purchase 50,000 tons of sugar. (There's no suggestion that ENAPAL or its employees indulged in any illegal or improper activities.) To do this, it signed a contract (no. 113/88) with Khema Trading Ltd., a small, reputable firm based in Gibraltar. Khema, in turn, used other go-betweens to find an apparently reliable supplier — a Spaniard who called himself German Anton Garcia and who had many contacts in the sugar business in the Caribbean.

Things started well. Barely three months after the deal was signed, word came from the Dominican Republic that ships carrying the sugar had sailed. Day by day, they steamed across the Atlantic, sending regular progress reports to Khema representatives in Europe. It was at this point that the fraudsters took advantage of the contract's method of payment — a letter of credit. Known as "the common lubricant of trade," it basically authorizes the purchaser's bank to pay the seller once the financial institution has satisfied itself that the contract's conditions have been met.[2] Shortly after the ships supposedly left the Caribbean, Garcia presented extensive documentation purporting to show that the sugar had been sent. The papers passed muster, and some $11.8 million US was duly released. After one of the middlemen took his cut of $1.3 million US, the rest ended up in Garcia's bank in Madrid.

Then the deal began to unravel. The vessels never arrived in Algeria. When Khema officials began to investigate, they learned to their horror that no shipments had left the Dominican Republic. Worse, no sugar had been purchased there in the first place. By March 31, 1989, it became clear that a fraud had been committed — and that the documents used to release the payment were forgeries. Garcia had been a phoney identity, too. Interpol was alerted. So were authorities in Spain, Belgium and Switzerland as well as the International Maritime Bureau, commercial shipping's London-based watchdog. The bureau cleared Khema and established that it had itself been a victim of the fraud. Thus began a huge international probe to try to find the missing money.

Tracing the payment proved particularly arduous and ultimately frustrating. From Madrid, the man who called himself

Garcia had rapidly shifted the $10.5 million US to Switzerland through a series of transfers. Speed was of the essence. The first transfer occurred on March 21, 1989, the final one on March 29, just two days before the fraud was confirmed. The money's destination was an account in the tiny Chêne-Bourg branch in Geneva of the Banque Populaire Suisse. This was certainly an out-of-the-way location: the branch had just seven employees and was in a shopping complex in an unremarkable neighbourhood. The money did not stay there long, however. On March 28, $2.5 million US was sent back whence it came — to Garcia's account in Madrid.

Around the same time, a further $2.657 million US went from Chêne-Bourg to another bank in Valencia, Spain. Garcia himself withdrew $460,000 US and three million Swiss francs in cash from the Chêne-Bourg branch. The balance — roughly 4.7 million Swiss francs — quickly went in and out of a mysterious bank account. Code-named "Eva," it was at a branch of the Swiss Banking Corporation in Geneva. Once withdrawn, these funds were also turned over to Garcia. Investigators found that "Eva" was opened solely for this transaction by a small-time Geneva architect, who also happened to be a close friend of the manager of the Chêne-Bourg branch of the Banque Populaire Suisse. The architect later admitted to police that he was introduced to Garcia by his friend, the bank manager, and was paid 30,000 Swiss francs for opening the account. By this time, however, the 4.7 million in Swiss francs was long gone. So were most of the rest of the funds.

Through a bit of clever snooping, however, some of the money was traced further. Investigators found that Garcia had another account in Geneva — at the Banque Scandinave. He held it jointly with another man, who is now suspected of planning the fraud. Shortly after withdrawing the $460,000 US and 3 million Swiss francs from the Chêne-Bourg branch, Garcia deposited virtually the same amount into the joint account at the Banque Scandinave. Most of the funds were subsequently withdrawn and also vanished. But there was a slip: a paper trail showed that about 1.7 million Swiss francs had gone to Romania.

When investigators followed up this lead, they discovered that the fraud's supposed mastermind was, in fact, a Western businessman with an office in Bucharest. He routinely exported to the West locally produced commodities like cement. What investigators suspected was that this was the final stage in a complex laundering operation: that is, illicit profits were brought to Romania and then used to buy goods that could easily be sold abroad. "He takes it in in cash and brings it out in something else. . . . [He] was using Romania like a Chinese laundry," said a source familiar with the inquiry. Picking totalitarian Romania for such a purpose was a good choice — the Ceausescu regime was adept at deflecting Western meddlers. This became apparent in the fall of 1989 when lawyers for the victims of the fraud went to court in Bucharest. They sought $18 million US that the suspected mastermind was thought to have in Romanian banks, but their efforts were to no avail. The creaking Romanian judicial system was unresponsive. A major roadblock was a regulation requiring a security deposit by the plaintiff of 50 percent of the claim. Such deposits, it turned out, could have been forfeited on a mere technicality, not a comforting prospect in view of the Ceausescu regime's avarice — and not a gamble the fraud's victims were willing to take.

And so the scam succeeded.

Since the end of the Cold War, similar accomplishments have been registered throughout Eastern Europe. Among them are feats pulled off by members of the Warsaw Pact's former ruling elites. Some of the region's security services, for instance, are reportedly resurrecting "their former import-export firms to keep their money-laundering and arms-dealing businesses going," says the *Economist*.[3] Fears of such activity are especially prevalent in contemporary Romania and Bulgaria. In Sofia, former secret policemen are suspected of having used corporate fronts to launder funds looted from the public treasury and hide them abroad. As one official told the *New York Times*: "Many millions of dollars are now outside the country, out of control."[4]

In the former Soviet Union, banks are said to have been used to launder "billions of roubles" on behalf of former communists or of the region's burgeoning organized crime groups. In the view of one senior Russian banker, "the transfer abroad of communist money is reminiscent of the Nazis' efforts to salt away cash at the end of the [Second World] war to provide for a future resurrection of the National Socialist idea."[5] Likewise with the disbanded Stasi, former East Germany's secret police. It is thought to have smuggled out more than $310 million US before the collapse of communist rule.[6]

The Stasi's masters in the former East German Communist Party pulled off a similar stunt nearly a year after the Berlin Wall collapsed. In October 1990, party officials used banks in Germany, Norway and Holland to transfer about $60 million US to a suspicious Soviet company, Putnik. At various times, they offered different explanations for the complex transaction. One was that the funds were to meet Putnik's request for financial help to build a centre for "the international workers' movement." Another, that they were paying off old party debts in the former Soviet Union. Neither held water. An investigation into Putnik — ostensibly registered in Moscow and linked to a Soviet bank — exposed the charade. Its premises, for one thing, were rather suspicious: They were in a derelict building. Moreover, there were no signs of supposed party debts or of a planned centre for international workers. The whole thing was simply a scam.[7]

Little can better illustrate Eastern Europe's fundamental vulnerability to financial manipulation — and thus to money laundering — than an audacious cheque-kiting scheme set up in 1990 in Poland. Cheque-kiters write cheques faster than banks can clear them, in order to get cash advances — which amounts to an unauthorized, interest-free loan.[8] Polish banks (like those in most other parts of Eastern Europe) are notoriously slow, which makes them excellent targets for cheque-kiters. Weeks can elapse before a cheque is cleared, thus presenting a great scamming opportunity — especially at a time of high interest rates. So realized two clever Poles. To initially raise funds, they developed a computerized system that baffled Polish banks by constantly shifting a large number of cheques through the banking system. The processing of cheques was so tardy that they had plenty of time to keep ahead of the game. Then, with their pool of capital in hand, they flew around the country in a helicopter. And according to the *Financial Times of London*, they deposited the same funds with different banks at the same time and then collected the interest on all the deposits. This was not illegal under existing Polish banking laws. The two men netted, by some accounts, hundreds of millions of dollars.[9]

The situation is much the same in neighbouring Czechoslovakia, where many people fear that the privatization of state industries is being used to sop up foreign dirty money. Though the evidence tends to be anecdotal, it is sufficient to alarm many people. Stories abound of millions of dollars in state assets being snapped up by people of apparently modest means who are suspected of being backed by either shady foreign interests, or, worse, by former Communists. This, in a country where the government reckons it would be impossible to legally set aside more than about $16,700 US in a lifetime. There is much talk in Prague of imposing rules and regulations against money laundering by Western criminals, "who, many allege, are treating Eastern Europe as the world's latest Wild West." But, as the *Economist* points out, how can such rules "be enforced in a country where it takes three weeks to transfer money from town to town?"[10] Thus, says Vaclav Klaus, the finance minister in Prague, "there is no such thing as 'dirty' or 'clean' money [in Czechoslovakia] — or at least no practical way of distinguishing between them."[11]

Many of his neighbours in Eastern Europe could say the same.

■ 12 PANIC ON THE RIVIERA

In the pre-dawn hours of February 11, 1988, a team of French officials quietly entered Mougins, a picturesque village in the hills above the Mediterranean resort of Cannes. Armed with a search warrant, they headed for the Villa Mohamedia at 204 chemin du Château. It was an address of some notoriety: Jean-Claude and Michele Duvalier had lived there for most of their two years in exile. For nearly as long, the couple had been the focus of efforts to recover the huge sums they had looted from Haiti. Thus far at least, the Duvaliers held the upper hand in this international game of cat-and-mouse. But thanks to the efforts of the fifteen French *magistrats* and *policiers*, the pendulum was about to swing the other way.

Such a shift in momentum had seemed remote barely eight months earlier. In June 1987, a tribunal in nearby Grasse had bolstered the Duvaliers' position by dismissing a potentially damaging case of embezzlement brought by Haiti. This did not mean that their legal woes were at an end, however. Some $8 million US in assets had been frozen by courts in the United States, including a $2.5 million US apartment in Manhattan's Trump Tower and a $100,000 US powerboat in Miami. Another $7 million US, including a $2 million US château, was tied up in French tribunals. Regardless, the June 1987 ruling meant that much stood in the way of Haitian authorities ever collecting those holdings. And even if worse came to worst and all $15 million US was lost, the Duvaliers had plenty more. Investigators in Haiti had documented how the Duvaliers had siphoned off a far greater amount — a minimum of about $166 million.

With barely $15 million US accounted for, where was the rest? No one was quite sure, though the exiled Duvaliers seemed to have more than enough money to meet their needs. One had only to look at the cars parked on the Mohamedia property: a Lamborghini, a Ferrari and a BMW. Or monitor the couple's regular visits to such purveyors of luxury goods as Dior, Givenchy and Boucheron. Or notice how the Duvaliers routinely settled their debts — no matter how extravagant — in cash.

As to the supposed source of their continuing affluence, Jean-Claude's own explanations varied. On some occasions, he told journalists it was the fruit of well-nurtured savings; on others, that it was the result of an inheritance. He was less forthcoming on the origins of either the supposed savings or the alleged bequest. Most incredible, however, were his declarations that the bulk of their fortune had remained in Haiti and that the rest had been frozen by authorities in France and the United States. So how did they pay their bills? Simple, Baby Doc told the French newspaper, *Le Figaro*: "We have friends all over the world who spontaneously came forward to help us."[1]

Though such reports might have regaled Haiti's investigators temporarily, the truth was less humorous, for they had been unable to discover either how the Duvaliers covertly remained solvent or, more importantly, where their secret cache was buried. To find the answers, they reckoned, the place to start was where the money trail stopped — behind the Mohamedia's high walls. That is why a team of French officials was headed for the villa early on the morning of February 11, 1988.[2]

The police burst in, startling and annoying the notorious couple, but they met with no resistance. The Duvaliers and the other bleary-eyed residents of the Mohamedia — mostly servants and hangers-on — were herded to the main living room while the mansion was combed from top to bottom. As expected, the police came across a large hoard of valuables — mainly jewelry and works of art. (Some paintings were stored in an unused sauna.) But none could be seized under the terms of the raid, which was conducted under a so-called rogatory, or information-gathering, judicial request from Haiti. That the raid was a success was due to a moment of ineptness on the part of Michele. At one point, she tried to conceal something in the folds of her nightgown. Unluckily for her, a French official noticed. A brief struggle ensued (accounts vary on its intensity) and in the end, Michele "volunteered" a pink and purple, suede-bound notebook.

What had she tried to hide? Nothing less than the Duvaliers' personal ledgers. Page after page in Michele's characteristic script detailed their profligacy. Take a four-day shopping spree to Paris in December 1987. The fate of every sou is dutifully recorded. Lodging at their favourite five-star Paris hotel, the Bristol, chewed up the equivalent of $5,000; dining, a further $5,000. Also recorded in the notebook was Michele's visit to Givenchy, the Paris couturier. For the sum of $192,000 US, she bought four suits, four dresses, four cocktail dresses, two belts and three pairs of gloves. A heftier tab was jointly rung up the same month at Boucheron, the Paris jeweler, where Michele's purchases were a moderate (for her) $83,000 US, including a $13,000 US cigarette holder. Jean-Claude's acquisitions, on the other hand, included earrings, brooches and cuff-links. They were listed in the notebook under the rubric *compte tonton*, or "uncle's account." Uncle was Michele's pet name for her husband. His total: $372,309 US.

When not in Paris, the Duvaliers indulged in spending habits that were just as impressive and just as diligently recorded. Large sums were doled out to favoured relatives and loyal servants got generous tips. Claude, the chauffeur, received a $400 US *pour-boire* in September 1987. There were purchases from a nearby vintner ($2,300 US in February 1988) and from a local antique dealer, Mouradian ($40,000 US in December 1987 alone). And there was a variety of sundry acquisitions — such as a hunting rifle for Jean-Claude ($1,000 US, also in December '87). Security at the villa carried a hefty price tag. The K.O. Security firm submitted an invoice for $16,011 US in February 1987.

From an ocean of such details, the suede-bound notebook gave up its most important information: references to two bank accounts, listed simply as no. 1 and no. 2. On November 11, 1987, the balance of the first stood at $19.36 million US, and the balance of the second clocked in at $6.7 million US. There was also a reference to a certain "Turner" receiving $62,000 US in October 1987. Who was this "Turner"? Investigators had long tried to identify the Duvaliers' secret money handlers. Perhaps "Turner" was behind the surreptitious cash deliveries that must have regularly replenished the Duvaliers' coffers? Though there were no further details in Michele's notebook, Haiti's sleuths sensed they were on to something significant. They squared the circle thanks to a slip by another member of Michele's family — her pampered brother, Ronald Bennett. When his private papers were seized, numerous references were found to the British bank, Barclays. Could accounts no. 1 and 2 be located at that financial institution?

Then came a pivotal discovery: tucked into his personal agenda was the business card of one John Stephen Matlin, complete with a handwritten private telephone number. Matlin, it turned out, was a lawyer who practised at a London firm called Turner and Co., which was a Barclays client. Matlin seemed to have taken a number of flights to Nice — the closest airport to Mougins — during the previous year and a half. Interestingly, he had left London on November 10, 1987, on a multicity trip that also took him to Nice. One day later, Michele scribbled into her notebook the current balances for account nos. 1 and 2. Had Matlin provided the information?

All in all, it was a promising haul. Perhaps, after two years of hard slogging, the tide was beginning to turn against the Duvaliers. Or so the couple's pursuers hoped.

From the start, theirs had been a hard task, if only because history provides little encouragement to those wanting to pry ex-dictators from their nest-eggs.

One of the few bright spots occurred in the early 1920s when the Costa Rican government eked out a small measure of justice for its citizens. After the fall of the corrupt dictator Frederico Tinoco, it denied responsibility for debts he had incurred with the Royal Bank of Canada. The reason, argued Costa Rica, was that Tinoco had used the money to build up a foreign nest-egg, not for legitimate purposes. In 1923, the bank demanded to be repaid and took its case to an international arbitrator, who ruled against it. The judgment stated: "The bank knew that this money was to be used by the retiring president . . . for his personal support after he had taken refuge in a foreign country. It could not hold his own government [responsible] for the money paid to him for this purpose."[3]

In spite of this one victory for justice, despots of Tinoco's generation and of the next one had few worries about being deprived of their secret fortunes. In the late 1950s, for instance, Juan Perón, the former Argentine strongman, seems to have had little anxiety about holding onto the $3 million US he had reportedly stashed away in Switzerland.[4] Of course, Perón's funds did eventually dry up. By the early 1970s, he was apparently forced to rely on the kindness of another dictator, Nicolae Ceausescu of Romania.[5]

In other cases, bad money handlers proved to be more of a problem than angry former citizens. Consider what happened to the fortune of Rafael Trujillo, the brutal dictator of the Dominican Republic assassinated in May 1961. The following year, his family put the Trujillo booty — said to total some $180 million US — into the hands of Julio Munoz, a Spanish financier who had built up a modest international financial organization. With banks in Switzerland, Lebanon and Luxembourg, it was knitted together by holding companies in

Panama and Liechtenstein. The problem was that Munoz was better at attracting the funds of a late dictator than at banking. His lending instincts were wretched: he seemed to have a weakness for ill-fated tourist developments. Disaster for Munoz (and for Trujillo's heirs) came in 1965 when his financial empire collapsed.[6]

The sixties and seventies saw the first concerted attempts by a number of countries to recover the illicit fortunes of their former despots. But these efforts proved largely unsuccessful. At the time, laws and banking conventions seemed to favour ex-dictators, not their ex-subjects. In the sixties, Iraq went after real estate bought in New York by the deposed King Faisal, but U.S. courts ruled that "confiscation decrees issued in Iraq could not meet American standards of due process."[7] Another instance occurred in 1974 after the ouster of Ethiopia's Haile Selassie. The new government tried to get access to his Swiss bank accounts, but again, no luck.[8] The Sandinistas in Nicaragua ran into comparable roadblocks. They had more success in overthrowing the Somoza regime in 1979 than in recovering any of the wealth of the former ruling family.

The dismal record carried into the next decade. The revolutionary government of Iran, which tossed out the Shah in 1979, was unable to get the Swiss to freeze his accounts there. And a multi-billion-dollar lawsuit launched against the Shah in the United States foundered in 1980 when the judge found that American courts did not have the authority to hear such cases.[9]

By the middle of the 1980s, however, attitudes began to change — kindled, in part, by a growing public outrage in the West over the apparent ease with which despots could loot their nations. American courts made an about-face and started ruling that they could hear such cases. Similarly in Switzerland, which was red-faced over its reputation (wholly unwarranted, claimed the Swiss) of blindly welcoming the funds of a Selassie or a Shah. Matters did not improve when a Swiss legislator, Jean Ziegler, published a stinging indictment of the country's banking system in 1990. Titled *La Suisse lave plus blanc*, or *Switzerland Washes Whiter*, it charged that "Switzerland today is the principal turntable for money laundering, for recycling the profits of death."[10] In the face of such assertions, the Swiss served notice that henceforth they would be far less genial hosts to corrupt leaders and, conversely, far more helpful to countries stalking their ex-dictators' loot. As one banker warned in 1990, "If you're a pig as a leader of a country, don't put your money here."[11]

Despite these signs of progress, the odds of recovering a former despot's treasure were barely improved. Many other obstacles remained, as shown by the Philippines' efforts to retrieve the wealth of the late Ferdinand Marcos.[12] (Marcos and his wife Imelda were exiled in February 1986 just weeks after the Duvaliers' fall — not a banner month for despots.)

The Marcoses are alleged to have looted at least $3.5 billion US during their twenty-year reign, though some estimates run as high as $10 billion US. To put this into perspective, consider that the dictator's legitimate salary was just under $13,000 US a year, and that in 1966, the couple listed total assets of $90,000 US in their joint income tax return.[13] Imelda Marcos' explanations for their affluence were often fanciful (much as Jean-Claude Duvalier's were).

Sometimes she even pleaded poverty.[14] These pronouncements were in sharp contrast to her lifestyle. In November 1991, for instance, she returned to Manila on a chartered Boeing 747. Her entourage occupied sixty rooms at the five-star Philippine Plaza Hotel. And Imelda herself took a $2,000-a-day suite. All accommodations were paid a week in advance.[15] Of the Marcoses's purported billions, Manila has managed to recover but a fraction — about $100 million US in cash and a like amount in assets. It is not certain whether the Philippines will acquire the only other known pool of money — a further $350 million currently frozen in Swiss banks.

Why the failure to get more? Ineptness, say some. Corruption and political in-fighting, say others. To be sure, pure intimidation was always a factor. Arsonists repeatedly tried to destroy the office and files of David Castro, head of Manila's asset recovery efforts, and they had better luck with his house, which mysteriously burned to the ground. While Castro himself bravely soldiers on, the impact of such coercion on others pursuing such a case is both hard to measure and impossible to dismiss.

"The Philippines was the best-situated country to recover money," says Severina Rivera, a Washington lawyer who advised Manila authorities until 1988. The evidence, she points out, was first-rate, compiled from the many files left behind by the fleeing Marcoses. And there was a strong sense of outrage around the world against the family — fuelled, in part, by Imelda's vast shoe collection and anecdotes of their absurb excesses (she once spent $6,000 on chocolates in a single afternoon). And, yet, says Rivera, it was all for naught. Time was wasted. Opportunities were frittered away, giving the Marcoses more time to hide their wealth. Disputed assets also lost value: a small California bank apparently owned by the Marcoses is reckoned to have lost more than 80 percent of its 1986 price. Rivera's gloomy verdict: "If a country does not recover in the first two years while the revolutionary fervour is strong, it will never recover."

It was against such historically poor odds that the operation to recover the Duvaliers' fortune began in March 1986. The first order of business was to get solid evidence on the extent of the pillage. Members of Haiti's New York law firm of Stroock and Stroock and Lavan — and the lead investigators, Manhattan-based Kroll Associates — were dispatched to Port-au-Prince. What greeted them was far from promising. Many records were incomplete; others, simply missing. Much of the pilfering had been done with a nod and a wink or through a simple phone call from a palace official to the Banque de la République d'Haiti, the central bank. Moreover, many Haitians remained terrified of speaking out. No one doubted that the much-hated Duvaliers still retained powerful friends in Haiti.

Little by little, however, evidence began to be compiled.

Despite the gaps and lapses, the central bank — and especially an efficient clerk named Madeleine Savain — had documented many withdrawals. On May 20, 1980, for instance, the bank filed a debit note (on the instruction of the President for Life) for $101,221 US. It was drawn from an official government account. The funds were directed to the Italian automaker Ferrari, which provided the sports car that Jean-Claude bought for himself a week before his wedding to Michele. The debit note was not an isolated case. Another dated April 11, 1984 (*"aux instructions . . . President à Vie"*) was drawn on the central bank's National Defence accounts. It was used to purchase a $100,000 cheque which was sent to Spritzer and Fuhrmann, the Curacao jewelers. Hundreds and hundreds of such documents were carefully assembled, cross-checked and indexed — a time-consuming, painstaking process.

By early 1987, a gargantuan effort by investigators had produced a seventeen-volume, 20,000-page dossier of documents and affidavits, including 9,000 exhibits. The report demonstrated how the Duvaliers had siphoned off (at the very least) about $166 million between 1980 and 1986. Investigators estimated that they had probably pilfered many times that amount, but the figure represented what could be conclusively established from the incomplete paper trail the Duvaliers left behind.

Such a sum may not rate as substantial in a Canada where the very rich, like media giant Ken Thomson or food products magnate Galen Weston, have fortunes estimated in the billions of dollars. But $166 million was more than Haiti's entire governmental budget for one year — an amount that could have made a tangible difference in the quality of life of its citizens. British reporter Michael Gillard estimated that it could have provided safe drinking water for the whole population — something 80 percent of Haitians don't have; educated 240,000 children for a year — nine out of ten Haitians cannot read; or made "a major inroad into malnutrition in a country where 25 percent of the country's children suffer."[16]

With the evidence assembled, the focus of Haiti's lawyers

turned to a common legal dilemma faced in such cases. It boils down to a problem of too many borders. That is, the exiled dictator lives in one country, the crimes were committed in another, and the assets are scattered all over the world. Recovering the money requires a court ruling that covers all those factors. First of all, the court would have to unequivocally determine that the despot — in this case, Jean-Claude Duvalier — had embezzled the sums in question. Second, the ruling would have to have sufficient legal weight to be widely respected — to be, for instance, just as applicable in seizing their apartment in Manhattan, as their château in France. It would also have to be flexible enough to deal with the unexpected. What if assets turned up on Mauritius in the Indian Ocean or in Thailand — in places never linked to the Duvaliers? Not an easy legal brief. Rules of evidence, for instance, vary from country to country. There is no point, after all, in getting a judgment in country "A" based on a kind of testimony — say, involving wiretaps — that could not be admitted into a court in country "B." And not every country's justice is universally held in high esteem. It would have been difficult, for instance, in the mid-1980s to have tried to enforce a ruling rendered by a communist court in Sofia against a Bulgarian anti-communist in exile in England.

So how can these obstacles be surmounted? There are two basic choices. Those seeking justice can either turn to the courts in the fallen despot's former home or, if that country's judicial system is deficient (through ineptness, corruption or a combination of both), seek a judgment in a country with a more respected judiciary. That country, in turn, must also be home to either the ex-dictator or to some of his assets. Historically, the second option has been the more attractive, but it has also often proved to be disappointing.

Take Iran's 1980 lawsuit in the United States against the deposed Shah. It sank when a New York judge ruled: "No court should be required to serve as a referee between dictators. . . . [How could] a New York court pass judgment on the perquisites of an emperor?"[17]

That setback did not deter officials in Manila in the late 1980s, however. Worried about the malleability of Filipino courts, they turned to the American justice system. U.S. courts proved more receptive than they had been to Iran and agreed to hear the matter — partly because the couple had extensive assets in the United States and were, at the time, living in exile in Hawaii. In spite of this initial progress, however, Imelda Marcos was acquitted in New York of racketeering charges in July 1990 (Ferdinand had died in 1989). Never known for her tact, Mrs. Marcos said at one point "It is so petty — this talk about a million here and a million there."[18]

A little over a year later, the Philippines agreed to drop all current and future lawsuits in the U.S. in return for a relatively modest sum — $1.2 million US in cash and up to $7 million in personal items, including jewelry.[19] In the end, Manila reluctantly returned to the first option: trying Mrs. Marcos on her native soil. That a criminal case was filed against her in September 1991, more than five years after their overthrow, had more to do with a looming Swiss deadline than anything else. A Swiss court in December 1990 ruled that unless criminal charges were brought within a year, it might lift the order blocking the Marcos funds known to be in Swiss banks.[20] With Imelda Marcos' return to Manila late in 1991, judicial efforts intensified against her, but it remains to be seen how successful they will be.[21] Indeed, there were indications in May 1992 that Mrs. Marcos, a distant also-ran in her country's 1992 presidential elections, was feeling quite confident: she began making noises about reclaiming assets already seized by the Filipino government.[22]

Haiti's lawyers also had qualms about Haiti's judiciary, with its many Duvalier appointees. Though the first criminal charge against the couple was laid in Port-au-Prince in April 1986, there was little hope that it would ever result in a conviction. Thus, Haiti's lawyers picked France as the primary legal battleground — a decision that, on the surface at least, seemed to favour their client. French public opinion was firmly on its side. Many French citizens were still incensed by the ex-dictator's extended stay on the Côte d'Azur. Also helping matters was the fact that Haiti's lawyers had settled on a practical strategy. As Curtis Mechling, a lawyer for Haiti, put it in 1987: "We have not cast the cases in political terms. We have not brought wide-ranging omnibus lawsuits, nor have we sought to put the entire Duvalier regime on trial. We have only gone after assets we have been able to tie to embezzled Haitian funds."[23]

After some preliminary skirmishes, the main judicial contest opened in April 1987 in Grasse, just a few kilometres from Mougins.[24] Though widely anticipated in the media, the case itself — the first of its kind in France — held remarkably little drama. Under the French legal system, it was a contest of documents and legal briefs. Duvalier himself did not have to testify or be cross-examined. Haiti, for its part, relied heavily on the seventeen-volume dossier of evidence, arguing that Duvalier had not acted as its legal head of state when he funnelled tens of millions of dollars from government coffers into foreign banks. His lawyers countered with what was basically a variation on the possibly apocryphal remark of Louis XIV: *L'État c'est moi*. They asserted that Jean-Claude Duvalier had embodied the Haitian state and had followed Haitian practice, tradition and law. Duvalier himself had made that point in a 1986 interview with American television journalist Barbara Walters: "There was never any embezzlement. It is simply and purely a lie, it is slander. You must know that all heads of state of my country have always had certain funds at their disposal for implementing policy. It was a paternalistic kind of system."[25] Duvalier's lawyers concluded that he should be accorded sovereign immunity, since a French court has no authority to hear a dispute between a deposed head of state and his former subjects.

This first round went soundly to the Duvaliers: the three-man tribunal in Grasse ruled in June 1987 that it did not have jurisdiction over such a case. With the passing of this legal storm, they settled back into their easy, extravagant life behind the high walls of the Mohamedia.

Then came the raid of February 11, 1988, which changed everything. For the first time in their exile, the Duvaliers faced a serious challenge to their ownership of a substantial portion of their fortune. Thanks to the clues contained in Michele's diary and in her brother's personal agenda, it was only a matter of time before Haiti's investigators tracked down the Duvaliers' "spending money" — $41.8 million laundered through Canadian banks in 1986. Decisive action was needed. And quickly.

The Duvaliers turned again to Matlin, the man who had acted as their money manager since the fall of 1986 and who had administered the 1986 laundering scheme. Since then, Matlin had been concerned with more mundane matters. For starters, he shifted the funds among a number of banks. The accounts were under either the name of Matlin's law firm, Turner and Co., or a corporate front — like Boncardo Ltd., which Matlin had set up in Jersey in October 1986. Though the details are sketchy, the largest chunks seem to have resided at Barclays in London for much of 1987.

Matlin also kept an eye out for good investments. According to Matlin's memos, the Duvaliers tended to prefer conservative ventures involving precious metals or real estate. A Matlin memo of January 29, 1988, for instance, discussed a possible deal in Campione, Italy: "It is agreed that I should process the negotiations on Campione on the basis of each party paying one half of the land cost but the Duponts putting in 100 per cent of the development finance . . ." (Dupont was the Duvaliers' code-name in Matlin's personal records.) Another Matlin memo, dated March 28, 1988, referred to a possible building project in Belgium: "There is no particular rush on this development. I am to investigate it as soon as convenient after the middle of April."

The bulk of Matlin's time, however, seems to have been spent either paying the Duvaliers' bills or disbursing huge sums to trusted vassals. His memos are thick with references to settling debts. Typical is one detailing a meeting with the "Duponts" on June 30, 1987. In it, he refers to drawing

"US $70,000 from [account no. 2] for Boucheron. This will keep until 18th July." All told, $494,000 US went to the jeweler Boucheron between April and August 1987. Transfers to family members were also common. Michele's brother Ronald Bennett received $1.344 million US between April 1987 and February 1988. Another sibling, Franz Bennett, got $1.15 million US between September 1987 and February 1988. Even Michele's first husband Alix Pasquet received $788,000 US between June 1987 and February 1988. Under such heavy demands, the pool of "spending money" inevitably shrank. The $41.8 million of January 1987 had dwindled to $30.8 million only thirteen months later when the second money laundering plan began to take shape.

The scheme's objective was a simple one — to create a gap in the paper trail and thereby stop investigators in their tracks. To do this, Matlin relied on a tried-and-true strategy — using unwitting Canadian financial institutions and especially the Royal Bank of Canada. Once again, the affair would be perfectly legal (though ultimately embarrassing to the financial institutions themselves). "When things were at risk, they were sent to Canada and moved around and back to where they came from, but in a cleansed and different form," said a source with intimate knowledge of the Duvaliers' finances.

The first task was to accumulate all $30.8 million in a single financial institution. Within days of the police raid on the Mohamedia, the funds began flowing into two accounts (nos. 0267–418846–014 and 0267–418857–014) that Matlin had opened at Crédit Suisse in Geneva. The funds arrived there from their most recent sanctuaries: some $21.47 million from the Banque Nationale de Paris's operations on Jersey; $9.35 million from Royal Trust Bank, also on Jersey. The Crédit Suisse accounts were in the names of two Panamanian shell corporations — Minoka Investments and Modinest Investments. Matlin had set them up on the Duvaliers' behalf in July 1987.

In the meantime, Matlin inquired about opening an account at the Royal Bank's main branch in Montreal — the same branch, ironically, that had acted as a key pivot in the 1986 laundering scheme. It would play a comparable role this time. On February 17, 1988, Matlin visited a Royal Bank office in London and filled out the necessary documents to set up the account in Montreal. He also completed a questionnaire intended to prevent money laundering. Similar ones are used by most other Canadian institutions. They are supposed to help ferret out suspicious deals by forcing clients to disclose the nature of the transactions. Matlin simply stated that funds for the Royal account would come from Turner and Co.'s "client accounts in Switzerland, Belgium, Jersey, Channel Islands, and elsewhere." Eight days later, the Royal Bank sent Matlin a telex confirming that account no. 386–860–1 had been opened. Similar arrangements were made with two other financial institutions in Montreal — the Union Bank of Switzerland and Royal Trust.

From this point on, the tempo sped up. Between March 3 and March 7, Matlin transferred the $30.8 million from Crédit Suisse in Geneva to the Royal Bank in Montreal. Then he instructed the Royal to use those funds to buy Canadian treasury bills. The bank complied. It spread out the purchases between March 11 and March 17 in order "to obtain the best rate possible," according to a telex sent by the Royal Bank to Matlin on March 16. (The Duvaliers themselves approved the purchase of the securities in statements signed in Nice during a Matlin visit on March 29, 1988.) Around March 19, Matlin himself flew to Montreal to personally handle the most crucial part of the operation — the actual breaking of the paper trail. To do this, he visited the Royal Bank's main branch in Montreal two days later, on March 21, and physically withdrew the $30.8 million in treasury bills. He also removed the balance of the account — $10,603 in cash. Had anyone followed the scent to the Royal Bank in Montreal, this would have represented the terminus. The final bit of evidence in the Royal Bank's possession would have been the receipts Matlin signed before putting the bonds and the cash into his briefcase. Nothing more.

Next, Matlin deposited those Canadian government treasury bills at the two other financial institutions in Montreal that he'd previously contacted. This occurred on the same day, March 21, a few hours after he had secured the treasury bills from the Royal Bank. At a nearby office of the Union Bank of Switzerland, he placed $21.4 million worth of the bonds into account no. 251-801-01. The rest — worth $9.4 million — went into account no. 321-659430 at a Royal Trust branch that was also in the vicinity of the Royal Bank.

Though the paper trail had been sheared, the "spending money" was not yet out of harm's reach. On April 25, 1988, there was a distressing (for the Duvaliers) legal ruling in France. Relying on evidence obtained as a result of the raid on the Mohamedia, a court of appeal in Aix-en-Provence reversed the previous year's decision in Grasse. It ruled that French courts did have the power to hear Haiti's case against the Duvaliers. Meanwhile, across the English Channel, the investigation of Matlin was intensifying. Before long, there were clear signs that Haiti's investigators were closing in on the British lawyer. Under such pressure, Matlin began to move the "spending money" once again. At first, only a portion was shifted. About a month after Matlin's trip to Montreal, $4.55 million worth of bonds were cashed between April 20 and May 4, 1988. The money was then transferred from Turner and Co.'s accounts at Union Bank of Switzerland in Montreal to Lloyds Bank in London.

The pace quickened in late May when it became clear that Haiti's lawyers in Britain were about to go to court seeking all Duvalier-related records held by Matlin. In short order, the rest of the "spending money" was transferred from Montreal in what appeared to be anxiety-provoking circumstances. On May 26, Matlin sent two urgent telexes to Montreal, one at 12:25 P.M. London time to Royal Trust and another at 12:33 P.M. London time to Union Bank of Switzerland. He asked them to cash the bills and rapidly transfer the funds to the Bank International of Luxembourg (account no. 3–176–923–550). There is a breathless quality to the message dispatched to the Swiss bank: "i have just received clients' instructions to sell immediately all canadian treasury bills and to convert the resulting funds into united states dollars. please have this carried out today. . . . these instructions have come as a surprise but i must comply with them." A few hours later, the two firms sent messages to Matlin: the $26.24 million had been safely wired to Luxembourg. Meanwhile, the funds at Lloyds Bank in London were also shifted out of Britain — $2.58 million went to the same account in Luxembourg, while $1.35 million was sent to the Amro Bank in Geneva. Matlin would later claim he did not know the owners of the accounts in Luxembourg and Geneva.

Barely one week later, judicial proceedings began in England. A preliminary court order was obtained on June 3, and Matlin began disclosing what he knew — including details of the money transfers that had occurred just eight days earlier. This was of little value, however. When Haiti's lawyers moved to seize the funds in Luxembourg, the account had been emptied. Worse, it was the end of the line. There was no subsequent spoor. This time, the paper trail had truly been cut. Matlin's laundering operation through Canadian banks had proved crucial for the Duvaliers. It afforded a margin of safety, one that had kept the "spending money" out of harm's reach.

The British court cases continued well into the next month — with tribunal after tribunal ruling in favour of Haiti's request for an order freezing the Duvaliers' assets in England. This culminated in a Court of Appeal decision on July 22, 1988, dismissing a final Duvalier appeal. In delivering the ruling, Lord Justice Christopher Staughton noted that while the defendants denied liability, they also claimed there had been a tradition in Haiti for over 180 years for a new government to take legal proceedings against the previous one. He said he was reminded "of the Roman historian who noticed that it was the practice of the later emperors to bring to justice the murderers of the previous emperor but one." In the same vein, he had little time for a Duvalier lawyer who had referred in evidence to "a worldwide campaign ... against them by the Haitian government supported by the United States government to persecute them. ... [a] campaign ... assisted by the international press which provokes prejudice against them." Lord Justice Staughton countered: "This case is most unusual. It is not the nature or strength of the [Haitian] republic's cause of action which puts it into this category. It is the plain and admitted intention of the defendants to move their assets out of the reach of courts of law, coupled with the resources they have obtained and the skill they have hitherto shown in doing that, and the vast amount of money involved." If the Duvaliers felt persecuted, he said, they should simply cooperate to get a quick trial instead of trying to hide "their assets where even the most just decision in the world cannot reach them."[26]

A terrific verdict for Haiti's investigators, but it was all too little, too late — there were no longer any British assets to freeze. By this time, the Duvaliers themselves seemed to sense they had regained the advantage after the five rocky months that began with the surprise raid in February. A sign of their renewed confidence came in August 1988. They sent an invoice to the Haitian government demanding $16.8 million US for properties left behind when they'd fled in February 1986. No detail was too small for this *facture*, which was reported in *Haiti-Observateur*, a respected expatriate newspaper published in New York City. The letter listed, in minute detail, the $3.5 million US worth of items the Duvaliers claimed to have left behind at the National Palace, including Limoges china, Baccarat crystal, a Rolls-Royce, two BMWs and Jean-Claude's Ferrari. Items at a ranch at Croix des Bouquets included "corn fields, cows, pigs and goats."[27]

The request did not get far with authorities in Port-au-Prince. No matter, the Duvaliers appear to have received a much better recompense on September 17, 1988, when General Prosper Avril took power in a *coup d'état*. He had been a close confidant of Jean-Claude Duvalier and had been repeatedly linked to the dictator's money-siphoning operations.

According to journalist Mark Danner, Avril had "kept an office in [Haiti's] National Bank, and . . . was sophisticated enough to take numerous trips to Switzerland and elsewhere to see to the young dictator's investments."28 Though Avril would later deny that he had been Duvalier's "bagman," a curious thing happened after he took power: efforts to track down the ex-dictator's funds faltered.

Haiti's Manhattan law firm, Stroock and Stroock and Lavan, certainly noticed the dramatic change. After the Avril coup, "cooperation from the Republic came to an abrupt end and significant outstanding bills were not paid," said Laurence Greenwald, a partner in Stroock, which had coordinated the international search for Duvalier assets since March 1986. He made the statement in an affidavit filed in September 1989 declaring that it was withdrawing from the case. The document listed instance after instance of phone calls not being returned by Haitian officials, of letters not answered, of court cases left in limbo because requests for documentation were ignored. (The Canadian investigators hired by Romania to find Nicolae Ceausescu's fortune would run into some of the same problems one year later.) Attached to the document was a March 1989 letter from Greenwald to Avril himself, noting forcefully that "when your government took office in September 1988, all support, all assistance and all cooperation immediately and totally ended."

For the Duvaliers, the withdrawal of Stroock and Stroock marked — for all intents and purposes — the end of their legal troubles. Their villa was raided one last time by French authorities in November 1988, but the couple seemed to have learned their lesson: no notebooks were found. And instead of the kinds of valuables spotted in February, "only worthless copies of jewels and paintings" turned up this time.29 After this, Haiti's case against the Duvaliers wobbled on in French courts, surviving only because of the tenacity and dedication of some unpaid lawyers. Yet the French proceedings also came to a dismal end. On May 29, 1990, the highest French court, the Cour de cassation, overturned the April

1988 Aix-en-Provence ruling — stating, once and for all, that French courts could not preside over a case against the former Haitian dictator and his wife.

The Duvaliers had won.

Victory, however, did not ensure happiness.[30] Jean-Claude and Michele are now divorced, though Michele is challenging the rupture in a French court. She's said to live in Paris with a Middle Eastern arms dealer. Jean-Claude, on the other hand, remains on the French Riviera. He now resides in a much smaller villa than the Mohamedia. He is said to suffer from diabetes. And his friends are dwindling in number. With each passing year, he seems to become an ever more pathetic and lonely figure, his money his only solace.

NOTES

CHAPTER 1: Rinsing Baby Doc's Loot

1. "Nightmare Republic" was the title of a brilliant Graham Greene essay on Haiti published by the *Sunday Telegraph* on 29 September 1963. It was reprinted in Graham Greene, *Reflections* (Toronto: Lester and Orpen Dennys, 1990).
2. Phil Davison, "Haitian Ruler Faces First Serious Threat," *Globe and Mail*, 30 January 1986.
3. Bella Stumbo, "The Woman Behind the Throne of Haiti," *Toronto Star*, 18 January 1986.
4. Elizabeth Abbott, *Haiti: The Duvaliers and Their Legacy* (New York: McGraw-Hill, 1988), p. 327.
5. Marlise Simons, "Duvalier's Haitian Property Nationalized by New Rulers," *New York Times*, 20 February 1986.
6. Michael Gillard, "The Great Haiti Heist," *The Observer*, 10 May 1987.
7. Phil Davison, "Duvalier Flees Haiti, Wild Celebrations in Streets," Reuters, 7 February 1986.
8. Peter Carlson, "Dragon Ladies under Siege," *People*, 3 March 1986.
9. William Lowther, "CIA on Trail of Baby Doc's Hidden Fortune," *Toronto Star*, 23 February 1986.
10. Details of the Duvaliers' departure and their chaotic final period in power are also drawn from Abbott's masterful *Haiti: The Duvaliers and Their Legacy*, and from Amy Wilentz's *The Rainy Season: Haiti Since Duvalier* (New York: Simon and Schuster, 1989).
11. Phil Davison, "Duvalier Flees Haiti, Wild Celebrations in Streets," Reuters, 7 February 1986.

12. Abbott, *Haiti: The Duvaliers and Their Legacy*, pp. 300–1.
13. *Background Brief: Haiti, a Year after Duvalier* (London: British Foreign and Commonwealth Office, 1987), p. 4.
14. Abbott, *Haiti: The Duvaliers and Their Legacy*, pp. 300–10.
15. "Haiti Uncovers Fiscal 'Irregularities,' " *International Herald Tribune*, 9 May 1986.
16. Julia Preston, "Haiti Seeks to Tie Losses to Duvalier," *Washington Post*, 12 May 1986.
17. "Bare, Brown and Barren," *The Economist*, 1 June 1991.
18. Patrick Bellegarde-Smith, *Haiti: The Breached Citadel* (Boulder, CO: Westview Press, 1990), pp. 115–16.
19. Bellegarde-Smith, *Haiti: The Breached Citadel*, p. 6.
20. Mark Danner, "Beyond the Mountains: Part 1," *The New Yorker*, 27 November 1989, p. 58.
21. Bellegarde-Smith, *Haiti: The Breached Citadel*, p. xviii.
22. Ibid., p. 35.
23. Abbott, *Haiti: The Duvaliers and Their Legacy*, pp. 10–11.
24. Bellegarde-Smith, *Haiti: The Breached Citadel*, pp 109–10.
25. Ibid., p. 109.
26. Mark Danner, "Beyond the Mountains: Part 3," *The New Yorker*, 11 December 1989, p. 104.
27. Mark Danner, "Beyond the Mountains: Part 2," *The New Yorker*, 4 December 1989, p. 139.
28. Mark Danner, "Beyond the Mountains: Part 2," p. 131.
29. Graham Greene, "Nightmare Republic," *Reflections* (Toronto: Lester and Orpen Dennys, 1990), pp. 224–25.
30. Abbott, *Haiti: The Duvaliers and Their Legacy*, p. 164.
31. *World Military and Social Expenditures 1989* (Washington, DC: World Priorities, 1989).
32. Marie Brenner, "Mythomania," *Vanity Fair* (December 1986).
33. Nicholas Faith, *Safety in Numbers: The Mysterious World of Swiss Banking* (London: Hamish Hamilton, 1982), p. 85.
34. Marie Brenner, "Mythomania."
35. Mark Danner, "Beyond the Mountains: Part 3," p. 105.
36. Ibid.
37. "Asylum Bid by Duvalier Rejected by Three Countries," *Toronto Star*, 6 February 1986.
38. Leslie Plommer, "France Rejects Duvalier's Bid for Status as Political Refugee," *Globe and Mail*, 20 February 1986.
39. Stephen Salisbury and Fawn Vrazo, "Lifestyles Of The Ousted Dictators," *Toronto Star*, 3 October, 1989.
40. Marlise Simons, "Switzerland Freezes Duvalier Accounts," *New York Times*, 16 April 1986.

41. Julia Preston, "Haiti Seeks to Tie Losses to Duvalier," *Washington Post*, 12 May 1986.
42. The RCMP investigation as well as a separate probe by the Superintendent of Financial Institutions, the federal banking regulator, were begun after a series of four articles by the author on Duvalier's money laundering activities. The series was transmitted by The Canadian Press, the national news service. The most complete versions appeared in two Quebec newspapers: "Duvalier a blanchi 42 millions$ au Canada" and "La règne de la plus folle extravagance" in Montreal's *La Presse*, 21 March 1990; and "Le Canada a permis de 'laver' l'argent de Bébé Doc" and "La vie de château aux frais des Haitiens pour les Duvaliers" in Quebec's *Le Soleil*, 22 March 1990.

CHAPTER 2: Why Is Money Laundering So Hard to Stop?
1. Oxford English Dictionary, 2nd ed. (Oxford: Clarendon Press, 1989), p. 702.
2. "Flushing Funny Money into the Open," *The Economist*, 5 May 1990.
3. Dennis Eisenberg, Uri Dan and Eli Landau, *Meyer Lansky: Mogul of the Mob* (New York: Paddington Press, 1979).
4. Tim Hindle, *The Economist Pocket Banker* (London: Blackwell and the Economist, 1985), p. 102.
5. *Oxford English Dictionary*, 2nd ed. (Oxford: Clarendon Press, 1989), p. 702.
6. I've generally relied on the definitions of "dirty money" and "black money" by the late Italian criminal financier, Michele Sindona. See Nick Tosches, *Power on Earth* (New York: Arbor House, 1986), pp. 87–98.
7. Jean-Marie Pontaut, "L'argent planque des dictateurs," *Le Point*, 8 April 1991.
8. "Private Banking: Arrivistes and Traditionalists," *The Economist*, 24 June 1989; Stephen Fidler, "Direct Investment Lifts Financial Inflows for Latin America," *Financial Times of London*, 5 September 1991.
9. *Forbes*, 24 July 1989, p. 123.
10. "Mobutu: 2,5 milliards de dollars au moins," *Le Point*, 8 April 1991.
11. Jonathan Friedland, "How to Be Inscrutable," *Far Eastern Economic Review*, 5 March 1992.
12. *Report of the Financial Action Task Force on Money Laundering*, prepared by a G7 task force, Paris, 7 February 1990.

13. "Flushing Funny Money into the Open," *The Economist*, 5 May 1990.
14. *Tracing of Illicit Funds: Money Laundering in Canada* (Ottawa: Ministry of the Solicitor General of Canada, 1990), p. xi.
15. *Hearing of the Standing Senate Committee on Banking, Trade and Commerce* (Washington, DC: U.S. Government Printing Office, 2 October 1985), pp. 11:24–11:25.
16. John Barham, "Bank Failed to Penetrate Latino Jungle," *Financial Times of London*, 29 August 1991.
17. "Cash at Any Price," *The Economist*, 9 May 1992.
18. "Marc Rich and Firm's Other Top Officer Won't Be Extradited to U.S., Swiss Say," *Wall Street Journal*, 26 October 1984.
19. *National Drug Intelligence Estimates 1990* (Ottawa: RCMP Drug Enforcement Directorate, 1991), p. 69.
20. Rupert Pennant-Rea and Bill Emmott, *The Pocket Economist* (London: Blackwell and the Economist, 1983), p. 118.
21. Adapted from the hilarious version by Martin Mayer in "International Drug Money Laundering: Issues and Options for Congress," Congressional Research Service Seminar, Washington, DC, 21 June 1990.
22. Ingo Walter, "The Market for Financial Secrecy," *Financial Times of London*, 8 August 1991.
23. *National Drug Intelligence Estimate 1990* (Ottawa: RCMP Drug Enforcement Directorate, 1991), p. 68.
24. James Cook, "But Where Are the Dons' Yachts?" *Forbes 400*, 21 October 1991.
25. *Tracing of Illicit Funds: Money Laundering in Canada* (Ottawa: Ministry of the Solicitor General of Canada, 1990), p. 310.
26. Marc Edge, "Downhill Slide Recalled," Vancouver *Province*, 4 July 1991.
27. *Organized Crime and the World of Business*, Quebec Police Commission, Quebec, Quebec, 2 August 1977.
28. Ingo Walter, "The Market for Financial Secrecy," *Financial Times of London*, 8 August 1991.
29. Raymond Farhat, *Le Secret Bancaire* (Paris: La librairie générale de droit et de jurisprudence, 1970), pp. 14–15.
30. "European Banking Secrecy and Disclosure Requirements: The Record," *Financial Times of London*, 29 March 1990.
31. Nicholas Faith, *Safety in Numbers: The Mysterious World of Swiss Banking* (London: Hamish Hamilton, 1982), pp. 49–87.
32. Ibid., p. 30.
33. Caroline Doggart, *Tax Havens and Their Uses 1990* (London: The Economist Publications, 1990), p. 45.

34. *Hearing before the Subcommittee on Consumer and Regulatory Affairs of the U.S. Senate Banking Committee* (Washington, DC: U.S. Government Printing Office, 1 November 1989).
35. "Private Banking: Arrivistes and Traditionalists," *The Economist*, 24 June 1989.
36. Alan Freeman, "A $1000 Question for the Bank of Canada," *Globe and Mail*, 19 August 1991; Greg Ip, "Where Are All Those $1000 Bills Going?" *Financial Post*, 2 July 1991.
37. "Private Banking: Arrivistes and Traditionalists," *The Economist*, 24 June 1989.
38. Cedric Ritchie, "Banks Must Balance Two Basic but Conflicting Responsibilities, *Toronto Star*, 3 February 1986.
39. Clyde Graham, "Financial Institutions Join War on Drugs," Montreal *Gazette*, 16 February 1990.
40. *Tracing of Illicit Funds: Money Laundering in Canada* (Ottawa: Ministry of the Solicitor General of Canada, 1990), p. 310.

CHAPTER 3: The Tricks of the Trade

1. *Tracing of Illicit Funds: Money Laundering in Canada* (Ottawa: Ministry of the Solicitor General, 1990), p. 184.
2. *International Drug Money Laundering: Issues and Options for Congress* (Washington, DC: Congressional Research Service, June 1990), p. 6.
3. Cited in speech by John Robson, Deputy Secretary of the U.S. Treasury Department, to American Bar Association and American Bankers Association, Washington, DC, 24 September 1990.
4. David Asman, "Colombia's Drug Capital Seeks a Lifeline from the North," *Wall Street Journal*, 1 May 1992.
5. "International Drug Money Laundering: Issues and Options for Congress," a seminar held by the Congressional Research Service, Washington, DC, 21 June 1990, p. 44.
6. *Tracing of Illicit Funds: Money Laundering in Canada* (Ottawa: Ministry of the Solicitor General, 1990), p. 19.
7. David Hogben, "Credit Bank Dropped Questions," *Vancouver Sun*, 1 August 1991.
8. *Drug Money Laundering, Banks and Foreign Policy*, report by the U.S. Senate Subcommittee on Narcotics, Terrorism and International Operations, Washington, DC: U.S. Government Printing Office, February 1990, p. 5.
9. Neal Hall, "Huge Sums Laundered in Vancouver," *Vancouver Sun*, 11 October 1989.

10. *Tracing of Illicit Funds: Money Laundering in Canada* (Ottawa: Ministry of the Solicitor General, 1990), p. 23.
11. Ibid.
12. "A Random Walk around Red Square," *The Economist*, 24 August 1991.
13. *Tracing of Illicit Funds: Money Laundering in Canada* (Ottawa: Ministry of the Solicitor General, 1990), pp. 221–22.
14. Ibid., p. 228.
15. Ibid., p. 130.
16. Dan Westell, a *Globe and Mail* reporter, came across an intriguing case in 1989. An FBI undercover agent, posing as a Colombian drug dealer, stung a Californian businessman who planned to use shares in two Canadian companies to launder $300,000 US in purported drug money. Dan Westell, "Toronto Firms Used as Pawns in Money Laundering Scheme," *Globe and Mail*, 28 April 1989.
17. *Tracing of Illicit Funds: Money Laundering in Canada* (Ottawa: Ministry of the Solicitor General, 1990), pp. 151–52.
18. See William L. Cassidy, "Fei-Ch'ien Flying Money: A Study of Chinese Underground Banking," address to the 12th Annual International Asian Organized Crime Conference, Ft. Lauderdale, Florida, 26 June 1990.
19. Ibid., p. 15.
20. Ibid.
21. William L. Cassidy, "Fei-Ch'ien Flying Money: A Study of Chinese Underground Banking," 26 June 1990.
22. "Sleeper Awakes," *The Economist*, 19 August 1991.
23. Richard Mangan, "The Southeast Asian Banking System," *The Quarterly*, U.S. Drug Enforcement Agency (December 1983).
24. Ibid.
25. *Tracing of Illicit Funds: Money Laundering in Canada* (Ottawa: Ministry of the Solicitor General, 1990), p. 249.
26. Richard Mangan, "The Southeast Asian Banking System," U.S. Drug Enforcement Agency (December 1983).
27. National Drug Intelligence Estimate (Ottawa: RCMP Drug Enforcement Directorate, 1988), p. 103.
28. R.T. Stamler, "Forfeiture of the Profits and Proceeds of Drug Crimes," *Bulletin on Narcotics*, vol. 36, no. 4 (1984).

CHAPTER 4: Dirty Money North of the Forty-Ninth
1. "Money Laundering and the Illicit Drug Trade" (Washington, DC, and Ottawa: U.S. Drug Enforcement Administration and the RCMP, June 1988).

2. Hearings of the House of Commons Standing Committee on Finance (Ottawa: Supply and Services Canada, 20 August 1991), p. 5:14.
3. *Ottawa Citizen*, 28 September 1989.
4. Diplomatic cable classified "protected." Drafted by D. Sherratt and approved by P. Dubois, from External Affairs to Canadian Embassy in Washington, DC. File no. 7009-1. Delivered 29 September 1989, 4:00 P.M.
5. See Canadian Press dispatch from Washington by Scott White, 4 October 1989.
6. Guy Gugliotta and Jeff Leen, *Kings of Cocaine* (New York: Simon and Schuster, 1989), pp. 87–88.
7. Nicholas Faith, *Safety in Numbers: The Mysterious World of Swiss Banking* (London: Hamish Hamilton, 1982), p. 219.
8. Ibid., pp. 218–19.
9. *National Drug Intelligence Estimate 1990* (Ottawa: RCMP Drug Enforcement Directorate, 1991), p. 68.
10. Relazione sull'attivita' svolta dalla Guardia di Finanza nella lotta all criminalita' organizzata di tipo Mafioso, Rome, August 1988, p. 28.
11. Tim Shawcross and Martin Young, *Men of Honor: The Confessions of Tommaso Buscetta* (New York: Collins, 1987), pp. 201–2.
12. Otto Obermaier, "RICO Works — For Example, in the Teamsters Case," *Wall Street Journal*, 26 September 1991.
13. United States of America, Appellee, against the Southland Corporation, S. Richmond Dole and Eugene Mastropieri, Defendants, and against the Southland Corporation and Eugene Mastropieri, Defendants-Appellants. Brief filed by the Office of the United States Attorney, Eastern District of New York, to the United States Court of Appeals for the Second Circuit. Docket Numbers 84-1284, 84-1307. New York City, 26 November 1984, p. 12.
14. Ibid.
15. Robert E. Powis, *The Money Launders* (Chicago: Probus Publishing Company, 1992), pp. 32–49.
16. *Interim Report on Organized Crime, Financial Institutions and Money Laundering* (Washington, DC: President's Commission on Organized Crime, October 1984), p. 35.
17. Gerald Posner, *Warlords of Crime* (New York: McGraw-Hill, 1988), p. 221.
18. *Interim Report on Organized Crime, Financial Institutions and Money Laundering* (Washington, DC: President's Commission

on Organized Crime, October 1984), pp. 44–45.

19. Kevin Rollason, "Drug Profits Overflow Box in City Bank Vault," *Winnipeg Free Press*, 16 June 1990.

20. *National Drug Intelligence Estimate 1990* (Ottawa: RCMP Drug Enforcement Directorate, 1991), p. 68.

21. *Tracing of Illicit Funds: Money Laundering in Canada* (Ottawa: Ministry of the Solicitor General, 1990), p. 14.

22. The case was first revealed by the enterprising reporter William Marsden in a two-part series that appeared in the Montreal *Gazette*, 7–8 April 1988.

23. René Laurent, "Bank Workers Tell Laundering Hearing of Bags of Musty Bills," Montreal *Gazette*, 6 December 1990.

24. Michael Hedges, "U.S. Indicts Mafia Leader as Top Heroin Smuggler," *Washington Times*, 26 April 1990.

25. *Tracing of Illicit Funds: Money Laundering in Canada* (Ottawa: Ministry of the Solicitor General of Canada, 1990), p. 107.

26. Powis, *The Money Launderers*, p. 193.

27. Hearings of the U.S. Senate Permanent Subcommittee on Investigations, 19 July 1991, pp. 12–13.

28. *National Drug Intelligence Estimate 1990* (Ottawa: RCMP Drug Enforcement Directorate, 1991), p. 68.

29. Robert Matas, "Kickback Schemes Brought Wealth," *Globe and Mail*, 4 July 1986, p. 4; Affidavit of John Horace Rahr, sworn 22 December 1988.

30. *Tracing of Illicit Funds: Money Laundering in Canada* (Ottawa: Ministry of the Solicitor General of Canada, 1990), p. 284.

31. Ibid., pp. 304–5.

32. Ibid., p. 304.

33. Ibid., pp. 281–82.

34. *National Drug Intelligence Estimate 1990* (Ottawa: RCMP Drug Enforcement Directorate, 1991), p. 68.

CHAPTER 5: Doing Laundry: Canadian Banks in the Caribbean

1. Some details on Lehder and Norman's Cay were drawn from: Guy Gugliotta and Jeff Leen's *Kings of Cocaine* (New York: Simon and Schuster, 1989); Insight team of *The Times* of London, "Paradise Lost" (September 1985); Sidney Kirkpatrick and Peter Abrahams, *Turning the Tide* (New York: Dutton, June 1991). Other details came from testimony at Lehder's trial and from interviews with former Lehder associate George Jung.

2. *Report of the Commission of Inquiry*, Nassau, Bahamas, 14 December 1984, p. 207.

3. Michael Bliss, *Northern Enterprise: Five Centuries of Canadian Business* (Toronto: McClelland and Stewart, 1987), pp. 57–58.
4. Ibid., pp. 112–13.
5. Ibid.
6. Ibid., p. 264.
7. Martin Keeley, "The Tax Haven That Jim Macdonald Built," *Canadian Business* (October 1979).
8. Steve Lohr, "Money Washes Up," *The New York Times Magazine*, 29 March 1992.
9. R.T. Naylor, *Hot Money and the Politics of Debt* (Toronto: McClelland and Stewart, 1987), p. 300.
10. Richard Blum, *Offshore Haven Banks, Trusts and Companies: The Business of Crime in the Euromarket* (New York: Praeger Publishers, 1984), p. 3.
11. Sidney Kirkpatrick and Peter Abrahams, *Turning the Tide* (New York: Dutton, 1991), p. 8.
12. George Pyke, "Angel for a Nymphet: Why Lou Chesler Owns Lolita," *Maclean's*, 14 July 1962.
13. Catherine Wismer, *Sweethearts* (Toronto: James Lorimer and Co., 1980), pp. 107–12.
14. Hank Messick, *Lansky* (New York: G.P. Putnam's Sons, 1971), p. 229.
15. James Dubro, *Mob Rule: Inside the Canadian Mafia* (Toronto: Macmillan, 1985), p. 69.
16. Barbara Hetzer, "The Wealth That Leaves No Tracks," *Fortune,* 12 October 1987.
17. Charles McCoy, "Halt in Drug Money Ends Bimini's Grand Party," *Wall Street Journal*, 5 May 1988.
18. *Report of the Commission of Inquiry*, Nassau, Bahamas, 14 December 1984, p. 13.
19. Athena Damianos, "Loss of Tourism and Drug Money Add to Bahamas Economic Woes," *Financial Times of London*, 27 April 1988.
20. Charles McCoy, "Halt in Drug Money Ends Bimini's Grand Party,"' *Wall Street Journal*, 5 May 1988.
21. Testimony of Leigh Ritch, U.S. Senate Subcommittee on Terrorism, Narcotics and International Operations, Washington, DC, 8 February 1988, p. 161.
22. "Dirty Laundry," CBC-TV's "the 5th estate," 13 May 1986.
23. "Crime and Secrecy: The Use of Offshore Banks and Companies," staff study by the U.S. Senate Permanent Subcommittee on Investigations, February 1983, p. 99.

24. *Tracing of Illicit Funds: Money Laundering in Canada* (Ottawa: Ministry of the Solicitor General of Canada, 1990), p. 32.

25. William Marsden, "Laundering 'Narco-dollars' in the Bahamas," Montreal *Gazette*, 26 January 1986.

26. Shana Alexander, *The Pizza Connection* (New York: Weidenfeld and Nicolson, 1988), p. 139.

27. William Marsden, "Mafia Informer Describes Link between Banks, Dirty Money," Montreal *Gazette,* 24 April 1986.

28. Cedric Ritchie, "Banks Must Balance Two Basic but Conflicting Responsibilities," *Toronto Star*, 3 February 1986.

29. Ingo Walter, *The Secret Money Market* (New York: Harper and Row, 1990), p. 275.

30. Cedric Ritchie, "Banks Must Balance Two Basic but Conflicting Responsibilities," *Toronto Star*, 3 February 1986.

31. "Crime and Secrecy: The Use of Offshore Banks and Companies," report by the U.S. Senate Permanent Subcommittee on Investigations, 16 July 1985, p. 70.

32. Cedric Ritchie, "Banks Must Balance Two Basic but Conflicting Responsibilities," *Toronto Star*, 3 February 1986.

33. *Tracing of Illicit Funds: Money Laundering in Canada* (Ottawa: Ministry of the Solicitor General of Canada, 1990), p. 32.

34. Testimony of Leigh Ritch, U.S. Senate Subcommittee on Terrorism, Narcotics and International Operations, Washington, DC, 8 February 1988, p. 161.

35. "An Honor System without Honor," *The Economist*, 14 December 1991; "After Maxwell," *The Economist*, 9 November 1991.

36. "An Honor System without Honor," *The Economist*, 14 December 1991.

37. "Cleaning Up the Rupees," *The Economist*, 25 April 1992.

38. Stephen Labaton, "Sale of Unregistered Bonds by Pakistan Barred in the U.S.," *New York Times*, 6 May 1992.

CHAPTER 6: Using and Abusing Offshore Tax Havens

1. Indictment of Robert E. Graven, James F. Foley, Jr., Gregory Long, and Cherie Long, U.S. District Court for the Middle District of Pennsylvania, 21 March 1990.

2. "Drug Money Laundering, Banks and Foreign Policy," a report to the Committee on Foreign Relations, United States Senate, February 1990, p. 26.

3. Bronwen Maddox, "Maxwell Recycled Seized Funds to Banks," *Financial Times of London*, 3 February 1992;

Bronwen Maddox, Ian Rodger and Robert Preston, "Swiss Links in Maxwell Share Deals," *Financial Times of London*, 17 January 1992.

4. "Oh, My Brass Plate in the Sun," *The Economist*, 16 March 1991.

5. Official statement issued 7 March 1991 by the Government of Montserrat.

6. Ron Suskind, "Second Invasion: Made Safe by Marines Grenada Now Is Haven for Offshore Banks," *Wall Street Journal*, 29 October 1991.

7. Christopher Byron, "The Panama Connection," *New York Magazine*, 22 January 1990.

8. "Burying BCCI," *The Economist*, 30 November 1991.

9. Steve Lohr, "Money Washes Up," *The New York Times Magazine*, 29 March 1992.

10. Richard Blum, *Offshore Haven Banks, Trusts and Companies: The Business of Crime in the Euromarket* (New York: Praeger Publishers, 1984), pp. 31–34.

11. Ibid.

12. "Crime and Secrecy: The Use of Offshore Banks and Companies," Staff study by the U.S. Senate Permanent Subcommittee on Investigations February 1983, p. 6.

13. Ibid., p. 160.

14. David Crane, *A Dictionary of Canadian Economics* (Edmonton: Hurtig Publishers, 1980), p. 333.

15. Helmut Becker and Felix J. Wurm, eds., *Treaty Shopping* (Deventer: Kluwer Law and Taxation Publishers, 1990).

16. *Catalogue of Publications 1991* (Amsterdam: International Bureau of Fiscal Documentation, 1991), p. 43.

17. "The Stateless Corporation," *Business Week*, 14 May 1990.

18. "Salting It Away," *The Economist*, 5 October 1991.

19. Richard Blum, *Offshore Haven Banks, Trusts and Companies: The Business of Crime in the Euromarket* (New York: Praeger Publishers, 1984), p. 8.

20. Rodney Gallagher, "Survey of Offshore Finance Sectors in the Caribbean Dependent Territories," (London: Coopers and Lybrand, 19 January 1990), p. 104.

21. *International Issues in Taxation: The Canadian Perspective* (Toronto: Canadian Tax Foundation, 1984), p. 118.

22. Edwin A. Finn and Tatiana Pouschine, "Luxembourg: Color It Green," *Forbes*, 20 April 1987.

23. Miville Tremblay, "Les profits que tire Montréal des Centres

financiers internationaux sont marginaux," *La Presse*, 17 July 1991; Bernard Simon, "A Tale of Two Tax Haven Cities," *The Financial Times of London*, 3 January 1991.

24. Rodney Gallagher, "Survey of Offshore Finance Sectors in the Caribbean Dependent Territories," (London: Coopers and Lybrand, 19 January 1990), p. 104.

25. "International Drug Money Laundering: Issues and Options for Congress," seminar held by the Congressional Research Service, 21 June 1990, p. 23.

26. Tim Shawcross and Martin Young, *Men of Honor: The Confessions of Tommaso Buscetta* (New York: Collins, 1987), p. 238.

27. "The High Roller," *Maclean's*, 17 December 1984.

28. Philip Mathias, "Argentina: Who Gave What to Whom?" *The Financial Post*, 19 November 1977; Robert Hutchison, "AECL Still Wonders Where Money Went," *The Financial Post*, 22 January 1977.

29. Ross Howard, "AECL's Argentine Deal over Nuclear Reactors Netted Minister Millions," *Globe and Mail*, 14 June 1985.

30. Caroline Doggart, *Tax Havens and Their Uses 1990* (London: The Economist Publications, 1990), p. 1.

31. Ingo Walter, *The Secret Money Market* (New York: Harper and Row, 1990), p. 186.

32. Caroline Doggart, *Tax Havens and Their Uses 1990* (London: The Economist Publications, 1990), p. 1.

33. Ingo Walter, *The Secret Money Market*, p. 186.

34. John Parker, *King of Fools* (New York: St. Martin's Press, 1988), pp. 210–11.

35. "Irving's Taxing Battle," *Maclean's*, 3 August 1987.

36. "Irving Oil Ltd., Plaintiff, and Her Majesty The Queen, Defendant," *Canada Tax Cases*, volume 1, ed. H. Heward Stikeman (Toronto: De Boo Publishers, 1988).

37. David Crane, *A Dictionary of Canadian Economics* (Edmonton: Hurtig Publishers, 1980), p. 343.

38. Donald Brean, *International Issues in Taxation: The Canadian Perspective* (Toronto: Canadian Tax Foundation, 1984), pp. 118–19.

39. David A. Dodge, "A New and More Coherent Approach to Tax Avoidance," *Canadian Tax Journal* (January-February 1988).

40. Margaret Studer, "In Liechtenstein, Supersecrecy Policy Benefits the Banks," *Wall Street Journal*, 21 April 1992.

41. "Drug Money Laundering, Banks and Foreign Policy," a report to the Committee on Foreign Relations, United States Senate (February 1990), pp. 27–29.

42. Richard Blum, *Offshore Haven Banks, Trusts and Companies*, p. 3.
43. Eliot Rosen, "Treasury's Blunder in Paradise," *The New York Times*, 4 October 1987.
44. Ibid.
45. "Drug Money Laundering, Banks and Foreign Policy," a report to the Committee on Foreign Relations, United States Senate (February 1990), pp. 28–29.

CHAPTER 7: The Canadian Pioneer
1. Dennis C. Gomes, "Investigation of the Background of Alvin Ira Malnik," Audit Division, Nevada Gaming Control Board, 5 March 1976, p. 13.
2. Robert Lacey, *Little Man: Meyer Lansky and the Gangster Life* (Boston: Little, Brown and Co., 1991), pp. 305–8; Dennis C. Gomes, "Investigation into the Background of Alvin Ira Malnik."
3. Ibid., p. 305.
4. This assessment lies at the heart of *Little Man: Meyer Lansky and the Gangster Life* by Robert Lacey (Boston: Little, Brown and Co., 1991).
5. James Cook, "But Where Are the Dons' Yachts?" *Forbes 400*, 21 October 1991.
6. Robert Lacey, *Little Man*, pp. 302–32.
7. Dennis C. Gomes, "Investigation into the Background of Alvin Ira Malnik"; Robert Lacey, *Little Man*.
8. James Cook, "But Where Are the Dons' Yachts?"
9. Robert Lacey, *Little Man*, p. 306.
10. Art Petacque, "Jury Probes Mob's Banker," *Chicago Sun-Times*, 9 April 1969.
11. *U.S.* v. *John Pullman*, court file no. 3624. U.S. District Court, Grand Rapids, Michigan, National Archives, Chicago.
12. Robert Lacey, *Little Man*, p. 305.
13. Michael Marrus, *Mr. Sam: The Life and Times of Samuel Bronfman* (Toronto: Viking, 1991), pp. 175–202.
14. National Archives of Canada, RG18, vol. 3547.
15. Michael Marrus, *Mr. Sam*, pp. 202–6.
16. Peter C. Newman, *Bronfman Dynasty: The Rothschilds of the New World* (Toronto: McClelland and Stewart, 1978), pp. 130–31.
17. National Archives of Canada, RG18, vol. 3547, p. 176.
18. James Dubro and Robin Rowland, *Undercover: Cases of the RCMP's Most Secret Operative* (Markham, ON: Octopus Books, 1991), pp. 291–92.

19. National Archives of Canada, RG18, vol. 3547, pp. 136–37.
20. Ibid., p. 326.
21. Ibid., p. 330.
22. Ibid., p. 330–35.
23. "Perri and His Wife Sent Up for Trial," Hamilton *Spectator*, 18 November 1927.
24. Cross-examination of John Pullman, in *Her Majesty the Queen* v. *John Pullman*, 7 April 1977, pp. 263–64.
25. Dennis C. Gomes, "Investigation into the Background of Alvin Ira Malnik," p. 7.
26. Sandy Smith, "Mobsters in the Marketplace," *Life*, 8 September 1967.
27. Dennis C. Gomes, "Investigation into the Background of Alvin Ira Malnik," pp. 7, 99–100; Sandy Smith, "Mobsters in the Marketplace"; Charles Grutzner, "Ex-Bootlegger Manages Money in Swiss Banks for U.S. Mobs,"*New York Times,* 2 March 1969, p. 241; Hank Messick, *Lansky* (New York: Putnam, 1971).
28. Reasons for judgment in *Her Majesty the Queen* v. *Joseph Burnett and Burnac Corporation, formerly Ruthbern Holdings Ltd.*, The Honourable Mr. Justice E.P. Hartt, 12 April 1991, p. 40.
29. Robert Lacey, *Little Man*, pp. 307–8; Dennis Eisenberg, Uri Dan and Eli Landau, *Meyer Lansky: Mogul of the Mob* (New York: Paddington Press, 1979).
30. Dennis C. Gomes, "Investigation into the Background of Alvin Ira Malnik," p. 7.
31. Quoted in Nicholas Faith, *Safety in Numbers: The Mysterious World of Swiss Banking* (London: Hamish Hamilton, 1982).
32. Examination of John Pullman in *Her Majesty the Queen* v. *John Pullman*, 16 May 1977, p. 90.
33. Ibid.
34. Dennis Eisenberg, Uri Dan and Eli Landau, *Meyer Lansky*, p. 273.
35. Peter Moon, "The Success of Joseph Burnett," *Globe and Mail,* 11 May 1974.
36. Dennis C. Gomes, "Investigation into the Background of Alvin Ira Malnik," p. 7.
37. Ibid., p. 7.
38. Dennis Eisenberg, Uri Dan and Eli Landau, *Meyer Lansky*, p. 276; Robert Lacey, *Little Man*, pp. 306, 402.
39. Stanley Penn, "Man Who Feds Think Handles Mob Money Is Caught in Canada," *Wall Street Journal*, 9 December 1975.
40. Examination of John Pullman in *Her Majesty the Queen* v. *John Pullman*, 16 May 1977, pp. 87, 109.

41. Dennis C. Gomes, "Investigation into the Background of Alvin Ira Malnik," p. 12.

42. Dennis C. Gomes, "Investigation into the Background of Alvin Ira Malnik"; New Jersey Department of Law and Public Safety, "Report to the Casino Control Commissioner with Reference to the Casino Licence Application of Resorts International Hotel Inc.," Division of Gaming Enforcement, 4 December 1978; James Cook and Jane Carmichael, "Casino Gambling: Changing Character or Changing Fronts," *Forbes*, 27 October 1990.

43. Dennis C. Gomes, "Investigation into the Background of Alvin Ira Malnik," pp. 12–13.

44. Hank Messick, *Lansky*, pp. 266–67.

45. Examination of John Pullman in *Her Majesty the Queen* v. *John Pullman*, 16 May 1977, p. 85.

46. Robert Lacey, *Little Man*, p. 305.

47. Dennis C. Gomes, "Investigation into the Background of Alvin Ira Malnik," Audit Division, Nevada Gaming Control Board, 5 March 1976, p. 6.

48. Charles Grutzner, "Ex-Bootlegger Manages Money in Swiss Banks for U.S. Mobs," *New York Times*, 2 March 1969.

49. Dennis Eisenberg, Uri Dan and Eli Landau, *Meyer Lansky*, pp. 277–81.

50. Catherine Wismer, *Sweethearts* (Toronto: James Lorimer, 1980), pp. 59–60.

51. Reasons for judgment in *Her Majesty the Queen* v. *Joseph Burnett and Burnac Corporation, formerly Ruthbern Holdings Ltd.*, The Honourable Mr. Justice E.P. Hartt, 12 April 1991, p. 39.

52. Peter Moon, "The Success of Joseph Burnett," *Globe and Mail*, 11 May 1974.

53. Examination of John Pullman in *Her Majesty the Queen* v. *John Pullman*, 16 May 1977, p. 66.

54. John Whitelaw, publisher, *Bimonthly Reports* (Toronto: February 1978), p. 3.

55. *John Pullman, plaintiff* v. *Her Majesty the Queen, defendant*, Amended statement of defence, 21 June 1977, p. 30.

56. Ibid., pp. 31–32.

57. Motion by John Pullman, plaintiff in *John Pullman, plaintiff* v. *Her Majesty the Queen, defendant*, Federal Court of Canada, 27 June 1977.

CHAPTER 8: Heavenly Bankers

1. Nick Tosches, *Power on Earth* (New York: Arbor House, 1986), p. 2.

2. Larry Gurwin, *The Calvi Affair: Death of a Banker* (London: Macmillan, 1983), pp. 10, 28, 36.
3. Michael Bliss, *Northern Enterprise: Five Centuries of Canadian Business* (Toronto: McClelland and Stewart, 1987), p. 462.
4. Robert Hutchison, "Sindona and the Canadian Connection," *The Financial Post*, 24 May 1980.
5. Nick Tosches, *Power on Earth*, pp. 37–38.
6. Robert Hutchison, "Sindona and the Canadian Connection."
7. Philip Mathias, "Sindona: 'No Involvement in The Pas,' " *The Financial Post*, 7 August 1971.
8. Nick Tosches, *Power on Earth*, p. 114.
9. Ibid., p. 98.
10. Interim Report on Organized Crime, Financial Institutions and Money Laundering (Washington, DC: President's Commission on Organized Crime, 1984), p. 84.
11. Carlo Bordoni, "Sindona e il suo clan," *Il Mondo*, 1 March 1978. Bordoni's full 158-page statement to Milan judge Ovilio Urbisci was reprinted in three issues of the magazine, 15 February 1978, 22 February 1978, and 1 March 1978.
12. Commissione Parlamentare D'Inchiesta Sul Caso Sindona E Sulle Responsibilita Politiche Ed Amministrative Ad Esso Eventualmente Connesse, Rome, 24 March 1982, p. 532.
13. Ibid., pp. 44–52.
14. Aubrey Sugar, "Seaway Dogfight May Have Chewed Up the Short Sellers," *The Financial Post*, 4 April 1970.
15. Tim Hindle, *The Economist Pocket Banker* (London: Blackwell and The Economist, 1985).
16. "Fiduciari diversi posti in essere da Banca Privata Finanziaria e da Banca Unione, per addurre a Mofi ed a Romitex i fondi necessari a sottoscrivere l'aumento di capitale dell'Interlakes Canada Holding S.A. Luxembourg," Estratto della Relazioni del Commissario Liquidatori arr. Giorgio Ambrosoli al Giudice Istruttore del Tribunale di Milano, pp. 28–37.
17. Ibid.
18. Commissione Parlamentare D'Inchiesta Sul Caso Sindona E Sulle Responsibilita Politiche Ed Amministrative Ad Esso Eventualmente Connesse, Rome, 24 March 1982, p. 712.
19. Robert Hutchison, "Sindona and the Canadian Connection," *The Financial Post*, 24 May 1980.
20. Philip Mathias, "Citizen Sindona," *The Financial Post*, 12 April 1986.
21. Ibid.

22. Item 1103.1, The Pas Inquiry Commission evidence, Provincial Archives of Manitoba, Winnipeg. Exhibit tabled 5 May 1972.
23. Larry Gurwin, *The Calvi Affair: Death of a Banker* (London: Macmillan, 1983), p. 31.
24. Philip Mathias, "Lugano, Surfacing Point for Canadian-bound Lire," *The Financial Post*, 8 July 1972, pp. 101–6; Claire Hoy, *Bill Davis: A Biographi* (Toronto: Methuen, 1985).
25. "Calvi Planned Move to Alberta, Son Says," *Globe and Mail*, 27 July 1987.
26. Nick Tosches, *Power on Earth*, p. 119.
27. Affidavit of Allen Gerald Paisley, partner in Touche Ross and Co. Filed in the Court of Queen's Bench of Alberta, 1 May 1987, p. 10.
28. Larry Gurwin, *The Calvi Affair: Death of a Banker*, p. 55.
29. Ibid., p. 20.
30. Affidavit of Allen Gerald Paisley, partner in Touche Ross and Co. Filed in the Court of Queen's Bench of Alberta, 1 May 1987, p. 27.
31. Ibid., pp. 11–12.
32. Ibid., pp. 23–24.
33. Ibid., pp. 29–30.
34. Affidavit of Allen Gerald Paisley. Filed in the Court of Queen's Bench of Alberta, 1 May 1987.
35. Ibid., pp. 51–62.
36. Ibid., p. 57.
37. Ibid., p. 35.
38. See Canadian Press dispatch by Gerry McNeil, 25 April 1988.
39. Cross-examination on Affidavit of Allen Gerald Paisley, Court of Queen's Bench of Alberta, 17 June 1987, p. 96.

CHAPTER 9: Of Bagmen and Slush Funds

1. For details on this case I am indebted to the skilful reporting of *Globe and Mail* reporter Richard Cleroux. See especially Richard Cleroux, "Evidence Offers Rare Glimpse at Montreal's Big Business-Political Links," *Globe and Mail*, 13 June 1979; Richard Cleroux, "Giguère Is Acquitted of Stealing from Fund," *Globe and Mail*, 21 July 1979.
2. Richard Cleroux, "Evidence Offers Rare Glimpse at Montreal's Big Business-Political Links."
3. Ibid.
4. Richard Cleroux, "Giguère Is Acquitted of Stealing from Fund," *Globe and Mail*, 21 July 1979.

5. Michel Vastel, *Trudeau, le Québécois: Mais la colombe avait des griffes de faucon* (Montreal: Les éditions de l'homme, 1989), p. 206.
6. Richard Cleroux, "Giguère Is Acquitted of Stealing from Fund."
7. Ibid.
8. Guy Bourdon, "Le sénateur Giguère est acquitté," *Le Devoir*, 21 July 1979.
9. Cleroux, "Giguère Is Acquitted."
10. Ibid.
11. Bourdon, "Le sénateur Giguère."
12. Khayyam Zev Paltiel, *Political Party Financing in Canada* (Toronto: McGraw-Hill Ryerson, 1970), p. 3.
13. Michael Bliss, *Northern Enterprise: Five Centuries of Canadian Business* (Toronto: McClelland and Stewart, 1987).
14. Claire Hoy, *Bill Davis, a Biography* (Toronto: Methuen, 1985), p. 85.
15. Conrad Black, *Duplessis* (Toronto: McClelland and Stewart, 1977), p. 606.
16. Jeffrey Simpson, *Spoils of Power: The Politics of Patronage* (Toronto: Harper & Collins, 1988), p. 135.
17. Stephen Handelman, "Soviets Secretly Paid Canada's Communists $2 million," *Toronto Star*, 14 March 1992.
18. Claire Hoy, *Bill Davis, a Biography* (Toronto: Methuen, 1985), pp. 101–6.
19. Ibid., p. 123.
20. Ramsay MacMullen, *Corruption and the Decline of Rome* (New Haven, CT: Yale University Press, 1988), p. x.
21. Jeffrey Simpson, *Spoils of Power*, p. 140.
22. Reginald Whitaker, *The Government Party: Organizing and Financing the Liberal Party of Canada, 1930–58* (Toronto: University of Toronto Press, 1977), p. 126.
23. Michael Bliss, *Northern Enterprise*, p. 471.
24. Philip Mathias, "How Widespread Are Political Kickbacks?" *The Financial Post*, 28 May 1977.
25. Jonathan Manthorpe, *The Power and the Tories* (Toronto: Macmillan, 1974), p. 135.
26. *Dictionary of Canadian Biography, Volume 12: 1891 to 1900* (Toronto: University of Toronto Press, 1990), p. 677.
27. Ibid.
28. The wording of the guideline for proper use of money was as follows: "[The minister's] certificate that the same or any part thereof has been disbursed for the service of the country shall

be a sufficient discharge and voucher for the payment of the same." "Proposed Amended Report of the Select Standing Committee of Public Accounts Relating to the Expenditure of Certain Secret Service Funds," 12 April 1877, p. 22.

29. "Proposed Amended Report of the Select Standing Committee of Public Accounts Relating to the Expenditure of Certain Secret Service Funds," Ottawa, 12 April 1877, pp. 19–21.

30. Norman Ward, *The Public Purse: A Study in Canadian Democracy* (Toronto: University of Toronto Press, 1951), p. 64.

31. W.A. Crockett, "The Uses and Abuses of the Secret Service Fund: The Political Dimension of Police Work in Canada, 1864–1877," M.A. thesis, Queen's University, 1982, p. 112.

32. "Proposed Amended Report of the Select Standing Committee of Public Accounts Relating to the Expenditure of Certain Secret Service Funds," Ottawa, 12 April 1877, p. 23.

33. Ibid., pp. 24–25.

34. Norman Ward, *The Public Purse*, p. 64.

35. Ibid.

36. W.A. Crockett, "The Uses and Abuses of the Secret Service Fund: The Political Dimension of Police Work in Canada, 1864–1877," p. 128.

37. Ibid., pp. 129–30.

38. Ibid.

39. Joseph Schull, *Laurier: The First Canadian* (Toronto: Macmillan, 1965), p. 223.

40. Undated, untitled study prepared by Professor Richard Clippingdale of Carleton University in the mid-1970s on request from The Honourable Robert Stanfield, then the leader of the federal Conservative party.

41. Khayyam Zev Paltiel, *Political Party Financing in Canada* (Toronto: McGraw-Hill Ryerson, 1970), p. 4.

42. J.L. Granatstein, "Was King Really Bribed? Diaries Cast Doubt on It," *Globe and Mail*, 18 January 1977.

43. Jeffrey Simpson, *Spoils of Power*, p. 138.

44. Reginald Whitaker, *The Government Party: Organizing and Financing the Liberal Party of Canada, 1930–58* (Toronto: University of Toronto Press, 1977), p. 18.

45. Ibid., pp. 18–19.

46. Peter Larkin to Wilfrid Laurier McDougald, 28 February 1922, National Archives of Canada, MG27, III, C24.

47. Peter Larkin to Wilfrid Laurier McDougald, 22 September 1927, National Archives of Canada, MG27, III, C24.

48. Reginald Whitaker, *The Government Party*, p. 18.

49. T.D. Regehr, *The Beauharnois Scandal: A Story of Canadian Entrepreneurship and Politics* (Toronto: University of Toronto Press, 1990), p. 139.
50. Ibid., pp. 59–60.
51. Ibid., pp. 138–40.
52. Khayyam Zev Paltiel, *Political Party Financing in Canada*, p. 7.
53. J.L. Granatstein, "Was King Really Bribed?" *Globe and Mail*, 18 January 1977. This was followed by a letter to the editor of the *Globe and Mail* from Bernard Ostry on 22 January, which sparked a reply by Granatstein on 26 January 1977.
54. Dale C. Thomson, *Louis St-Laurent* (Toronto: Macmillan, 1967), pp. 213–16.
55. Denis Smith, *Gentle Patriot: A Political Biography of Walter Gordon* (Edmonton: Hurtig, 1973), p. 28.
56. Letter to the editor signed by Alex Inglis and John Munro, *The Ottawa Citizen*, 5 December 1973.
57. See Canadian Press dispatches, 6–7 September, 1988.
58. Susan Delacourt, "Tories Giving PM Extra Expense Payments," *Globe and Mail*, 19 July 1991.
59. Kevin Cox, "Financial Sins Haunt N.S. Grits," *Globe and Mail*, 22 October 1990.
60. Susan LeBlanc, "Political Stipends Not Something New," Halifax *Chronicle-Herald*, 19 April 1991.
61. Kevin Cox, "Financial Sins Haunt N.S. Grits," *Globe and Mail*, 22 October 1990.
62. Brian Ward, "Grit Funds Ruled Exempt from New Conflict Act," Halifax *Chronicle-Herald*, 28 December 1991.
63. Brian Underhill, "Tories Paid $588,059 to Buchanan," Halifax *Chronicle-Herald*, 22 April 1991.
64. "Sweet Sound of a Whistle," Halifax *Chronicle-Herald*, 16 April 1991.
65. John Sawatsky, *Mulroney: The Politics of Ambition* (Toronto: Macfarlane, Walter & Ross, 1991), p. 227.
66. Rae Murphy, Robert Chodos and Nick Auf der Maur, *Brian Mulroney: The Boy from Baie-Comeau* (Toronto: Lorimer, 1984), p. 104.
67. Robert McKenzie, "Wagner Given Cash before '72 Election, Former Aide Says," *Toronto Star*, 7 February 1976.
68. John Saywell, ed., *Canadian Annual Review of Politics and Public Affairs* (Toronto: University of Toronto Press, 1977), p. 151.
69. "The High Roller," *Maclean's*, 17 December 1984; Rod McQueen, "Watch Out for Walter Wolf," *Canadian Business*

(November 1984); David Hatter, "Multimillionaire Wolf Linked to Mulroney Aides," Montreal *Gazette*, 6 July 1984; Robert Matas, "Jetsetting Financier Hates to Take Risks, Values His Privacy," *Globe and Mail*, 7 February 1987.

70. Jeffrey Simpson, *Spoils of Power*, pp. 357-58.

CHAPTER 10: Nicolae Ceausescu and the Looting of Romania

1. Biographical details on Ceausescu are drawn from: Edward Behr, *Kiss the Hand You Cannot Bite* (New York: Villard Books, 1991); John Sweeney, *The Life and Evil Times of Nicolae Ceausescu* (London: Hutchison, 1991); Robert Cullen, *Twilight of Empire* (New York: The Atlantic Monthly Press, 1991); Robert Cullen, "Down with the Tyrant," *The New Yorker*, 2 April 1990; Roger Thurow, "The Dictator Lied through His Teeth — and His Tusks," *Wall Street Journal*, 26 April 1991.

2. "The Hole in the Map," *The Economist*, 12 August 1989.

3. Mireille Duteil, "Mobutu: 2,5 milliards de dollars de moins," *Le Point*, 9 April 1991.

4. Julian Ozanne, "Mobutu's End Game," *Financial Times of London*, 5 September 1991.

5. Charles Parmiter, "The Red Aristocrats," *Reader's Digest* (Montreal: October 1990).

6. Edward Behr, *Kiss the Hand You Cannot Bite*, pp. 221–25.

7. "The Bad Couple," *The Economist*, 11 January 1992.

8. Roger Thurow, "The Dictator Lied through His Teeth — and His Tusks."

9. Sorin Dumitrescu, "In the Hands of the Securitate," *The Unesco Courier* (Paris: August 1990).

10. The ensuing text is a summary of the views Patricia Adams eloquently expresses in *Odious Debts* (Toronto: Earthscan, 1991).

11. Ibid., p. 164.

12. Ibid., p. 194.

13. "The Hole in the Map," *The Economist*, 12 August 1989.

14. Ibid.

15. Ion Mihai Pacepa, *Red Horizons* (New York: Random House, 1987), p. 73.

16. Ibid., p. 79.

17. Yossi Melman and Dan Raviv, *The Imperfect Spies* (London: Sidgwick and Jackson, 1989), pp. 251–53; and Tad Szulc, *The Secret Alliance* (Toronto: HarperCollins, 1991), pp. 277–79.

18. Tony Patterson, "KoKo Scandal Net Closes," *The European*, 24–26 May 1991; John Elson, "Anyone Want a Pariah?" *Time*, 1 July 1991.

19. "Bulgaria Probes Fake Companies Involving Communist-Era Police," *New York Times*, 15 January 1992.
20. "Enquête sur les armes secrets de Saddam Hussein," *Le Nouvel Observateur*, 31 janvier 1991; "Give a Little, Take a Lot," *The Economist*, 30 March 1991; Alan Friedman, Richard Donkin, George Graham, "Saddam Linked to $1bn Share Stakes in European Companies," *Financial Times of London*, 25 March 1991; Fred Bleakley, "Saddam Is Said to Have Assets Hidden in Over 40 Banks World-wide," *Wall Street Journal*, 25 March 1991.
21. Gerald Seib and John Fialka, "How Saddam Hussein Survives Sanctions and Dissent for a Year," *Wall Street Journal*, 16 January 1992.
22. Petre Bacanu, *Romania Libera*, 8 November 1991.
23. William McPherson. "Who 'Won' Romania's Mysterious Revolution?" *The Washington Post*, 17 November 1991.

CHAPTER 11: The Wild West in the East

1. Peter Fuhrman, "The Bulgarian Connection," *Forbes*, 17 April 1989.
2. Ruppert Pennant-Rea and Bill Emmott, *The Pocket Economist* (London: Blackwell and the Economist, 1982), p. 197.
3. "Behind Democracy's Façade," *The Economist*, 18 April 1992.
4. "Bulgaria Probes Fake Companies Involving Communist-Era Police," *New York Times*, 15 January 1992.
5. John Lloyd, "Russian Commercial Banks under Attack," *Financial Times of London*, 28 September 1991.
6. Leslie Colitt, "Hunt for Stasi Funds Stepped Up," *Financial Times of London*, 29 November 1991.
7. "The Lolly Factor," *The Economist*, 27 October 1990; Tony Patterson, "How the Missing Millions Have Rocked Gysi's Reformed Party," *The European*, 7 November 1990.
8. Ingo Walter, *Secret Money* (New York: Harper and Row, 1990), p. 128.
9. Christopher Bobinski and Hugh Carnegy, "Poles Charged in Financial Scandal," *Financial Times of London*, 14 November 1991.
10. "Seeking Clean Capital," *The Economist*, 9 November 1991.
11. Ibid.

CHAPTER 12: Panic on the Riviera

1. Catherine Delsol and Francis Puyalte, "Baby Doc: 'Je N'ai jamais détourné d'argent public,'" *Le Figaro*, 6 May 1988.

2. Bertrand Le Gendre, "La vie en or des Duvalier," *Le Monde*, 24–25 April 1988; Christian Lionet, "Le magot de Bébé Doc retrouvé à Londres," *Libération*, 20 June 1988.

3. Cited in Patricia Adams, *Odious Debts* (Toronto: Earthscan, 1991), pp. 167–79.

4. Standford Brown and Arnaud de Borchgrave, "Anybody's Money Pours In," *Newsweek*, 15 June 1959.

5. Ion Mihai Pacepa, *Red Horizons* (Washington, DC: Regnery Gateway, 1987), p. 78.

6. Nicholas Faith, *Safety in Numbers* (London: Hamish Hamilton, 1982), pp. 190–98.

7. Alan Tomlinson, "Manila and Haiti Get Dictators' Hidden Plunder," *The Times of London*, 25 November 1987.

8. Rone Tempest, "Ex-Despots Can't Bank on the Swiss," *Los Angeles Times*, 3 January 1990.

9. "Booty of Dictators Usually Falls through the Cracks," *Wall Street Journal*, 2 December 1986.

10. Jean Ziegler, *La Suisse lave plus blanc* (Paris: Editions du Seuil, 1990), p. 13.

11. Edward Cody, "Swiss Show More Readiness to Freeze Assets of Despots," *Washington Post*, 31 January 1990.

12. Jean-Loup Reverier, "Marcos: Une iceberg en or massif," *Le Point*, 8 April 1991; Jean Ziegler, *La Suisse lave plus blanc* (Paris: Editions du Seuil, 1990); Lawrence Macdonald, "Philippines, with New Data, Acts Today to Get Marcos Funds Held in Swiss Bank," *Wall Street Journal*, 11 September 1991; Seth Mydans, "Hunt for Marcos' Billions Yields More Dead Ends Than Hard Cash," *New York Times*, 31 March 1991.

13. Jean-Noel Cuenod, "Près de 500 millions en attente," *La Tribune de Genève*, 4 June 1991.

14. "The Iron Butterfly Flies Home," *The Economist*, 9 November 1991.

15. Ibid.

16. Michael Gillard, "The Great Haiti Heist," *The Observer*, 10 May 1987.

17. "Booty of Dictators Usually Falls through the Cracks," *Wall Street Journal*, 2 December 1986.

18. "A Million here, a Billion there . . . ," *The Economist*, 10 November 1990.

19. Nicholas Cummings-Bruce, "Marcos Baubles Buy Immunity in U.S. Courts," *Guardian Weekly*, 10 November 1991.

20. William Dullforce, "Court Rejects Marcos Appeals on Assets," *Financial Times of London*, 28 December 1990.

21. José Galang, "Ramos Widens Lead in Manila Polls amid Fraud Claim," *Financial Times of London*, 19 May 1992.
22. "Marcos Set to Launch Suit over Assets," *Globe and Mail*, 26 May 1992.
23. Alan Tomlinson, "Manila and Haiti Get Dictators' Hidden Plunder," *The Times of London*, 25 November 1987.
24. Michael Gillard, "The Great Haiti Heist," *The Observer*, 10 May 1987.
25. ABC Television's "20/20," 12 June 1986.
26. Raymond Hughes, "Duvalier Millions 'Must Stay Frozen,' " *Financial Times of London*, 23–24 July 1988.
27. "Duvaliers Demand $16.8 Million," *Haiti-Observateur*, 12–19 August 1988.
28. Mark Danner, "Beyond the Mountains: Part 3," *The New Yorker*, 11 December 1989.
29. "Police Uncover Nothing of Value in Raid on Duvalier French Villa," *Globe and Mail*, 26 November 1988.
30. " 'Baby Doc' Duvalier, Wife Divorced in Santo Domingo," *Jet,* 2 April 1990. "Divorced for Life," *The New York Times,* 24 June 1990. Fred Dannen, "Lifestyles Of The Rich and Infamous," *Vanity Fair*, April 1992.

INDEX

PERMISSIONS

Excerpts from the following were used by permission:

"After Maxwell" (November 9, 1991). Copyright *The Economist,* London.

"Bank Failed to Penetrate Latino Jungle" (August 29, 1991) by John Barham. Copyright *The Financial Times of London.*

"Behind Democracy's Facade" (April 18, 1992). Copyright *The Economist,* London.

Bill Davis, A Biography by Claire Hoy, Methuen, 1985. Copyright Claire Hoy.

"Burying BCCI" (November 30, 1991). Copyright *The Economist,* London.

"Cash at Any Price" (May 9, 1992). Copyright *The Economist,* London.

"Citizen Sindona" (April 12, 1986) by Philip Mathias, Copyright *The Financial Post,* Toronto.

Duplessis by Conrad Black, McClelland and Stewart, 1977. Copyright Conrad Black.

"Illicit Funds: Money Laundering in Canada." Copyright Solicitor General of Canada, 1990. Reprinted with permission of the Minister of Supply and Services Canada, 1992.

International Issues in Taxation: The Canadian Perspective, Canadian Tax Paper no. 75 (Toronto: Canadian Tax Foundation, 1984), 118-119. Reproduced with the permission of the Canadian Tax Foundation.

Little Man: Meyer Lansky and the Gangster Life by Robert Lacey. Copyright 1991, Little, Brown and Company, Boston.

"Lugano, Surfacing Point for Canadian-bound Lire" (July 8,